## Africa in the New Millennium

ABOUT THIS SERIES

The books in this new series are an initiative by CODESRIA, the Council for the Development of Social Science Research in Africa, to encourage African scholarship relevant to the multiple intellectual, policy and practical problems and opportunities confronting the African continent in the twenty-first century.

CODESRIA in association with Zed Books

Titles in the series:

*African Intellectuals: Rethinking Politics, Language, Gender and Development*
Edited by Thandika Mkandawire (2005)

*Africa and Development Challenges in the New Millennium: The NEPAD Debate*
Edited by J. O. Adesina, A. Olukoshi and Yao Graham (2005)

*Urban Africa: Changing Contours of Survival in the City*
Edited by A. M. Simone and A. Abouhani (2005)

*Liberal Democracy and Its Critics in Africa: Political Dysfunction and the Struggle for Social Progress*
Edited by Tukumbi Lumumba-Kasongo (2005)

*Negotiating Modernity: Africa's Ambivalent Experience*
Edited by Elísio Salvado Macamo (2005)

*Insiders and Outsiders: Citizenship and Xenophobia in Contemporary Southern Africa*
Francis B. Nyamnjoh (2006)

## About CODESRIA

The Council for the Development of Social Science Research in Africa (CODESRIA) is an independent organization whose principal objectives are facilitating research, promoting research-based publishing and creating multiple forums geared towards the exchange of views and information among African researchers. It challenges the fragmentation of research through the creation of thematic research networks that cut across linguistic and regional boundaries.

CODESRIA publishes a quarterly journal, *Africa Development*, the longest-standing Africa-based social science journal; *Afrika Zamani*, a journal of history; the *African Sociological Review*, *African Journal of International Affairs* (AJIA), *Africa Review of Books* and *Identity, Culture and Politics: An Afro-Asian Dialogue*. It co-publishes the *Journal of Higher Education in Africa*, and *Africa Media Review*. Research results and other activities of the institution are disseminated through 'Working Papers', 'Monograph Series', 'CODESRIA Book Series', and the CODESRIA Bulletin.

TUKUMBI LUMUMBA-KASONGO | editor

# Liberal democracy and its critics in Africa

Political dysfunction and the struggle for social progress

CODESRIA Books
DAKAR

*in association with*

Zed Books
LONDON | NEW YORK

University of South Africa Press
PRETORIA

*Liberal democracy and its critics in Africa: Political dysfunction and the struggle for social progress* was first published by Zed Books Ltd, 7 Cynthia Street, London N1 9JF, UK and Room 400, 175 Fifth Avenue, New York, NY 10010, USA in 2005

www.zedbooks.co.uk

and in South Africa by UNISA Press, PO Box 392, Pretoria RSA 0003
www.unisa.ac.za

in association with CODESRIA, Avenue Cheikh Anta Diop, X Canal IV, BP3304 Dakar, 18524 Senegal
www.codesria.org

CODESRIA would like to express its gratitude to the Swedish International Development Cooperation Agency (SIDA/SAREC), the International Development Research Centre (IDRC), Ford Foundation, MacArthur Foundation, Carnegie Corporation, the Norwegian Ministry of Foreign Affairs, the Danish Agency for International Development (DANIDA), the French Ministry of Cooperation, the United Nations Development Programme (UNDP), the Netherlands Ministry of Foreign Affairs, Rockefeller Foundation, FINIDA, NORAD, CIDA, IIEP/ADEA, OECD, IFS, OXFAM America, UN/UNICEF and the Government of Senegal for supporting its research, training and publication programmes.

Cover designed by Andrew Corbett
Set in Arnhem and Futura Bold by Ewan Smith, London
Index: ed.emery@britishlibrary.net
Printed and bound in Malta by Gutenberg Press Ltd

Distributed in the USA exclusively by Palgrave Macmillan, a division of St Martin's Press, LLC, 175 Fifth Avenue, New York, NY 10010.

A catalogue record for this book is available from the British Library.
US CIP data are available from the Library of Congress.

CODESRIA edition  ISBN 2 86978 143 1 cased
Zed Books edition  ISBN 1 84277 618 5 hb
                   ISBN 1 84277 619 3 pb

# Contents

# About the contributors

*Joseph-Marie Zambo Belinga* obtained his doctorate in 1994 from the University of Yaoundé I, Cameroon. The title of his thesis was *Les Groupes de Pression au Cameroun: Du Parti Unique au Multipartisme*. He is a lecturer in the Department of Sociology and Anthropology at the University of Yaoundé I.

*Emmanuel Debrah* is a lecturer in the Department of Political Science, University of Ghana, Legon, where he teaches Public Administration, Public Policy Analysis, Local Government and Development Administration. He previously worked with the Electoral Commission of Ghana as a senior electoral officer, and consults for the Centre for Democratic Development (CDD) Ghana. He was a visiting research scholar in the Department of Political Science and Public Administration, North Carolina State University, USA, 2002–03; a participant in the Democracy and Diversity Summer Institute, Cape Town, South Africa, 2002; and a Laureate in Democratization and Electoral Process at the Institute of Governance, Council of Development for Social Science Research in Africa (CODESRIA), Dakar, Senegal, 2001. His research interest covers democratization, elections and the electoral process; political parties; grassroots/local governance.

*W. Alade Fawole*, Associate Professor of International Relations at the Obafemi Awolowo University, Ile-Ife, Nigeria, holds a PhD in Political Science from the George Washington University, Washington, DC, USA. His areas of research interest are: African politics and development; Nigerian politics and foreign policy; democratization in Africa; conflict mediation in Africa. He was visiting senior lecturer in Political Science, University of Ibadan, Nigeria, 1998–99; visiting fellow, African Studies Centre, Leiden, the Netherlands, 2000; and resource person, CODESRIA Institute of Governance, Dakar, Senegal, August 2001. His recent publications include: *Beyond the Transition to Civil Rule: Consolidating Democracy in Post-Military Nigeria* (editor, 2001); *Military Power and Third-Party Conflict Mediation in West Africa: The Liberia and Sierra Leone Case Studies* (Research Monograph, 2001); *Nigeria's External Relations and Foreign Policy under Military Rule, 1966–1999* (2003); *Understanding Nigeria's Foreign Policy under Civilian Rule Since 1999: Institutions, Structures, Processes and Performance* (Monograph, 2004).

*Joachim Emmanuel Goma-Thethet* is Professor of Contemporary History in the Department of History of the Faculty of Letters and Human Sciences at the Université Marien Ngouabi of Brazzaville in Congo. He is a specialist on the ongoing history of Africa, particularly pan-Africanism. He successfully defended his thesis in France in 1984, entitled *L'idée de nation africaine chez les leaders panafricains de la Première Guerre Mondiale à la naissance de l'OUA*. He is conducting a research project on human rights in Central Africa from the First World War to the 1990s.

*Tukumbi Lumumba-Kasongo* is Professor of Political Science at Wells College; visiting scholar, Department of City and Regional Planning, Cornell University; visiting research fellow, Center for the Study of International Cooperation in Education (CICE), Hiroshima University, Japan; co-founder and director of CEPARRED; and a research associate at the Institut d'Ethno-Sociologie, University of Cocody, Côte d'Ivoire. He has published extensively on democracy and political change in Africa, international relations, social movements, higher education and politics in Africa, and world politics. His books include: *The Dynamics of Economic and Political Relations between Africa and Foreign Powers: A Study in International Relations* (1999); *Rise of Multipartyism and Democracy in the Global Context: The Case of Africa* (1998); *Political Re-mapping of Africa: Transnational Ideology and the Re-definition of Africa in World Politics* (1994). He is the editor of *African and Asian Studies* (journal) and co-editor of *International Studies in Sociology* and *Social Anthropology* (books). His forthcoming book is entitled: *Who and What Govern in the World of the States?: A Comparative Study of Constitutions, Citizenry, Power, and Ideology in Contemporary Politics*. He is also the vice-president of the African Association of Political Science, representing the Central African region.

*Beatrice N. Onsarigo* teaches in the Department of Sociology at Egerton University, Njoro, Kenya. She participated as a laureate at the CODESRIA Institute of Governance, Dakar, Senegal, August 2001.

*Aimé Samuel Saba*, from the Central Africa Republic (CAR), has studied Environmental Sciences and Sociology and is working towards his doctorate in these fields. He is a lecturer at the University of Bangui where he is also working on qualitative methods in social and environmental sciences. He has conducted many studies on the socio-economic impact of HIV/AIDS on children. He is also interested in external and internal migration in Africa, especially the problems of population movements as they are related to the environment. Currently, he is the Chief of Staff of the African Agency of Environmental and Social Research.

*Rachid Tlemçani* is Professor of International Politics at the University of Algiers. He has been a visiting scholar at Georgetown University, the European Institute University (Florence), and Harvard University. He has published extensively on Algeria, namely *State and Revolution in Algeria* (1986), *État, Bazar et Globalisation* (1999), *Elections et Elites en Algérie* (2003) and an entry in *Dictionnaire du vote* (2001). He has also published on world politics in *MERIP, Middle East Quarterly* and *Etudes Internationales* as well as in the Algerian newspapers, especially *El Watan* and *Le Matin.*

# Preface

Who wins or loses the presidential, legislative, local, regional and national elections in Africa? What factors and conditions influence the electoral decisions, the behaviour of the candidates and the process of producing the elected officials? What are the social significance and policy implications of the elections for the majority of the African people?

Based on international activism for human rights, judicial activism, the magnitude of the demand for democracy, some successful cases in presidential and legislative elections in Africa, and people's expectations about what democracy should do to improve their social and economic conditions, some people believe that Africa is now in a transition towards liberal democracy. Others argue that the full realization of this democracy depends on the quality of the democratic processes that have been created. These processes include the establishment of independent national electoral commissions; rules governing voting, nomination of candidates, the nature of competition among the candidates, and political parties; and the general level of political education. Thus, the underlying question behind the arguments advanced in this book and the analytical preoccupation of the authors is: Do democracy and democratic process matter, as currently practised by the African state structures and people, and are they reflected in the economic, social and cultural conditions of the African struggle for progress?

This book is a collection of research projects, more or less empirical, that were developed out of the work of the Governance Institute 2001 of the Council of Development for Social Research in Africa (CODESRIA) on the topic 'Democracy and Democratic Process in Africa'. The authors focus on the practices of democracy, the values that they represent in each specific case, the meaning and implications of such practices in the policy arena, and the issues of whether these practices and values may pave the road to social progress. All the authors are African scholars who want to see social progress happen on the continent. They are teachers and researchers in their respective institutions of higher learning. The studies in this collection challenge both tourist-knowledge paradigms and the assumptions related to the plantation mentality of some Africanists who use their research data for purposes other than those of African development. The authors are not armchair scholars; they are actors-participants in their own social contexts. That does not mean that their perceptions and definitions cannot be scientifically challenged. It means only that, for the most part, their perceptions and definitions are strongly rooted in, and conditioned by, a commitment to seeing things as structurally different for the betterment of the African people.

What has been studied in this collection? How did we produce the articles included in this book? In August 2002, Professor Adebayo Olukoshi, the executive secretary, and Professor Jean-Bernard Ouedraogo, the deputy executive secretary of CODESRIA, asked me to review and edit the research papers that were produced and presented by the laureates and the resource persons for the Governance Institute 2001. They also asked me to write my own contribution for the work of the Institute. I enthusiastically accepted this work after discussing my perspectives with them and because of the importance of the subject matter, namely, democracy and the democratic process in the struggles of the African people to liberate themselves from poverty, social and gender inequality, new imperialist forces embodied in liberal globalization and militarization. Their main objective was to see whether these papers could be recommended, upon their revisions, for publication in the CODESRIA book series or in *Africa Development*. Thus, the process of reviewing the papers started in September 2002 and ended in January 2003. Some authors with a high level of enthusiasm revised their manuscripts two or more times, depending on the nature of what needed to be done. Although I did not impose the development of a single analytical methodology on the authors, I worked to ensure that the whole project developed some common theoretical elements and a broader intellectual framework.

On 24 May 2004, I was contacted by Dr Francis Nyamnjoh, the Head of Publications and Communication at CODESRIA, who enthusiastically informed me that the project on 'Democracy and Democratic Process' was scheduled for publication in a new series: Africa in the New Millennium, a co-publication initiative by CODESRIA and Zed Books in the United Kingdom. Dr Nyamnjoh explained further that 'The series targets sound scholarship by distinguished scholars.' The authors are delighted to be part of this new series. The four chapters written in French, concerning Algeria, Cameroon, Central African Republic (CAR) and Congo-Brazzaville, were translated into English by CODESRIA. All the articles were updated, and in some cases revised, based on the new guidelines.

Since January 2003, when we finalized the first version, the African political landscape in many countries has not significantly changed. However, the political situation has not been static either. Electoral process continues its course, producing more or less predictable outcomes. In 2004 in Algeria, Abdelaziz Bouteflika was re-elected president in relatively peaceful

xi

conditions, and in South Africa, Thabo Mbeki was also re-elected for the second and final term as president without any disruption. In the Sudan, the war has intensified between the freedom fighters and the government; since February 2003, the Sudanese government and its allied Arab militias have waged a brutal war against the so-called 'rebel insurgency and innocent people in Darfur', destroying villages, raping girls and women, and causing one of the worst humanitarian crises in Africa with massive displacement of the people towards Chad. The northern and southern parts of Uganda continue to fight Museveni's military dictatorial management (totalitarian approach) of the country. In the Democratic Republic of Congo, a 'giant' and fragile transitional government composed of a president and four vice-presidents, former rebel chiefs and their clients was established; and this government was set up to start the process of building political institutions which should pave the road to the presidential and legislative elections in 2005. However, the war has not ended in the country. Political intrigues among the lumpen-intellectuals, leaders of militia groups, and the neighbouring countries continue to weaken possibilities for any serious institutional building to take place in the country.

There are some tendencies towards reversals or setbacks: for instance, President Gnassingbe Eyadema (then sixty-seven) in early January 2003 in Togo succeeded in amending Article 59 of the constitution on the term limit of the elected president from 'five years renewable once' to 'five years renewable', which poses worrisome and serious problems related to the nature of the democratic process (electoral management and organization; candidacy declarations; the role of money, military and civil society), as examined by each author in this book. Nevertheless, if one uses elections as the single most important factor for determining democratic expression, then, in 2003, African countries could no longer be singled out as undemocratic when compared to their behaviour and the state structures that existed in the 1970s and 1980s. It should be noted, however, that even in the 1970s and 1980s, there were periodical presidential and legislative elections organized within the framework and structures of the one-party state in Algeria, Côte d'Ivoire, Egypt, Nigeria, Togo, Zaïre (the Democratic Republic of Congo), to cite only a few countries. What makes the current elections different from those that took place during the Cold War era or between the Second World War and the independence years? The international context, the local dynamics, especially the people's struggles for democracy, and the global challenges to the content of what democracy is help to identify some major differences between what is taking place currently and what occurred in the past.

'Democracy and the Democratic Process', the theme of the 2001 Institute of Governance, has become one of the most popular topics in Africa since the rise of multi-partyism in the early 1990s. As articulated in this book, the debate on what democracy is, how it is produced, and what it can do for citizens in Africa has taken different forms, which in most cases depend on the social-class basis of the forces involved. This debate is important for understanding the nature of African democratic values and their policy implications. I articulate in general terms that the popularity of democracy and its processes in Africa is partly due to the fact that the majority of people believe and expect that, if effectively and correctly used, democracy can produce good and responsible leadership. 'Good' leadership is leadership that exercises power properly and legally on people's behalf in the process of formulating policies needed to solve the immense social problems of Africa.

The chapters in this book are the products of individual research projects of young scholars and resource persons (most of whom are generally senior scholars in social sciences) who were selected to participate in the Institute of Governance 2001. It should be noted, however, that 'democracy' as articulated in this project at large and in specific research projects (case studies) is about understanding how various dimensions of liberal democracy have been working in Africa.

Based on my participation in the 2002 Institute, both in selecting the laureates and teaching in the programme, it can be generalized that the laureates who participate in these institutes are selected mainly on the quality of their research proposals and their pertinence to the main theme of the Institute. These proposals are generally evaluated on the basis of their originality, the clarity of their methodologies, the regional and gender representation, the coherence and consistency of their arguments and hypotheses, and the feasibility of their projects. How does an individual, specific project fit into the logic and assumptions of the main theme? Some of these issues are addressed by the director of the Institute in collaboration with the executive secretary and the deputy executive secretary and the Scientific Committee.

With the exceptions of Chapters 1 and 2, each chapter in this book is a distinct empirical research project that raises specific methodological issues. In fact, each chapter is a case study with its own particularities and historical and social context. At the same time, however, one of the objectives of the Institute is to generate a critical comparative study in which the laureates can learn from one another. Out of this comparative analysis, some generalizations have been made to explain the nature of political behaviour in Africa. These case studies were built on strong local observations supported by solid theoretical interpretations. Some of the common sub-topics related to democracy and democratic process, which were identified and discussed by the authors include: the issues of corruption of leadership; its authoritarian behaviour within the ruling parties; the involvement of militarism in elections; the role of opposition parties and ethnicity in social and political mobilization; the nature of the relationships among the constitutional commissions, the ruling parties and the behaviour of the incumbent presidents; the quality of political alliances within and among various political parties; and the quality of the people's participation. What is interesting is that each author makes a contribution towards differentiating between what democracy and democratic process *are* and what they have not been or what they are not in Africa. That is to say, another perspective of understanding and appreciating democracy and democratic process in Africa is to analyse the lack of democracy and democratic process and the existence of weak political opposition and institutions in Africa.

In Chapter 1, Tukumbi Lumumba-Kasongo introduces and discusses theoretical and conceptual issues related to how liberal democracy is defined by the realist school of thought. The issue concerning the relevance of liberal democracy in weak African social and economic conditions is also examined. The major question behind the theoretical mapping of liberal democracy is: Why is it that liberal democracy and its processes have not effectively and productively expanded in most African countries?

In Chapter 2, 'Reflections on the question of political transition in Africa: the police state', Rachid Tlemçani examines the behaviour of African states, parties and citizens at large within the intellectual framework of an emerging new sub-field in political science in the United States, namely, comparative democratization. While the third wave of democratization was flourishing in South America in the 1980s, authoritarian regimes were still consolidating their power in African and Arab countries. It is only since the collapse of the Berlin Wall and the Soviet Union that a new wave of political pluralism has emerged in the African and Arab world. Furthermore, the author analyses the nature of the crisis of the African state, which is manifested in ethnic violence, refugee problems, illiteracy and HIV/AIDS. He also discusses how the electoral process is directly affected in the African and Arab world by inefficiency and lack of transparency of functioning of the administrative and political apparatuses of the state in delivering services to the public. Further, he uses the case of Algeria to examine the role of the military in the national liberation movement and after independence from a historical perspective. *L'état sécuritaire*, the original French sub-topic, is characterized by three essential elements in the African and Arab world, namely, a state of emergency, the privatization of national patrimony and a high level of corruption.

Chapter 3 is 'An explanation of electoral attitudes in Cameroon 1990–92: towards a new appraisal'. It should be mentioned that very few empirical studies have been conducted on Cameroon that examine the attitudes of voters in relation to the objectives of their political parties. Using various theoretical frameworks and different explanatory models of the electoral behaviour developed by sociologists and political scientists, Joseph-Marie Zambo Belinga examines how ethnicity has been instrumentalized historically since the time of colonization based on its anthropological and sociological perspectives, which limited political behaviour (voting) to ethnic imperatives. He also touches on some epistemological questions related to the sociological significance of ethnicity. What really is ethnicity? Challenging and also clarifying the classical affirmation of the existence of a positive relationship between the vote and ethnicity, the study focuses on the voting patterns in major parties in specific regions of Cameroon during the legislative and presidential elections of 1992. The findings of the study tend to support the hypothesis that the vote is influenced by numerous factors and ethnicity is only one among different key variables.

In Chapter 4, Beatrice N. Onsarigo examines 'Factors influencing women's participation in democratization and electoral processes in Kenya: a case study of Gusii women'. She has explored and analysed the factors influencing women's participation in democratization and the electoral process in Kenya at large since Kenya gained its political independence from the United Kingdom in 1963. This is an empirical study analysed from historical and sociological perspectives. The author examines specifically how political parties, the politics of money and a culture of violence have influenced the electoral process and had a negative impact on women's participation in democratization. Although the author has drawn a significant amount of information from the general history of colonial and post-colonial politics in Kenya, the core of this study focuses on Gusii women (1992 and 1997). Women are the majority in Kenya, yet their representation in the parliament has been very limited. Women's rights, which are part of human rights, have been abused in Kenya due to the history of cultural bias and the nature of the Kenyan state. However, the author shows that Kenya's politics are not static. In 1997, two women ran for the presidency. One key issue the author analyses is the influence of money in determining the outcome of elections. She established a clear relationship between having access to the financial resources and the electoral process in Kenya. The study revealed that in Kenya economic empowerment is a prerequisite to political participation and leadership.

Chapter 5 concerns 'Alliances in the political and electoral process in the Republic of Congo 1991–97'. It deals with the processes and mechanisms used to produce political coalition with the main objective of obtaining and controlling state power. Using three major political parties as illustrations, namely, le Parti Congolais du Travail (PCT) of Dénis Sassou-Nguesso, l'Union Panafricaine pour la Démocratie Sociale (UPADS) of Pascal Lissouba, and le Mouvement Congolais pour la Démocratie et le Développement Intégral (MCDDI) of Bernard Kolélas, Joachim E. Goma-Thethet examines political alliances historically and shows how they were articulated in France as well as in Congo-Brazzaville (1945–63) prior to the new movement of alliance-formation in the 1990s. The study indicates how ethnic factors and regional consciousness firmly became the tools of this movement. The role of ideology in this alliance was weak and was not a determining factor in the struggle for power.

In Chapter 6, 'The electoral process and the 2000 general elections in Ghana', Emmanuel Debrah shows how popular the practice of liberal democracy has become in many parts of Africa. He also takes a historical approach to identify how liberal democracy has been defined by various political parties in Ghana, and argues that Jerry Rawlings and his party made a political mockery of liberal democracy in that the electoral process was full of intrigue, manipulations and irregularities. It was with the intended objective of staying in power that Rawlings outmanoeuvred the opposition. The author also examines how Rawlings and the NDC underestimated the strength and potency of the opposition. He develops the argument that in Ghana by 2000, the initial burst of popular enthusiasm ignited by the flame of democratization in 1992 had given way to widespread disillusionment. Thus, what is interesting is that the outcome of the presidential elections was not predicted through the high level of manipulations and corruption promoted by the ruling party.

Chapter 7, 'Voting without choosing: interrogating the crisis of "electoral democracy" in Nigeria', W. Alade Fawole analyses the nature of the electoral process in Nigeria since independence. Using the political theory analysis of the Hobbesian state, the author argues that for the past forty years Nigerians have been 'regularly called out, through intimidation, blackmail, bribery and even deployment of threats and occasional use of state terror, to participate *en masse* in the electoral ritual of voting for contestants for state power without actually choosing or determining who the winners and losers are. The vast majority of the Nigerian electorate do not really exercise the power of choice since they are often coerced, intimidated or blackmailed into merely confirming the candidates for office that had been pre-selected for them.' The electoral process in Nigeria has been defined as an essentially fraudulent exercise. Most of the Nigerian people during the First and Second Republics did not believe in the effective functioning of liberal democracy. The author analyses the nature of the crisis of liberal democracy and its social policy implications in Nigeria as reflected in the electoral process, including the role of the national electoral commission, the nomination of candidates and the voting process. In most cases, the outcomes of the elections are known in advance. The author concludes: 'One inescapable conclusion from the preceding analysis is that the generality of Nigerians do not actively participate in the actual choice of those who rule them. Taking part in the charade of elections is only a façade that disguises popular dis-empowerment of a more invidious type.'

In Chapter 8, 'The electoral process in the Central African Republic in 1993 and 1999: protagonists and challenges', Aimé Samuel Saba locates his analysis of the electoral process within the context of the nature of the history of colonial state formation in Africa. He deals historically with the methods of the French colonization and the evolution of politics. He examines issues such as ethnicity, the army, personality politics, the charismatic dimensions of political leaders, the types of regimes, how the country became an empire with Bokassa as emperor, the adoption of structural adjustment programmes, and electoral behaviour. He shows that the elections, which took place in the so-called democratic era, never respected the rules of the game of democracy. As in the case of Nigeria, irregularities, fraud and manipulation have become rooted in the electoral process. In the Central African Republic today, only those who have raw power win or rule.

In the Conclusion, Chapter 9, Tukumbi Lumumba-Kasongo identifies common characteristics, similarities and trends within various aspects of the democratic process in Africa. Why is it that the democratic process has been essentially dysfunctional in the cases examined in this book? The answer has to come partly from the nature of the political economy of democracy and the democratic process itself, and that of the African political culture.

In this book, which can be characterized as a veritable political mapping of the ideas and thoughts enveloped in optimism and scepticism related to the functioning of democracy and democratic process, the authors challenge the common assumptions and nearly universal views about liberal democracy and its various processes in Africa.

*Tukumbi Lumumba-Kasongo*

To all the African people who are struggling to establish a real democracy as a social tool for articulating a progressive functioning society for all.

# 1 | The problematics of liberal democracy and democratic process: lessons for deconstructing and building African democracies

TUKUMBI LUMUMBA-KASONGO

## Introduction: objectives and issues

Africans are seeking democracy as a matter of survival; they believe that there are no alternatives to this quest, that they have nothing to lose and a great deal to gain. This awareness has grown in recent years, as it has become more and more obvious that neither the indigenous political elites nor the multilateral development agencies are capable of dealing with the African crisis. Insofar as the democracy movement in Africa gets its impetus from the social and economic aspirations of people in Africa yearning for 'a second independence from their leaders,' it will be markedly different from liberal democracy. In all probability, it will emphasize concrete economic and social rights rather than abstract political rights; it will insist on the democratization of economic opportunities, the social betterment of the people, a strong welfare system. (Ake 1996: 139)

We cannot deconstruct a system that we do not know or understand. The political system that has been adopted in most parts of Africa since the early 1990s is that fragment of liberal democracy known as multi-partyism. Therefore, deconstruction will be of liberal democracy as it has been experienced in Africa. This book examines both practical and theoretical interpretations of liberal democracy in order to critique this theory and explore what we can learn during this transitional period.

There is a widely held conviction that democracy can produce the best social systems, ruling classes, citizenry, social and gender relationships and governing systems as reflected by their decision-making processes. The assumption behind this reasoning is sociologically controversial because it perceives democracy as normatively good. As is shown in this chapter, the above philosophical meanings of democracy have been historically constrained and contradicted by the power of the state. The relevant question is, what kind of democracy can embody the above characteristics of the best system in Africa?

Given the fact that by 2004 most African states have adopted liberal democracy as their system of governance, my first objective is to clarify theoretically the issues raised in the case studies analysed in this book. For this purpose, I examine theoretically and conceptually the major philosophical assumptions of liberal democracy, identify elements associated with its various processes and discuss its dominant social and political characteristics.

Another related objective is to critique liberal democracy from a historical-structural perspective focusing on why a social phenomenon behaves and reproduces itself the way it does. Using the theory of liberal democracy as a causal explanatory theory (science) as well as an ideological phenomenon (value system) which relates and shapes science in a dynamic manner, I have argued that science and ideology are complementary tools to be used to understand the nature of the relationship between the state and society.

The first part of this chapter deals with the theory of liberal democracy and the second is a reflective discussion of some specific problems related to liberal democracy as reflected in the African conditions. It synthesizes and clarifies thoughts, ideas and issues about democracy and the democratic process written in the form of a critical essay.

The following intellectual guidelines include: What is liberal democracy? What social values does it articulate at large? What are the processes that produce this democracy? What role do citizens, as voters and consumers, play in this democracy? All these questions lead to the main questions, which are: What kind of liberal democracy has been adopted in Africa? How does it function organizationally, legally and behaviourally? How can it be an effective social process? What kind of democracy can be socially and economically progressive, philosophically and ideologically relevant, and technologically appropriate in Africa? How can such a democracy be produced?

It is argued that no contemporary nation-state, individual or social class has a monopoly over democracy and that democracy and its processes are historically and socially learning processes or cognitive human experiences. Democracy can be practised if a people have a relatively high level of social consciousness about their social conditions. It is correct to generalize that after the collapse of the Soviet Union the majority of the world perceived democracy as an instrument of social progress. Yet why is it that liberal democracy has produced some positive social, economic and political effects in some regions but not others? How can these successes and failures be measured? Do the processes that produce or sustain democracy matter in terms of their impact in a given society?

Deconstructing and reconstructing democracy in Africa are both historical and philosophical processes. This is a reflective exercise with both paradigmatic and policy assumptions and implications. Research and change are the main foci of this essay, a reflective work in that it critiques liberal democracy philosophically and socially while exploring the possibility of inventing an alternative. Democratic processes are not natural as they embody social forces and ideological purposes with concrete objectives about what kind of society is to be built for the people involved. Who are the agents of these processes? How do they operate and what instruments do they use to promote these processes? What are the philosophical assumptions behind this democracy in terms of its main normative values such as justice, freedom, and social and gender equity and equality?

The study of deconstructing democracy in Africa must be framed with the logic of the broader ideological foundation of the power struggles that have shaped and characterized African politics for more than forty years. In 1995, CODESRIA published a major work in which this author participated, *African Studies in Social Movements and Democracy*, which examined various cases of the struggle for democracy that took place in Africa between the 1970s and 1990s. This study is an important reference work in the process of deconstructing the current structures of the African states and societies.

The polarization of the world by the ideological, military and power struggles between the Soviet Union and the United States did not contribute to the development of liberal democracy in Africa. On the contrary, these struggles inhibited possibilities for the rise and expansion of both centralized democracy and liberal democracy models by controlling the agencies of social change, including the people, their history and their culture, in the name of state ideology and security. In most situations in Africa, these models were used predominantly as the instruments of control and manipulation. In most cases during the Cold War era, state apparatuses, especially ruling political parties and executive branches of government, essentially served as national intelligence agencies for the superpowers to investigate, recruit and intimidate progressive forces and halt their agendas.

This polarization contributed to the establishment of the most notorious dictators in Africa, including Idi Amin of Uganda, Joseph-Désiré Mobutu of the Democratic Republic of Congo, Macias Nguema of Equatorial Guinea and Gnassingbe Eyadema of Togo. Both social and political rights, which are the foundation of democracy, were limited and constrained by the dicta of the dominant ideologies. The international conflict created a non-democratic world, especially in the southern hemisphere, heavily armed and policed by the United States and the Soviet Union.

As of the end of 2002, electoral democracies existed in more than 180 countries. In the 1970s, one-party regimes and military dictatorships, supported by multinational corporations including the World Bank and the International Monetary Fund (IMF), the United States and the Soviet Union, held power over Africa, South America, Asia and Eastern Europe.

In Africa, since the presidential elections in Benin where Mathieu Kérékou was defeated and replaced by Nicéphore Soglo in 1991, new electoral democracies have produced new presidents and parliaments. The emerging trend in electoral democracies is reflected in the role of coalitions in the democratic process. The formation of coalitions or the alliances with opposition parties is having some success in winning presidential and legislative elections by defeating the old ruling parties in Ghana, Kenya and Senegal, despite resistance by the state apparatuses and ruling parties. In Mali in the 2002 elections, the transition was smoother than anticipated with the election of General Amadou Toumani Touré, former head of state, as president, as in Benin with the re-election of Mathieu Kérékou in 1996 and 2001. The re-election of Thabo Mbeki as president in April 2004 is a testimony to the consolidation of democracy in South Africa.

Despite its shortcomings as an ideological rather than pragmatic phenomenon, coalition-building is seen by Africans and African analysts as an encouraging sign in the transfer of state power. Coalition-building has contributed to avoiding violent power struggles in countries where it has been used effectively. It also embodies elements of newness and inspiration, which are expected to be part of liberal democracy. Not only have the claims of this democracy become global, but democracy itself is being perceived as a global value. For many people in developing countries, democracy is the saviour. It is defined either as a dimension of development or a force complementary to development. As Claude Ake wrote:

> Democracy requires even development, otherwise it cannot give equal opportunities to all, it cannot incorporate all to articulate their interests to negotiate them. It cannot produce a political community in which all are able to enjoy rights, nor avoid compromising justice because it takes the development of consciousness and capabilities to seek and enjoy justice. That is why development, especially even development in this broad sense, is an integral part of the process of democratization. (Ake 1992: 50)

At the same time, many lumpen-intellectuals and lumpen-proletarians have used foreign-sponsored arms against regimes in their countries in the name of liberal democracy. Both in Côte d'Ivoire and the DRC the so-called rebels have used liberal democracy, human rights and constitutional arguments to challenge regimes that kill civilians and cause massive destruction of fragile social infrastructures.

Liberal democracy has had massive support among various groups in

Africa since the 1990s and there are high expectations about what it can produce for society. In most cases, these expectations have taken the form of almost magic solutions to poverty, political instability, vicious power struggles and internal and sub-regional wars.

Nevertheless, there is a paradox between what is expected of liberal democracy and its implications for social and economic conditions in Africa. While Africa is adopting liberal democracy as the most promising formula for unleashing individual energy and generating political participation, African social and economic conditions are worsening.

Despite the historical and cultural particularities, and the extreme exploitative role characterized as marginalization in international political economy, Africa will not be able to progress collectively and sustain its progress without some kind of democracy. One of the factors that has significantly contributed to the lack of social progress in Africa is not that it is too marginalized in international relations, commerce, trade, financial capital and technology, but that it is too highly integrated into the global economy and is thus too open to the vagaries of the capitalist economy. The nature of Africa's integration and its openness are among the most important reasons for the underdevelopment of the continent. Thus, the logical consequence of my reasoning is that Africans should invent their own form of democracy as a means for social progress. The question is, what kind of democracy can best serve as a tool of social mobilization and social participation?

The post-depression and post-Second World War eras in Africa represented new trends in the nature of the relationship between the colonial powers with their 'liberal democracy' and the efforts of their colonized subjects to advance the decolonization process. I characterize this period as the second effective colonization period. Boundaries, which had been shifting since the Berlin Conference of October 1884 and January 1885 as a result of new deals or negotiations between the European powers, became more clearly defined in West Africa, the Great Lakes region, and Eastern and Southern Africa. In North Africa the question of Western Sahara became a central issue in the redefinition of Morocco. This redefinition was based on the exploitation of raw materials for European industries and their markets. Furthermore, as a result of contradictions related to war, including the psychological disposition of Africans who fought and died to defend Europe, new knowledge gained by the conditions of war contributed to the acceleration of various struggles of political independence. The spirit related to the liberation of Europe from Nazism and fascism is directly linked to the dynamics of decolonization that occurred in Africa.

Additionally, the rise and the activism of leftist movements in Europe,

5

especially the expansion of International Socialism, created possibilities for new social and ideological alliances to take place in metropolitan Europe, with implications for its colonies. This is how someone like Félix Houphouët-Boigny of Côte d'Ivoire formed an alliance with the French Communist Party after the formation of the Rassemblement Démocratique Africain (RDA). The demand for democracy in Europe by the working classes supported the decolonization movements in Africa. The colonial state was no longer perceived as 'immortal', even in the case of Belgium, which thought otherwise in its historically anomalous attempt permanently to isolate the Belgian Congo from other European colonial experiences. Thus, colonial state reforms, which took various forms with local elections in the British and French colonies, fostered new political and social negotiations that would redefine colonial politics in Africa. A key element here is the projection of electoral democracy as part of the decolonization process. The question is, did this electoral process imply or signify the practical existence of democratic norms and values? Between the post-Second World War era in the 1940s and the collapse of the Soviet Union in the early 1990s, many different social groups systematically engaged in various struggles for political independence in Africa. The wars of liberation, popular movements and class-based power struggles took place in most parts of Africa with the main objective of obtaining state power by any means.

I will not elaborate on the normative assessment of what liberal democracy and its processes ought to be. Various social classes have differing expectations concerning what they think liberal democracy should do. The general discussion on the significance of liberal democracy has to take into account the social-class base of its advocates. Do African peasants, farmers, petit-bourgeois intellectuals and organic intellectuals all have the same concept of liberal democracy and its policy implications? Does liberal democracy effectively operate the same way among various social classes, regardless of the social status of the people involved?

## Liberal democracy and democratic process: a general perspective

*General principles of liberal democracy within the framework of the realist school of thought* One can conceptualize liberal democracy from idealist or realist perspectives and reach relatively the same conclusions. Liberal democracy has become an almost magic word among various social groups around the world, including Africa. Is there any conceptual consensus concerning its definition and usage? In this section, I define liberal democracy in its classical sense, identifying its major characteristics. The main objective is to interpret liberal democracy theoretically in order to understand the case studies analysed in this book.

6

In the West, the realist school of thought providing the framework for this section has been dominant in analysing state formation and international relations since the Second World War. Liberal democracy as adopted in Africa was produced partially as a part of the state-centric reforms and agenda.

It should be emphasized that liberal democracy is primarily the product of western political thought and the evolution of western societies through the bourgeois and technological revolutions in England, France and the United States. However, liberal democracy is not the monopoly of western society as struggles outside the West have shaped its content and contributed to its redefinition. Thus, it is argued that if certain social and education conditions are met in accordance with people's vision, political organization and level of social progress, it can be redefined by people according to their norms and exigencies. The maturity of the state and the level of social and economic conditions have been determining factors in the development and functioning of liberal democracy. Western political thought has been influenced by the Hobbesian state-of-nature perspective, theories of anarchism and libertarianism, and by the Hegelian divine foundation of statehood.

One of the main differences between the realists and idealists in political science is that realists tend to define the world mainly in a state-centric paradigm while idealists perceive multiplicity and diversity as being essential to the development of equilibrium in both society and state. Idealists argue that there are other actors that should equally participate in the management of world politics. Also called power-politics theory, the realist school of thought, as reflected in the works of Thucydides, Thomas Hobbes, Niccolò Machiavelli, G. W. F. Hegel, E. H. Carr, Hans Morgenthau and Henry Kissinger, is essentially state-centric. States are fundamentally self-interested and competitive phenomena (Newman 1996: 17).

As an irreducible element in international politics, the underlying condition for state development is conflict. In international relations, state expansionism is the motive for the interactions among nations. It is in the name of 'national interest' that states interact. In theory, it is in the name of those interests that they also take arms against one another. These interests are defined as natural and organic. Humanity is secondary to the interests and actions of the actualization of state power. In classical western scholarship, Aristotle discussed the conditions that ought to be conducive to the 'immortality' of the state in the *polis*. In this limited democracy, the citizens' participation in the *agora* (the market, or the public place) was perceived to be the most important condition for the advancement of society and the simultaneous promotion of the 'immortality' of the state, even if women, slaves and traders were not qualified to be citizens (Lumumba-Kasongo 2000). In this tradition, the state is then perceived as a rational political entity, despite contradictions that may emerge from its actions and means. As Ann Kelleher and Laura Klein stated:

> While the state primacy perspective of the world does not define the superiority of types of systems, it does privilege a specific type of political organization: The state is viewed as the most important unit for both national and international interaction. According to those who hold this perspective, the primary political identity for all groups and individuals should be as citizens of the state of their birth or adoption. The state primacy perspective does not argue for universal similarity in cultures or centralized power between states. In fact, it gives states a tremendous amount of autonomy in deciding the nature of their realms. (Kelleher and Klein 1999: 41)

Within the concept of state primacy, realists emphasize the sovereignty of the state. No matter how it was created, the state is a self-centred entity. As David Held wrote:

> Modern liberal and liberal democratic theories have constantly sought to justify the sovereignty power of the state while at the same time justifying limits on that power. The history of this attempt since Thomas Hobbes is the history of arguments to balance might and rights, power and law, duties and rights. On the one hand, states must have a monopoly of coercive power in order to provide a secure basis on which trade, commerce, religion and family life can prosper. (Held 1993: 18)

To discuss how realists define and characterize some elements of liberal democracy, it is necessary first to describe the classifications of the functions of government as reflected in the structures of western industrial societies. Without examining the historical configurations of how a government has been created and what the social forces behind its formation were, realist scholars have defined the role of government in a 'perfect competitive society' in the following manner:

1. to protect our freedom from the enemies outside our gates
2. to preserve law and order
3. to enforce private contracts
4. to foster competitive markets
5. to undertake those few public projects like road construction, that are clearly of general value to the whole society and cannot be readily undertaken under private auspices (Franklin 1977: 47)

First, it should be noted that the concept of a 'perfect competitive society' is ahistorical, even in the United States after the great depression. Second, there is the notion of government as an entity that should function like a balance wheel through appropriate monetary and fiscal policies. This idea is important for the functioning of any government in the capitalist world as it also relates to another notion that realists, and in particular the mainstream economists, have produced government as a neutral entity and impartial institution. The executive power of the state can represent the general interest of society as a whole and hence steer capitalism in the social interest (Franklin 1977: 48). The best government should be the government that does not govern or that governs least. In the United States, for instance, the ideas of 'small government' or 'take the government off people's backs' are frequently part of the political lexicon before elections. Nevertheless, despite controversies, the United States qualifies the notion of the strong government paradigm. Contrary to the arguments related to the laissez-faire principle of realists, the United States government has significantly intervened in the mobilization of resources and sponsorship of development projects, including banking systems, since the 1940s.

As Ned Boudreau said:

> The United States, for example, this year passed what *The Economist* ( June 29–July 5 2002 issue) called 'an appalling new farm bill,' which raised subsidies to American farmers to $170 billion over ten years – a staggering rise of 80%. In Europe, the Common Agricultural Policy (CAP) shows little sign of changing any time soon. The CAP eats up 48% of the European Union's annual budget on farm subsidies. In 2002, CAP subsidies totaled $39 billion. The issue of agricultural subsidies in the industrialized North and West are so fraught that even mainstream conservative business media are predicting subsidies could and most likely will de-rail the Doha Round of negotiations for further expansion of free trade based on neo-liberal principles. (Boudreau 2002)

Without subsidies from the government, American farmers would not be able to compete with European farmers who have been until recently sup-ported by welfare states.

What are the characteristics of liberal democracy from a realist's per-spective? How does a citizen interact with the state? How should a citizen pursue his or her interests? How should his or her interests be protected within the framework of state sovereignty?

Citizens in this historical context are individuals who are legally born or naturalized in a country. They have obligations to the society in terms of respecting laws, paying taxes, and working to maintain the equilibrium of the society. They also have rights or entitlements to pursue a good life and happiness as part of the sovereignty principle of the state. From a realist perspective, these individuals are also buyers and sellers, and producers and consumers. Within the logic of the self-regulated market or the 'invisible hand' of Adam Smith, buyers and sellers are free to buy and sell whatever and whenever they want. What is important is that the quality of their goods should allow them to compete effectively. Citizens should be able to participate freely in order to sell and buy their services and to sell their labour according to their abilities.

The liberal democracy is the system of governance that, in principle, protects citizens' rights and privately-owned instruments of production (land, machinery, factory buildings, natural resources and the like). The state should produce social equilibrium. This democracy is called 'procedural democracy'. As Robert D. Grey, citing Joseph Schumpeter, stated:

> The democratic method is that institutional arrangement for arriving at decisions in which individuals acquire the power to decide by means of a competitive struggle for the people's vote (1942). Scholars who adopt this procedural, or elitist, version of democracy tend to be concerned primarily with stability of the system. Once the rules are in place, is the system able to maintain itself without experiencing outbursts of violence or becoming oligarchies? Rule of law and constitutionalism help regulate both government and citizens' activity to limit abuses of power and keep the system running. (Grey 1997: 83)

Do the people matter in this type of democracy? In general terms, people, as consumers and voters, matter. Elections should bring the political elite and the electors closer. But mass values are articulated through elitist filters, the process by which important issues are elevated from their individualistic origins to a broader local or national agenda. As Grey indicates:

> Central to procedural definitions of democracy is the free and fair competition among political parties for the power to make public decisions. This regular competition for power keeps conflicting groups from engaging in violence, much like individuals in conflict might 'settle it' through a coin toss or an arm-wrestling match rather than in a fist fight. Hence, in a procedural democracy, conflicts are legitimate and adverse to public interest. (Gray 1997: 87)

With its concern for reason, law and freedom of choice could be upheld only by recognizing the political equality of all mature individuals; this democracy limits the power of the state (Held 1993: 18). As Beetham wrote:

> Democracy is a political concept, concerning the collectively binding decision about the rules and policies of a group, association or society. It

claims that such decision-making should be, and it is realized to the extent that such decision-making actually is, subject to the control of all the collectivity considered as equals. That is to say, democracy embraces the related principles of popular control and political equality. In small-scale and simple associations, people can control collective decision-making directly through equal rights to vote on law and policy in person. In large and complex associations, they typically do so indirectly, for example through appointing representatives to act for them. (Beetham 1994: 28)

The question of whether or not liberal democracy effectively functions the way liberal theorists intend is not the object of this study. Individualism or individual rights, free choice, freedoms or civil liberties, and democratic accountability are the most important characteristics of liberal democracy. However, the ideal of liberal democracy and the practices of liberal democracy have historically presented significant contradictions, some of which are touched on in the next section.

## A democratic process

*General issues and perspectives* Julius Nyerere said:

The machinery through which a government stays close to the people and the people close to their government will differ according to the history, the demographic distribution, the traditional culture (or cultures), and the prevailing international and economic environment in which it has to operate. For democracy means much more than voting on the basis of adult suffrage every few years; it means (among other things) an attitude of tolerance, and willingness to operate with others on terms of equality. An essential ingredient of democracy is that it is based on the equality of all the people within a nation's boundary, and that all the laws of the land apply to all adults without exception. The nation's Constitution must provide methods by which the people can, without recourse to violence, control the government, which emerges in accordance with it and even specify the means for its amendment. (Nyerere 1999: 3)

The democratic process is the machinery that produces elected officials and general rules that should govern the people. It should reflect how they would like to govern themselves. No democratic process is perfect. Considered as a corrective social system, however, the democratic process should embody democratic values. Democratic cultures have considerable capacity for correcting their own failures (Dahl 1989: 180). As Dahl stated:

No solution, procedural or substantive, can guarantee that no one's interests will ever suffer in any way. Neither the democratic process nor any other feasible process for arriving at collective decisions can always, or even often, satisfy the requirement that no one should be made worse off. The important point is, however, that if the process by which these decisions are made gives equal consideration to the interests of everyone, and then though the interests of some persons were harmed the principle wouldn't be violated. (Dahl 1989: 166)

Attention must be paid to the democratic process as it relates to the origin and nature of the democratic system. From a systems analysis perspective, it is logically correct to say that the nature of the democratic process in a given country is very likely to inform the quality of democracy to be established in such a country, as Dahl appropriately argued:

In the actual world, as Advocate and Critic agree, 'democracies are never fully democratic: they invariably fall short of democratic criteria in some respects'. Yet our judgment about feasible alternatives depends in part on how well the democratic process functions in practice. A solution that would be appropriate for a country in which democracy functions barely and badly we might reasonably reject for a country where the democratic process functions well. (Dahl 1989: 177)

Democracy and democratic process are dialectically interrelated phenomena. Although they are two scientifically separate parts of a democratic society, the dynamics of one may help in understanding the other. In order to understand liberal democracy, it is imperative to understand its process. My intention is to raise general conceptual issues as tools for analysing how various dimensions of the democratic process function and how they may also fail to produce democratic behaviour in some countries. The discussion focuses briefly on some characteristics of the process and their general societal significance.

The democratic process implies a certain order in the way the rules of democracy are interpreted and implemented. In the West, democracy technically means rule by the people, of the people and for the people. Democratic process therefore also implies the way in which people set up the agencies and rules to govern themselves. It is a process through which people's interests and their willingness to be governed are reflected in the way collective decision-making is made. According to Dahl:

The process for making binding decisions includes at least two analytically distinguishable stages: setting the agenda and deciding the outcome. Setting the agenda is part of the process during which matters are selected on which decisions are to be made ... Deciding the outcome, or the decisive stage, is the period during which the process culminates in an outcome, signifying that a policy has definitely been adopted or rejected. If the first setting the agenda is the first say, the decisive stage is the last say, the moment of sovereignty with respect to the matter at hand. Until the decisive stage is completed, the process of decision-making is tentative. It may lead to discussion, agreements, even outcomes of votes; but these are all preliminary, may be overruled at the decisive stage. Decisions become binding only at the conclusion of the decisive stage. (Dahl 1989: 107)

The process implies effective participation, voting equality, enlightened understanding of the issues involved and control of the agenda as criteria for a democratic process. In this process it is assumed that each member of the society is capable of thinking and acting democratically. Fairness, respect for rules and the like will be produced by equal consideration, a doctrine that stems from the idea of intrinsic equality. This idea implies that some rights are fundamental to the existence of human life and should not be alienated by any institutions or individuals. The democratic process is, in principle, the actualization of the theory of political equality. The process must reflect citizenship (rights), competence and participation (collective decision-making) and freedom of self-determination (autonomy).

Democratic process is a process in which the primary political rights, or 'inalienable rights', are expressed through decision-making. It must promote effective participation, enlightenment and final control over the agenda. Whoever controls the agenda defines the process and also predicts its outcome.

*A critique of liberal democracy and its processes* It is argued that a critical knowledge of liberal democracy and its processes, as clearly reflected in African objective conditions, a knowledge which is inspired by the dynamics of African culture and history, can be beneficial to the African people and their leaders as they search for the chance to invent the developmental democracy and new democratic state's paradigms needed for progressive social change.

A critique of liberal democracy can be made by examining the nature of the relationships between what they ought to do in society and what they actually do. The contradictions between the theory and the practice of liberal democracy can also reveal much about the substantive issues of this democracy. One may also critique the nature and process of liberal democracy by analysing its linear historical origins, claims and values, societal projections and individualistic philosophical bases as well as the origin, nature and function of its institutions. These institutions include constitutional agencies, presidencies, parliaments, national assemblies and political parties.

Such an analysis might examine how they define and promote citizenship, rights, liberties, power and justice. What kind of society and human being has liberal democracy been articulating in Africa, both economically and politically? Although this critique is theoretically general, it should help localize the discussion of African democracies and their democratic processes within the broader context of globalized liberal democracy.

Another dimension of this critique is to discuss the theoretical weaknesses of liberal democracy within the structuralist perspectives. My main question is: Why have the elements of liberal democracy not become an integral part of African political culture despite efforts by African intellectuals and segments of the bureaucratic and technocratic structures of some African societies?

As analysed in the case studies included in this book, Africans and their political figures have been fighting, and in some cases have been forced, to adopt some values of the existing dominant western liberal democracies known as representative democracy (the United States' model) or the parliamentarian model (basically the European model). Both types of democracy have similar democratic processes but with different political meanings and expectations. Their political cultures are the reflections of how democracy was produced, the political history of struggles for independence, the role of churches and the working classes. The major issue is that neither of these two models has been fully integrated into the African social systems of governance. The current regime changes have not yet registered any significant political or cultural changes at the institutional and individual behaviour levels.

Important ideological forces such as African socialism, anarchism, libertarianism and Marxism have critiqued liberal democracy by relating it to human nature and its role in defining and defending the development of the global political economy, capitalism. Marxism has been the single most important systematic and scientific method of analysis used to understand the evolution of capitalism and its contradictions. Although politics and economics are the most interrelated subjects in the social sciences, in this section I do not expand on the critique of capitalist political economy. For further references to this question, I refer readers to some of the author's previous works, for instance, those published in *Politics Administration and Change* (vol. 34, 2000) and *African Association of Political Science, Occasional Paper Series* (vol. 5, no. 1, 2001).

In this book, the point is made that only in relation to the world political economy can one fully appreciate and understand the functioning of liberal democracy and its assumptions. Although the advocates of capitalism historically did not link it to political liberalism for centuries, in the past ten to fifteen years, especially in Africa, the free-market logic and privatization as the dominant paradigms of global capitalism have been working hand-in-hand with liberal democracy. Citizenship, defined as a right, and consumerism are interrelated identities; namely, one is a citizen in liberal democracy and a consumer in capitalism. A citizen is thus also a consumer. The vote serves as a common good or a superior interest of society. In the real world of liberal democracy and capitalism, however, the vote is a commodity that embodies individual interests. It can be sold or manipulated with a monetary value. The calculation for obtaining a vote, or selling it, in the electoral process is fully influenced by the power of money in all liberal democracies, with the extreme case being the United States.

Despite its popularity and a few success stories in some aspects, this democracy has not been functionally effective in most parts of Africa, as is shown in the articles included in this book.

One of the weaknesses of the democratic process is that it tends to minimize the influential power of an external agency in determining human behaviour. It also neglects to appreciate and to take into account the nature of the impact of the external on the collective decision-making process, an intrinsic part of governance. Yet social class, economy and geography are more determining factors for shaping human behaviour than internal disposition, reason and biology, as part of human objective conditions. Poverty, illiteracy, low social status, ethnicity, cultural dispositions and gender inequality work against the growth and development of democracy as is the case in the United States.

Another characteristic of liberal democracy is the centrality of individualism. Individual rights and values are vital to its definition of a citizen. In the United States, for instance, this dimension is perceived as a divine right. Individualism implies autonomy and, in its extreme interpretation and form, can lead to anarchism. In a moderate way, it is expressed in 'limited' government. In modern terms, it is 'Reaganomics', in the context of deregulation. In this doctrine, the human being is fully developed, free from the imperatives of the organizational structures of the state or government. As Samir Amin (1989) demonstrated, individualism is the invention of western society. Its metaphysics is linked to the struggle against nature and its constraints. The West has also developed a dualism that separates the reason/mind from the body and the corollary that freedom reflects the struggle with evil associated with the impurity and imperfection of the physical world. Despite changes mostly triggered and supported by western influences through colonization, rapid urbanization and its constraints and liberal globalization, African societies maintain a more monistic, rather

15

than dualistic or individualistic, cosmology in their definitions of what it is to be human and in their social configurations.

Although African societies are culturally, geographically and historically diverse, and colonial and neocolonial experiences have added new political and educational elements to their complexity, the metaphysics of African societies are characterized more by the principle of collective existence than that of individualism. Politically and psychologically, an individual vote has more meaning in relationship to others. Liberal democracy has been challenged in Africa when it preaches individual rights as opposed to those collective rights that are part of African value systems. Individual consciousness is emerging because of economic imperatives; however, it has not found a solid social base. Thus, despite social and economic changes, the social philosophy of interdependent coexistence is still well reflected in the African extended family system. This system is still a functioning sociological and economic unit of analysis in African social-relations and productive systems. In some villages and regions, inhabitants tend to define themselves as being related or as people with some common sociological or historical origin, reflecting an effective notion of 'global village'. From this perspective, the vote of an individual can have more meaning within an ethnic, clanic or caste-consensual affiliation than within an institutional ideological basis, if one exists. The notion of a sister, a brother or a cousin is far more elastic and broader in Africa than in the West.

Another characteristic of liberal democracy is competitiveness among the voters, candidates, parliamentarians or members of congress in articulating their public views, developing consensus, or also in having access to resources. Competition over human and material resources implies that only clever or more 'intelligent' well-informed people, more aggressive or persuasive individuals with greater political clout, are more likely to have such resources. As in the *agora* in fifth-century BCE Greece, in the liberal democracy today only those citizens or representatives who are skilled in public discourse will be listened to or heard from. There is a certain egotism associated with this dimension of liberal democracy. African systems of social coexistence, with their emphasis on the collective self, tend to discourage the development of egotism. Competition is generally perceived negatively, as a sign of vanity. Although this dimension has been changing and many social groups in Africa are defined as essentially competitive in their cultural fabric and the marketplace, competition in general is still seen as a tool of greed. As stated elsewhere:

> In some generalized terms, I would like to argue that competition that is translated as an instrument of the political market has not been well

16

adopted in the African liberal democracy because: (1) most African cultures do not honor grit and heroism of individual achievement in relationship to personal hedonism; and (2) political liberalism has not yet developed its base in the African economic liberalism. Individual showing off, admiration of personal skills, and individual intuition that are associated with competition seem not to have been consistently encouraged. In fact, in some cases competition is perceived as an enemy of social harmony. (Lumumba-Kasongo 2000: 46)

While advocates of liberal democracy may try to minimize cultural and social differences, African societies struggle to maintain their differences in historical terms. Particularism, as part of primordial systems, is perceived and defined as one of the enemies of both liberal democracy and the free-market economy. These two dogmas claim to teach universal values, which are viewed as being progressive and good in themselves. Yet particularism, viewed as a positive inspirational source, can contribute to democracy as a collective affirmation of the self.

Another issue that should be mentioned is the nature of the relationship between economic development and the adoption of liberal democracy. Scholars have expressed the view that the level of development informs the quality of liberal democracy. Robert Packenham, in discussing four premises of the United States' foreign policy and aid – (i) change and development are easy; (ii) all good things go together; (iii) radicalism and revolution are bad; and (iv) distributing power is more important than accumulating power – also emphasized this point when he stated: 'There is a positive correlation between level of economic development and the chances of democracy. More precisely, the higher the per capita GNP, the more frequent the competitive political systems and polyarchies. Often, in the approach, economic development was seen as the main requisite or cause of political democracy' (Packenham 1976: 210).

The United States believes that economic assistance should lead to 'political stability'. Stability is the capacity of state apparatuses and bureaucracies to maintain their equilibrium without major disruption. It does not necessarily include their distributive mechanisms. Why is it that the United States has not yet effectively and genuinely supported the establishment of liberal democracy outside Western Europe?

The electoral process is heavily influenced by the power of money. All the studies in this book indicate that there are direct connections between monetary contributions and election outcomes. The winners are generally the candidates who spent the most money, except in the presence of a strong coalition formed by opposition parties.

Every electoral system has regulations regarding funding. In the United States, despite some efforts to control money given to the candidates since the Federal Elections Campaign Act (FECA) of 1974, the issue of funding has not been solved. This Act and its amendments created a loophole through which money is given to political candidates (Herrnson 2000: 15). In the United States, there are two types of money that are given to the candidates, 'soft money' and 'hard money'. Soft money can come from a variety of sources, such as corporations, special clubs, individuals, families; and hard money comes from the FECA.

In a liberal democracy, especially one following the United States representative democracy, there is no such thing as a 'free lunch'. Financial contributors have interests and agendas. In the 1972 Richard Nixon re-election campaign, a donation of 1.7 million dollars was given by a group of people later rewarded with ambassadorships (Drew 1999: 47). A similar situation occurred in 1988 when certain Republicans were rewarded with ambassadorships for financially supporting the candidacy of George H. W. Bush. These were members of the Team 100 who each donated 100,000 dollars (Makinson 1992: 16). The issue becomes more complicated when monetary donations are equated with freedom of speech as granted in the First Amendment. The argument states that a monetary contribution should not be limited unless it infringes on the free speech of another citizen. In short, money is effectively used to buy representation and support special interests.

As reflected in the cases in this book, money influences election outcomes in Africa also. This is not a normative statement as to the acceptability of such practices. The main differences can be localized, for instance, at the level of the economic development of the electorates, the quality of social and political infrastructures and the maturity of state apparatuses such as the court. Notions such as choice, competition, monetary contributions, campaigns, voting processes and the organization of political parties, as used in Africa, are filtered through elements of African cultures, shaped by the level of economic underdevelopment and defined, in practical terms, by ethnicity and educational values. These values are perceived as universal, but in terms of evaluating the outcomes of democratic process, they are dysfunctional. As Claude Ake wrote:

> Even at its best, liberal democracy is inimical to the idea of people having effective decision-making power. The essence of liberal democracy is precisely the abolition of popular power and the replacement of popular sovereignty with the rule of law. As it evolved, liberal democracy got less democratic as its democratic elements, such as the consent of the gov-

erned, the accountability of power to the governed, and popular participation, came under pressure from political elites all over the world as well as from mainstream social science, which seemed even more suspicious of democracy than political elites. On the pretext of clarifying the meaning of democracy, Western social science has constantly redefined it, to the detriment of its democratic values. (Ake 1996: 130)

## Conclusion

Given the extreme level of underdevelopment and the exploitative, peripheral and parasitical nature of the role of Africa's international relations, there is a need to invent a democracy that would function as a tool of social progress. It must mobilize human and material resources, promote genuine participation, and develop theories, policy and politics of gender and social equality. Despite affirmative action in the United States, quota representation is not appreciated by most Americans as a good way of promoting the principle of equal consideration of interests.

In the area of gender equality, African women are not well represented in parliaments and national assemblies or at executive levels of political parties, making their real political participation in the decision-making process almost non-existent. Yet, if African democracies are instruments of change, we cannot tolerate the marginalization of central social forces, particularly women. The first step towards changing this unjust situation is to use quota representation (or parity) of gender at all levels until the value of equal representation is incorporated in the governance and the political culture. To guarantee its protection and minimize the chance of its abuse, this formula must be supported by constitutions. Women's demand for equal participation in Africa is a human rights and development issue. After justice has been realized in terms of political representation, the quota system can be revisited through referenda. Representative democracy, in its classical sense, fails at this because its ethos is based on extreme individualism. It is founded on a bias against the masses, the poor, women and other social groups perceived as followers and thus expected to cast their votes to legitimatize those who run for the elections. Furthermore, this democracy does not deal effectively with the question of unequal causal social relations among people and the origins of social phenomena in societies.

The above issues were also critically analysed in the presentations made by African women researchers who met in Cape Town, South Africa, in November 1999 for the African regional meeting on 'Political Restructuring and Social Transformation'. In the synthesis of their works, liberal democracy is defined as:

Liberal definition of democracy is more concerned with reason, law, and freedom of choices but overlooks the position of different social categories in the social space where power is located. Evidently, this definition ignores the fundamental premises upon which democracy is based. This conception of democracy does not take into account the historical contingencies that have limited women's chances to exercise their freedom. To the contrary, in the case of Africa, political organizations, prior to colonialism, were characterized by the existence of democratic rule even among people governed by monarchic rules in highly pyramidal political structures. Political organizations were also characterized by gender balance in formulation and implementation as well as women's participation in the political process. (Taylor 2000: 14)

The theory of liberal democracy has serious epistemological problems as a tool of analysis as well as a model for building a society. As a tool of analysis, its topologies are against history and against particularism. Yet, if critically examined, history and traditions can be used as inspirational objects in reconstructing societies. In addition, universalism projected by liberal democracy, as fully expanded by the western-supported human rights organizations, is indeed Eurocentric, despite the fact that in its evolution and development, European liberal political thought has been influenced by other cultures. Africans and other people also defended this system, militarily and culturally, as the European nation-states were collapsing during the 1930s and 1940s.

Conceptually, liberal democracy has been shaped by dualistic metaphysics that characterize western society at large. The ideals of liberal democracy have a mission of 'enlightening' or 'civilizing' the group, a duality reflected in the theory of social class. A dynamic middle class should save the civilizing society; and with the protection of property owners, this class can invent, consume and be happy, the ultimate goals of a citizen. This model of the middle class has failed in Africa but I am not discussing the factors and causes of its failures. An elite theory of liberal democracy is very much atomistic and dichotomous in its application. As Claude Ake wrote:

Africans have a communal consciousness; we do not think of ourselves as atomized in competition and potential conflict with others, but as members of an organic whole. African traditional democracy lies in a commitment to the desirability and necessity of participation as a collective enterprise. In the African tradition, participation does not merely enjoy rights, but secures tangible benefits. It entails active involvement in the process of deciding on common goals and how to realize them. (Ake 1990: 49)

Africans need to establish developmental democracy as elaborated by Olu-koshi (2002) and the developmental state (Amuwo 2003) in order to deal effectively with extreme poverty, political instability, violent power struggles and civil wars. Democracy will not be possible unless we capture the African state, bring it to the public domain, democratize it and transform it into an instrument of social progress (Lumumba-Kasongo 2002b). The author's own perspective on the kind of democracy that Olukoshi proposed can be summarized as follows:

> Democracy is not a menu prepared from the outside of a given culture. It is a political means through which social contradictions, with respect to col-lective and individual rights, should be solved at a given time and in a given society. There cannot be real democracy if a concerned society does not have any consciousness of its own contradictions, does not allow political debate, and does not outline a social practice to provide rules for the society to manage its interests and objectives with equity and justice. Democracy should be a struggle against social inequality, injustices, exploitation, and social miseries. That is to say, democracy is more than formal political pluralism or the process of producing an electoral code or an electoral commission ... Democracy is both a process and a practice that involves equal economic and social opportunities for the citizenry. It is a corrective process in which a given society, especially a formerly colonized society, is born again ... It is a ritual processing of new ideas and policies in a given society. (Lumumba-Kasongo 1998: 34)

To realize this kind of democracy, its process must be guided by the principle of equal consideration for the interests of all. This democracy is essentially social. It implies that its process should produce a social agenda rather than promote an individualistic agenda. As the author has explained elsewhere:

> We have to search for some forms of working multipartyisms and demo-cracies. In the absence of guided revolutions, a combination of politics of consensualism and consociational democracy (Lijphart 1984) can contrib-ute to the process of producing a human, productive, and a transformative multipartyism and democracy. This working multipartyism has to be constructed on a genuine premise of 'politics of compromise.' Within the existing levels of social and economic cleavages, this compromise will not be actualized until the African systems of governance provide and secure basic rights and needs for all. The sine qua non condition for a better functioning multipartyism and democracy is that the state has to provide social security, improve the standards of living, and provide advancement of

all. I have argued that African states should be recaptured and transformed so that they can be able to subsidize liberties and rights. This can be done if social protection is codified. There is a need to create a leadership that is nationalistic and understands the dynamics of the world economy and its contours. (Lumumba-Kasongo 2002a: 221–2)

In short, it is difficult for representative democracy to succeed in current African social and economic conditions. Access to basic resources is needed to promote active participation in the political process and belief in the political system. Africans must firmly establish the systems of checks and balances which would limit the chances of personalization and individualization of power, corruption, military ambition, political charlatanism and opportunistic politics. Political participation should guarantee the protection and collective security of citizens. One thing to be carefully observed and examined is whether Africa's multi-partyism contributes to opening the wounds of political intolerance and to the exaggeration of ethnic and religious differences. African democracies should be guided by principles of cultural diversity, social equality and equitable access to resources. It is only through a strong social state that alternative democratic practices can be fully articulated. As Julius Nyerere stated:

> In advocating a strong state, I am not holding a brief for either an overburdened state or a state with a bloated bureaucracy. To advocate a strong state is to advocate a state, which, among other things, has power to act on behalf of the people in accordance with their wishes. And in a market economy, with its law of the jungle, we need a state that has the capacity to intervene on behalf of the weak. No state is really strong unless its government has the full consent of at least the majority of its people; and it's difficult to envision how that consent can be obtained outside democracy. So a call for a strong state is not a call for dictatorships either. Indeed, all dictatorships are basically weak because the means they apply in governance make them inherently unstable. (Nyerere 1999: 3)

## References

Adeleye-Fayemi, B. and A. Akwi-Ogojo (eds) (1997) *Report of the First African Women's Leadership Institute* (22 February–14 March) (Kampala, Uganda).

Agyeman, O. (2001) *Africa's Persistent Vulnerable Link to Global Politics* (Jose, New York, Lincoln, Shanghai: University Press).

Ake, C. (1990) 'Democracy and Development', *West Africa*, 49 (April).

— (1992) *The New World Order: The View From the South* (Lagos, Nigeria: Malthouse Press).

— (1996) *Democracy and Development in Africa* (Washington, DC: Brookings Institution).

Amin, S. (1989) *Eurocentrism* (New York: Monthly Review Press).

Amuwo, K. (2003) 'Globalisation, NEPAD, and the Governance Question in Africa', submitted to *JEDIRAF*.

Baradat, L. P. (1994) *Political Ideologies: Their Origins and Impact*, 5th edn (Englewood Cliffs, NJ: Prentice Hall).

Barkan, D. J. (ed.) (1994) *Beyond Capitalism vs. Socialism in Kenya and Tanzania* (Boulder, CO and London: Lynne Rienner).

Beetham, D. (1994) 'Key Principles and Indices for a Democratic Audit', in D. Beetham (ed.), *Defining and Measuring Democracy* (London: Sage Publications).

Boudreau, N. (2002) 'The Coming Death of Globalization', *Znet/Global Economics Oxymorons* (December) <http://www.zmag.org>.

Dahl, R. (1971) *Polyarchy: Participation and Opposition* (New Haven, CT: Yale University Press).

— (1989) *Democracy and Its Critics* (New Haven, CT and London: Yale University Press).

Diamond, L., J. J. Linz and S. M. Lipset (1995) *Politics in Developing Countries: Comparing Experiences with Democracy* (London and Boulder, CO: Lynne Rienner).

Di Palma, G. (1990) *To Craft Democracies: An Essay on Democratic Transition* (Berkley, CA: University of California Press).

Drew, E. (1983) *Politics and Money* (New York: Macmillan).

— (1999) *The Corruption of American Politics: What Went Wrong and Why?* (NJ: Carol Publishing).

Fall, Y. (ed.) (1999) *Africa: Gender, Globalization and Resistance* (Dakar, Senegal: African Association of Women for Research and Development).

Federation of Transvaal Women (1988) *A Woman's Place is in the Struggle, Not Behind Bars!* (New York: Africa Fund).

Franklin, S. R. (1977) *American Capitalism: Two Visions* (New York: Random House).

Grey, R. D. (ed.) (1997) *Democratic Theory and Post-Communist Change* (Upper Saddle River, NJ: Prentice Hall).

Held, D. (1993) *Prospects for Democracy: North, South, East, West* (Stanford, CA: Stanford University Press).

Herrnson, P. S. (2000) *Congressional Elections: Campaining at Home and in Washington* (Washington DC: CQ Press).

Kelleher, A. and L. Klein (1999) *Global Perspectives: A Handbook for Understanding Global Issues* (Upper Saddle River, NJ: Prentice Hall).

Lijphart, A. (1984) *Democracies: Patterns of Majoritarian and Consensus Government in Twenty-One Democracies* (New Haven, CT: Yale University Press).

Lumumba-Kasongo, T. (1995) 'Social Movements and the Quest for Democracy in Liberia: The Case of the Movement for Justice in Africa (MOJA)', in M. Mamdani and Wamba-dia-Wamba (eds), *African Studies in Social Movements* (Dakar: CODESRIA), pp. 409–61.

— (1998) *The Rise of Multipartyism and Democracy in the Context of Global Change: The Case of Africa* (Westport, CT and London: Praeger).

— (2000) 'Capitalism and Liberal Democracy as Forces of Globalization with a Reference to the Paradigms Behind the Structural Adjustment Programs in Africa', *Politics and Administration and Change*, no. 34 ( July–December): 23–52.

— (2001) 'Political Parties and Ruling Governments in Sub-Saharan Africa', in R. Dibie (ed.), *The Politics and Policies of Sub-Saharan Africa* (Lanham, MD: University Press of America), pp. 133–63.

— (2002a) 'Reflections on Liberal Democracy and International Debt Issues in Post-Cold War Africa', paper presented to the 10th General Assembly of CODESRIA, 8–12 December, Kampala, Uganda.

— (2002b) 'Reconceptualizing the State as the Leading Agent of Development in the Context of Globalization in Africa', *African Journal of Political Science/ Revue Africaine de Science Politique*, vol. 7, no. 1 ( June): 79–108.

Mclellan, D. (ed.) (1971) *Karl Marx's Early Texts* (Oxford: Oxford University Press).

Makinson, L. (1992) *The Cash Constituents of Congress* (Washington, DC: Center for Responsive Politics).

Martin, G. (2002) *Africa in World Politics: A Pan-African Perspective* (New Jersey, Trenton, NJ and Asmara, Eritrea: Africa World Press).

Marx, K. (1967) *Capital*, vol. 3. ed. F. Engels (New York: International Publishers).

Newman, M. (1996) *Democracy, Sovereignty and the European Union* (New York: St Martin's Press).

Ninsin, K. A. (1985) *Political Struggles in Ghana 1967–1981* (Accra: Tornado Publishers).

Nyerere, J. (1999) 'Governance in Africa', *African Association of Political Science Newsletter*; New Series, vol. 4, no. 2 (May–August).

Nzongola-Ntalaja, G. and M. C. Lee (eds) (1997) *The State and Democracy in Africa* (Harare, Zimbabwe: African Association of Political Science).

Olukoshi, A. 'Towards Developmental Democracy', *New Agenda*, no. 5: 76–82.

Olukoshi, A. and L. Laakso (eds) (1996) *Challenges to the Nation-State in Africa* (Uppsala: Nordiska Afrikainstitutet).

Onimode, B. (ed.) (1989) *The IMF, the World Bank and the Africa Debt: The Social and Political Implications*, 2 vols (London: Zed Books).

Packenham, R. A. (1976) *Liberal America and the Third World: Political Development Ideas in Foreign Aid and Social Science* (Princeton, NJ: Princeton University Press).

Przerworski, A. (1991) *The Market: Political and Economic Reforms in Eastern Europe and Latin America* (New York: Cambridge University Press).

Rustow, D. A. (1970) 'Transitions to Democracy: Toward a Dynamic Model', *Comparative Politics*, vol. 2, no. 3: 337–63.

Schmitter, P. (1991) 'What Democracy is and is not', *Journal of Democracy*, vol. 2, no. 3: 75–88.

Schumpeter, J. (1942) *Capitalism, Socialism, and Democracy*, 2nd edn (New York: Harper).

Shlomo, A. (1968) *Karl Marx on Colonialism and Modernization: His Dispatches and Other Writings on China, Mexico, the Middle East and North Africa* (Garden City, NY: Doubleday).

Taylor, V. (2000) *Marketisation of Governance: Critical Feminist from the South* (Cape Town, South Africa: Development Alternatives with Women for a New Era).

United Nations (1995) *African Women and Leadership*, 4th World Conference on Women, Beijing, China (Addis Ababa, Ethiopia: UN Economic Commission for Africa).

Wallerstein, I. (1979) *The Capitalist World Economy* (Cambridge, Cambridge University Press).

# 2 | Reflections on the question of political transition in Africa: the police state

RACHID TLEMÇANI

Nowadays, all social and political life is governed by elections, from meetings of business partners to communal and presidential elections. In the 1970s and 1980s, a certain form of democratization, strongly encouraged by the United States, was instituted in Latin America. Following the collapse of the Berlin Wall, electoral processes were also put in place in several countries in Eastern Europe, the Middle East and Africa. The vote within multilateral institutions such as the IMF, the World Bank and the World Trade Organization (WTO) has even become a basic demand of the World Social Forum.[1]

Procedural democracy is gradually replacing other procedures for designating representatives of political, social and economic communities. Not only are elections used by all groups governed by rules and regulations, but they are also part of the deliberation procedures for enacting laws. Universal suffrage is trying to make this procedure the only means of legitimating political power. Elections have become the mechanism of choice for facilitating change or transition from authoritarian regimes to democratic regimes. They also play a crucial role in upholding the rule of law in a constitutional state. They have undoubtedly become the underpinning of democracy in most countries. Global democracy has become a reality in world business. The colonialist Victor Hugo once said in regard to a war of liberation : 'On peut résister à une armée mais jamais à une idée dont le temps est venu' (One can resist an army, but never an idea whose time has come). But is it wise to endeavour to put European democracy into full effect in Africa and in the most underdeveloped regions of the world when the process of state formation has not been achieved?

Models seeking to explain this new phenomenon vary widely, to such an extent that a new discipline termed Comparative Democratization has recently been introduced in political science departments in US universities. The principal thesis conveyed in the abundant literature on the subject, referred to as the 'democratic transition', supports the idea that authoritarian and totalitarian regimes are being replaced by democratic regimes. Political democracy is the most effective tool for changing or transforming authoritarian and totalitarian regimes.

Many competing theories are available to suggest 'how to do it'. However, very few researchers have taken the trouble to undertake an in-depth analysis of the political transition underway in several developing countries. The absurdity of equating capitalism with democracy has rarely been questioned. Triumphalism has indeed permeated theoretical reflection in the literature. This lucrative new industry has significantly contributed to changing the course of political struggles in the countries of the South. The prestigious *Journal of Democracy*, founded in 1983 by the American Congress, has contributed enormously to the abundant literature on democratic transition (Chomsky 1998). In the early 1990s, even those international and state institutions that supported the most abject dictatorships in the South suddenly developed programmes to promote democracy, human rights and good governance.[2] Ironically, the US State Department, known for its violations of human rights during the Cold War era, has suddenly become the champion of free elections in authoritarian states.[3] Many activists associated with the Third World movement for fundamental freedoms changed camps overnight to become producers of 'recipes' for promoting democracy in government and multilateral institutions (Guilhot 2001). The social question is no longer on the agenda.

The fundamental hypothesis of this school of thought, which soon came to prevail in the field, is based on the idea that peaceful political change, the rotation of elites and renewal of political staff are possible through the ballot box. Proponents of this hypothesis claim that since democratic transition has been very successful in some countries, it ought to be consolidated in all poor and developing countries by any means, including, paradoxically, the use of force. Subsequently, authoritarianism would evolve naturally into systems closely approximating those of the industrialized world. In reality, such a theory is hard to apply in Africa and in the Arab and Muslim world. It raises more problems than it can solve. We do not consider its main paradigm very relevant in terms of explaining the new socio-economic and political reality emerging in these countries. Paradoxically, political power in this region has, in some cases, become more repressive than under the old regime, in spite of the institutionalization of multi-party politics or the organization of multi-party elections. Decision-making has become less transparent than before. The political class is more concerned about organizing elections than putting in place an enabling environment for the rule of law and the fight against corruption. The current security situation at both national and regional levels does not seem to be conducive to operating a system whereby political officials are accountable before the courts and citizens for their management of national resources. Contrary to this thesis, which has been unanimously endorsed by the political establishment, we argue that a new type of state is emerging in several developing countries. Economic growth can hardly be achieved in a political setting in which the leadership is weak, such is the main assumption underpinning this theory. Furthermore, the second war against terrorism[4] has been a new stage in the formation of this state. European powers acting under the banner of the United States are also in favour of the establishment of a powerful state – not in the consensual, but in the repressive sense. For the time being, we prefer to call such a regime a 'security state', as opposed to a 'rogue state', 'outlaw state', 'pariah state' or even a 'bunker praetorian state', to borrow Henry Clement's (2001) expression. These latter expressions are used more in diplomatic parlance than in political sociology. Furthermore, they are more ideological and selective than our concept, though it needs to be refined in other case studies.

In spite of the apparent state disengagement that is taking place to the detriment of new actors, the question of the state remains central when approaching African politics. The security state is waging a war against society and people. The new intensified efforts to accommodate or to exclude certain groups from the political arena have led, in contradistinction to the main hypothesis in the literature, to state redeployment at the cost of state retreat. The state function of distributing patronage remains important since political participation is restricted by the formal mechanisms of elections. As a result, political processes are dominated by the state's agenda of intervention in the political and economic sphere as well as in the security sphere. We will focus exclusively on state redeployment in the security sphere in this chapter. This aspect has been neglected in the abundant literature about the democratic transition.

## The question of democratic transition in Africa and the Arab world

The theory of democratic transition applied to this region in fact raises more questions than it can solve. We shall succinctly list a few well-known cases that are a cause for concern and will help us examine the main features of the security state. Other case studies will, it is hoped, examine this working hypothesis more thoroughly.

Elections in Africa and the Arab countries are often characterized by boycotts by opposition parties, low voter turnout[5] and massive fraud. Vote-rigging and falsification of election results are frequent.[6] The principle of changeover of political power through 'free elections' has not yet been accepted by elites moulded in a culture of misogyny, authoritarianism and conspiracy. Multi-partyism has not developed to a stage where all political groups agree to compete with one another on a level playing field (Oliver de Sardan 2000).

Contrary to the argument advanced in the literature on democratic transition, political change is determined not by the ballot box but by coups and vote-rigging. In the final analysis, elected officials are often chosen not by citizens and the consent of the governed, but by government and 'occult' powers. They do not feel that they are accountable to their constituencies. Thus, parliament has no legislative or decision-making authority, and is a mere transmission channel for rubber-stamping.

Actors who held high the banner of totalitarianism and its excesses cannot overnight become architects of the rule of law. There is no modern-ist political will to lay the foundations of a national state and the rule of law. In the face of disorder and violence, there can be no justification for the use of force, however well organized it is. Democracy cannot be built without democrats, just as socialism could not have been built without socialists.

For many political leaders, the holding of multi-party elections is nothing but an alibi aimed at qualifying them for the benefits of 'bene-volent globalization' (Cassen and Clairmont 2001). The harmful effects of the neoliberal Washington consensus[7] on the political practices of local elites have not been studied carefully in such paradigms by the 'crossbreeds of democracy'.

New forms of praetorian power are justified with a view to ending the political impasse resulting from multi-party elections. In most cases, African armies are commanded by clans that control all the forces of law and order. Posts of responsibility within such forces are entrusted to close relatives of the supreme commander. Such a situation accounts for the political and institutional instability of the regimes in question. The political system is closely related to a network of corrupt military superiors. In sub-Saharan Africa, local conflicts have claimed more than 7 million lives. The 'rite of war' has also caused the displacement of whole populations. More than 10 mil-lion of the world's 14 million displaced persons are in Africa. According to the US State Department, 120,000 African teenagers out of a total of 300,000 worldwide are involved in various local conflicts. According to this report, published in July 2001, it is very unlikely that arms trafficking will reduce in these regions since no sanctions are imposed on arms traffickers.

Sierra Leone and Liberia are uneasily pacified after their wars. Côte d'Ivoire, West Africa's economic powerhouse, has been in a state of chaos since 19 September 2002. These three countries have overlapping and rival ethnic groups, exploited and manipulated across artificial frontiers by ruthless or reckless leaders to sequester and exploit the products of the region's natural wealth.

Since the political and humanitarian disaster of the 1994 Rwandan genocide, France has seemingly refrained from intervening militarily in Africa. After distinguishing itself as the only colonial power with military bases in Africa, it was invited to redeploy its forces in Côte d'Ivoire, apparently to quell the armed rebellion in that country. Meanwhile, President Laurent Gbagbo, who in October 2000 proclaimed himself winner of the most highly contested election in the history of his country, sought military support in Angola. The rebels, in turn, appealed for popular support in neighbouring countries. To put an end to the unrest, France decided to grant President Gbagbo military assistance 'by way of military cooperation'. Such assistance was deemed necessary to enable Gbagbo's army to redeploy nationwide. However, paradoxically, various forces that support Gbagbo perceive the French military assistance as having a dual role. It tries to pacify the government and at the same time supports, through its deliberate inaction, the rebels.

It is ostensibly very difficult to apply a western electoral model in a region where illiteracy is rising in spite of worldwide technological progress. The African continent is the only region in the world where the school attendance rate continues to drop significantly.[8] For instance, in Morocco, a country whose economy has taken off successfully, according to IMF reports, 62 per cent of the electorate during the September 2002 election was illiterate. In such a context, voters cannot understand the political programmes of candidates. A certain literacy threshold is required for European-type elections to be free and fair.

More critically, famine has substantially increased in Africa while it has decreased in other regions in the world. It is not decent to compel hungry people to put into full effect a law prepared from the outside of a given culture. Democracy should be a political struggle to cut hunger and a fight against socio-economic inequality, injustice and alienation.

The question of democracy is exacerbated by another social scourge which is eating into the fabric of African society: AIDS. This pandemic continues to claim victims in Africa whereas countries such as Brazil have succeeded in containing it. As a matter of fact, more than 70 per cent of the world's HIV-carriers are in Africa. The world pharmaceutical industry is still refusing the production of retroviral drugs in Africa. Unless the international community lends a hand, the AIDS pandemic could exterminate an entire population and lead to the so-called natural selection of humanity. Health security is therefore far more crucial than the outcome of an election, be it the most democratic. A sick population is not in a position to vote freely.

Regarding the institutional framework, political and administrative systems in African and Arab countries are incapable of functioning with even the minimum efficiency, transparency and fairness expected of a public service. The situation is therefore much more serious than is generally believed. Diplomatic make-believe and judicial or institutional shams tend to minimize the phenomenon of state decadence. States continue to deteriorate in spite of the holding of multi-party elections. The helplessness of state officials has reached such a degree that the public sector is no longer capable of disposing of refuse, whereas enormous sums are allocated for the organization of elections whose results are known in advance. There is an ever-growing disparity between the state's claim to act in all areas of the social sector and the reality of its poor performance. Is it not more salutary to sweep before one's door than to fabricate armchair strategies that take into account all parameters except the aspirations of people?

Paradoxically, political liberalization has sped up state privatization and consequently the plunder of national patrimony. For instance, the elections held in Senegal in 2000, considered as a milestone for African democracy, have had no positive impact on the socio-economic situation of the Senegalese; this is not to say that it has continued to deteriorate significantly. Such an outcome was foreseeable since state privatization was intensified perniciously while institutional mechanisms considered conducive to market economies were hastily put in place.[9] The plunder of public resources by senior state officials in collusion with foreign powers tends to be openly perpetrated on a large scale in police states. Africa's external debt currently stands at 500 billion dollars.[10] Paradoxically, the continent has lost the equivalent of its external debt as a result of capital flight. Approximately 50 per cent of local savings in Africa are deposited abroad while this capital flight does not exceed 5 per cent in Asia or 20 per cent in Latin America. If only 20 per cent of the capital lost were returned in the form of direct investment, African countries would not need the structural adjustment programmes (SAPs) of the World Bank and International Monetary Fund (IMF) and, consequently, the current socio-economic and liquidity crises would have been reduced to a great extent.

The more this phenomenon develops, the more corruption becomes ingrained in our social habits. Its spread produces a quasi 'culture of corruption' which eats into the fabric of all state institutions, both formal and informal, in the works. It is very difficult to change a country's general orientations when there is no development strategy involving all social protagonists. Procedural democracies do not permit people to influence major decisions even when new presidents, governments and members of parliaments are produced. In this type of 'karaoke democracy' the visible actors come and go, but the songs remain unchanged, selected from a very limited menu.

The tailoring of electoral models to different socio-economic and cultural realities has often yielded contested results. Thus, in some countries, 'free elections' have further exacerbated political and institutional instability. In other countries, they have simply fanned latent armed conflicts instead of alleviating them. Such new conflicts, categorized as 'low-intensity crises', have led to humanitarian military intervention, now considered an absolute necessity if genocide and ethnic cleansing are to be avoided. Most countries of the South are not perceived as stakeholders in the new security order on the horizon but rather as stakes coveted by economic and geo-strategic powers. Major financial and other interests are at stake in these 'Lame Leviathans' (Callaghy 1987: 87–116).

Strangely enough, supporters of democratic transition have not been very interested in Africa and the Arab world, as compared to Latin America and Eastern Europe. However, there exists 'an armada of experts' in those countries. One cannot talk of democratic transition success without first examining thoroughly the electoral experiences of those countries. Algeria, for instance, remains a fascinating case study for those interested in multiparty elections, electoral fraud, civil society, Islamic fundamentalism, terrorism and liberalization in general. It is therefore difficult to build a grand theory without rigorously studying this country which has challenged, as we all know, so much conventional wisdom. Though Algeria deserves careful attention, it still is not a deviant case.[11]

## From historic legitimacy to electoral legitimacy in Algeria

Violence has indeed been a privileged tool in the transition from historic or revolutionary legitimacy to electoral legitimacy in several countries. In Algeria, it was the bloody events of October 1988 that shattered the revolutionary legitimacy which had been the basis for a tacit consensus within the army general staff, security services and powerful interest groups. The delicate balance within the inner circle which political leaders knit and unknit with the financial flows was upset once and for all after the riots.

Since the date when the Popular Liberation Army, later known as the People's National Army, opened fire on young demonstrators, paradoxically born during the post-colonial period, the government has indeed been trying to acquire a new form of legitimacy. However, the military and its allies continue to think, in spite of profound global changes, that they are the builders of democracy, as was the case during the industrialization of the 1960s and 1970s. In Algeria, it was not the state that shaped the army, but the army that shaped the state. Strangely, the army has its state but the state does not have its army. Liberalization has been a great opportunity for security redeployment in a rapidly changing environment.

Soon after the riots, electoral processes were instituted in Algeria and coincidently elsewhere. Algeria organized, against all odds, about ten elections during the decade of terrorism and terror so as ultimately to secure electoral legitimacy; but in vain. Meanwhile, the Algerian crisis deepened to a considerable extent. A 'dirty war', erroneously termed a 'civil war' in the media to depict the phenomenon of security redeployment across the country, has accompanied elections.[12]

Paradoxically, the violence has continued unabated, in spite of a significant increase in security forces, the setting up of new structures and the acquisition of technologies more adapted to the new challenges. To fulfil its new mandate, the Algerian army has, for instance, set up a new special force consisting of units of elite soldiers,[13] a force of communal guards, GLD (legitimate self-defence groups) and patriots. The GLD are supposed to assist the state forces in isolated rural areas whereas the communal guards are created to control the city centres.

In addition to this, there is the CCLAS (Anti-Subversion Command Centre) and the reactivated ASP (Security and Prevention Assistants).[14] In addition to all these structures, the Algerian elite – a unique phenomenon in the world – have been carrying weapons since they became a specific target of terrorist bands. According to estimates by the FFS (Front of Socialist Forces), there is one soldier to every thirty Algerian inhabitants. If we add to these estimates all professional groups likely to carry arms as part of the fight against terrorism, it is possible that each household possesses a weapon. In comparison, in France, the most militarized country in Europe, there is one police officer per 120 inhabitants. Insecurity is, however, more rampant in France than in other countries of the European Union. The question of security in France remains first on the agenda of every electoral campaign. Contrary to this thesis, the greater the incidence of arms proliferation in a country, the less safe the country is.

In addition to that, police and gendarme posts have substantially increased, in particular, in the shantytowns that have mushroomed around the metropolis as a result of rural exodus and terrorism. The number of police officers has increased from 21,000 to 120,000 between 1992 and 2000, and from 16,000 to 120,000 for the gendarmerie. In spite of that, thefts, robberies, house-breaking, pickpocketing, shoplifting and delinquencies have considerably increased. According to the 2003 official report, for example, 56,103 thefts were reported across the country, of which 15,396 took place in Algiers. The redeployment of police units has not reduced the prevailing insecurity.

Last but not least, the day after Bouteflikla's second electoral victory, an executive order was issued to create the CONAD (Centre opérationnel national d'aide à la decision/National operational centre for assistance to the decision). This centre ultimately aims to control events that may threaten the forces of law and order and national security. Rioting has become a widespread phenomenon in 'democratic' Algeria. The centre is seen as another organization which will attempt to police marches and other public protests.

This security apparatus is reinforced by an imposing legal superstructure and other instruments, as part of the fight against terrorism and other threats. The new security legislation is integrated with the special provisions of the anti-terrorism decree. In the aftermath of the events of 11 September 2001, many governments in Africa and Europe have enacted an anti-terrorist bill, as Algeria suggested long ago. Security redeployment has gained momentum in Africa and elsewhere. Algeria has influenced this decision in some way which has intensified security redeployment. As a reward for Algeria's 'success story', the USA has granted it military assistance for the first time, though Washington accuses the country of human rights violations. The Bush administration has decided to sell a large package of military equipment which includes night-vision gear for use by individuals or on military vehicles. A radical regime has moved overnight from ideological confrontation to military co-operation. In the near future, the security state will reach a very crucial step in its formation: it will be integrated in NATO while playing an important role in the neo-Mediterranean order.

Unsurprisingly, President Abdelaziz Bouteflika was re-elected in April 2004. On the eve of the electoral campaign, he clearly appeared to have surmounted opposition from influential sections of the army. The rejection of Taleb Ibrahimi's candidacy in the presidential race, a serious rival, indicates that the military establishment has granted its blessing for a second term. More critically, Bouteflika's landslide victory is widely seen as a blow to fifteen years of superficial multi-partyism and a clear indication of a rampant neo-authoritarianism. Bouteflika has effaced the bitter memory of his first election, in 1999, when he was the army's clear choice; his rivals withdrew on the eve of the vote citing, among other claims, the military's bias. During his first mandate, the security redeployment was intensified ultimately to crack down on Islamist bands and others. Furthermore, he has been successful in refashioning himself in the international fora as a protector rather than *protégé* of the military.

As organized, multi-party elections are used as new tools for co-opting civilian elites entrusted with a mission to guide the administration, the state and diplomacy. Elections are not capable of alleviating the legitimacy crisis and containing clan warfare. Quite on the contrary, elections tend further to exacerbate the conflict since it has permeated the public sphere. More critically, it is nowadays very difficult to distinguish the public from the private exercise of violence.

The first criterion for selecting candidates is not competence, but 'obedience and willingness to cooperate under all circumstances with the government', wrote retired General Rachid Ben Yelles (2002). And he added, 'Only candidates approved by the security service' are appointed. More than four decades after independence, the government implements policies chosen by the army. From then, the power is retained by the army, which mandates a government to run the administration to achieve a state-inward model of development. Saïd Sadi, Secretary General of the RCD (Movement for Culture and Democracy), has asserted on several occasions that 'the army remains the only authentic party in Algeria'. In retrospect, this testimony has great empirical validity. To recap: it was not procedural democracy that defeated political Islam, but the security forces. 'Washington has much to learn from Algeria on ways to fight terrorism,' said William Burns, Assistant Secretary of State for Near East Affairs, when he ended his visit in Algiers.

## Instruments of the security state

The state of emergency, the privatization of national patrimony and corruption constitute three essential instruments for the setting up of the security state in several African and Arab countries.

Shortly after the cancellation of the first round of the legislative elections, Mohammed Boudiaf, President of the HCE (Supreme State Council), on 9 February 1992 decreed a nationwide state of emergency lasting for one year. This presidential decree provides, however, that the state of emergency may be lifted before the expiry of that period. Twelve years later, the state of emergency is still in force, as is the one in Egypt decreed in 1981 following the assassination of President Anwar Sadat. Over ten elections have been organized in Algeria in the meantime, yet the legitimacy crisis is still unresolved. On the contrary, political liberalization initiated under pressure from western states has made the situation more untenable than before because it has opened the door to new contenders from the post-independence generation.

The HCE in ordering the state of emergency relied on Article 86 of the 1989 Constitution. The article was incorporated in Article 91 of the 1996 Constitution. It states that a state of emergency or state of siege can be ordered by a decision of the president of the republic 'in case of absolute necessity' and for 'a fixed duration'. Article 91 further stipulates that 'the duration of the state of emergency or state of siege may only be extended after the approval of parliament sitting in a joint session of both chambers'. Although the CNT (National Transitional Council), the unelected parliament, 'approved' the decree on the state of emergency, the text has to date not been formally debated either by the National Assembly or by the Senate.

As a general rule, a state of emergency is defined as an exceptional measure, 'limited in time', pursuant to which, 'in time of danger', civilian authorities are endowed with exceptional powers 'to limit the exercise of public freedoms'. It is different from a state of siege in the sense that police powers are exercised by civilian and not military authorities. The 1992 decree granted the Minister of Interior and the *wali* (governor) exceptional powers although, according to the final report of the commission in charge of investigating the events in Grande Kabylie, the 1992 decree was 'supplemented' by another text kept secret: the inter-ministerial order of 25 July 1993 which clearly mandates the regional military commanders to carry out 'operations to restore order'. The chairman of the commission in charge of investigating the events in Great Kabylia remarked: 'the chronology of the said texts shows a subtle slide from a state of emergency toward what looks rather like a state of siege.

The powers granted by the 1993 Order to regional military commanders are exclusive, which is characteristic of a state of siege.' Such new authority 'stopped being exercised since the reinforcement of the police and the *gendarmerie* enabled these forces to meet public order needs', stated Ali Benflis, Head of Government, to the Agence de Presse Officielle (l'APS). Khaled Ziari, former senior officer at the General Delegation of National Security, in an interview in *Le Matin* (3 March 2002), pointed out that 'the broadening of the area of intervention of the police service and the numerous unquestionable professional powers of National Security allow the police to maintain public order under optimal conditions, in all places and circumstances'. According to General Larbi Belkheir, a director at the Presidency of the Republic, interviewed in *Le Monde* (7 March 2002), 'the state of emergency does not make sense'. Most surprisingly, terrorist violence has intensified at a time when leaders are talking of lifting the state of emergency. Its maintenance cannot be justified by any reason other than that of security redeployment, since the process has not yet been completed nationwide.

Events in Algeria since the institution of the state of emergency have placed the army on high alert. Its role in society has become a contentious issue. For some, like Islamists of the ex-FIS (Islamic Salvation Front) and parties affiliated to the reconciliatory movement, namely the FFS or the PT (Workers' Party), the state of emergency has paved the way for authoritarian normalization of the regime, while advocates of the eradication movement are of the opinion that the army absolutely ought to have intervened after the first round of the 1991 legislative elections to prevent authoritarian excesses. According to the RCD, the MDS (Social Democratic Movement) and the ANR (National Democratic Alliance), authoritarianism is perceived as indispensable to the salvation of the Algerian Republic. This political debate fuelled by the 'crossfire of democracy' has not really shed any light on the nuts and bolts of the political transition in Algeria.

Regarding the institutional framework, the state of emergency has helped put in place conditions congenial to the emergence of neo-authoritarianism with an 'islamo-democratic' face, to borrow an ideological notion very much in fashion in the francophone press. It is scrupulously described in the main state reform document. This document provides for the devolution of greater prerogatives and powers to state officials to the detriment of local and national elected officials as well as political parties. This new approach is based on the Tunisian model which received the 'blessing' of the United States and European governments even before the events of 11 September 2001. According to the said approach, a repressive, but strong and therefore stable regime has to be encouraged in Africa and the Maghreb.

### Privatization and corruption

The dominant class, by broadening its security intervention range, has also succeeded in extending the scope of its economic intervention. The state privatization process is gathering momentum while the people are caught in the crossfire of Islamic armed groups and the forces of law and order. This dual-state restructuring process entered a new phase with the organization of the 10 May 2002 elections. The appropriation of state revenue and its derivatives is at the root of conflicts within the political class and its internal and external clientele. In Algeria, a tidy sum of 10 billion dollars is injected into the import chain every year. Its distribution at the helm of the state is extended to the emerging class of elected representatives at the local level. The latter, allied to the bureaucrats, work at the limit of legality in the allocation of housing and plots, and the award of public contracts. The economy is understood only in terms of state revenue, distribution and consumption. Economic agents become predators and kleptomaniacs. Brute force becomes the principal regulatory factor when intermediary institutions are mere screens. Influence is exerted *in camera*, outside government institutions and popular assemblies. Elective and other institutions are only shadows of the places where power is wielded.

As in Russia and elsewhere in the other 'controlled economies', elites and their allies have reconverted to business. Finance groups appear, as if by magic, without any clue as to the origin of their wealth. Some fifteen business tycoons have mushroomed in Algeria. Apart from Rafik Khalifa, the following are worth mentioning: Issad Rebrav (metallurgical, food-processing and car dealing business sectors and the media), Mustapha Ait Adjedou (pharmaceutical laboratories), Hadjas Brahim (Union Bank), Abdelkader Habchi (diamonds), Mohammed Sahraoui (property), Mahfoud Belhadj, President Bouteflika's current chief of protocol (air transport). Khalifa is active in the pharmaceutical sector (Khalifa Pharma), banking (Khalifa Bank), car rentals (Khalifa Rent), the media (Khalifa TV and ANN), construction (Holzmann), and he plans to build a new town at the gates of Algiers, designed by the architect Ricardo Bofill. Strangely, Khalifa Airways, which was formed only a few years ago, has more passenger planes than the state corporation, Air Algeria. In addition to its thirty-five planes, it has placed an order for a dozen Boeing aircraft. With the opening up of Air Algeria's share capital, we should expect the Khalifa Group to become a dominant shareholder in that corporation. This group is in the process of setting up a state within the state founded on a peculiar form of capitalism that the Russians describe as mafia capitalism.

According to many observers, the origin of Khalifa's fortune is mysterious. Some people say he acquired part of the war chest of the FLN (his father, Laroussi Khalifa, was in charge of the Algerian secret service), while others allege that he benefited from the fortunes of his emir friends in the Gulf states. Still others claim that his 'empire' is 'the biggest money laundering network at the service of Algerian generals'. Khalifa grooms his public image; he offered a water purification system worth 70 million dollars to the city of Algiers and became the principal sponsor of Olympique de Marseilles, the biggest soccer club in France. Rafik Abdelmoumene Khalifa, whose companies employ 12,500 persons in Algeria and have an annual turnover of 1 billion dollars, has, in less than ten years, become Algeria's leading private employer. Thus, Algerians are wont to say good-humouredly that after ten years of civil war, 'Algeria has escaped from the *califat* only to fall into the *Khalifa*'. French and Swiss newspapers have tried to probe the mysterious origins of the Algerian billionaire's fortune, all to no avail. As a result of serious factional struggles, his empire collapsed overnight in 2003, causing a loss to the national budget of approximately 20 billion dollars.[15]

## Conclusion: the security state and riots

President Abdelaziz Bouteflika admittedly rekindled great hopes shortly after his inauguration on 15 April 1999. But the hopes of peace and social prosperity which he so quickly raised fizzled out with the new unfolding crisis of legitimacy triggered precisely by his election. Indeed, just before the second anniversary of his election, clan warfare at the helm of the state entered a new phase in complexity and confusion. At the same time, a large popular protest movement which had gained ground with the implementation of the structural adjustment reform erupted violently in the social domain. This movement reached a climax when rioting broke out in Kabylia in April 2001.

The 'socialist' state tried as best it could to implement the social policy, which is no longer the case with the security state. Under the new system, there is no longer any room for a social policy to meet growing demand, on the one hand, and changes in the world economy, on the other. Today, Algerians are discovering that they are 'naked' in the face of efforts to contain both the security redeployment and the security order in the Mediterranean region.

The *hogra* (injustice, contempt), hunger, unemployment, insecurity and insufficient housing are today forcing entire populations, even in the most remote areas of the country, to come out on the streets to express their anger and frustration. The deteriorating social situation is promoting an atmosphere of open rebellion nationwide. Mutual mistrust between public authorities and citizens is such that rioting has become the order of the day in Algeria. It has spread at an alarming rate throughout the country. All sectors of activity are affected by the social conflicts: strikes in the primary and secondary education, higher education, health, finance, industrial, judicial and transport sectors have been organized by angry workers together with walk-outs, sit-ins and hunger strikes. There is gunfire, hostage-taking, burning of tyres and the setting up of roadblocks all over the country.

This already explosive situation is aggravated by a renewed spate of killings nationwide, while Kabylia has for the past three years remained in a state of dissidence. Rioting is becoming the only instrument of dialogue between citizens and public authorities. Algeria is getting caught in a cycle of widespread rebellion, which poses a serious threat to national unity, already weakened by a decade of violence and terror.

The lack of intermediary institutions between the government and the people, and between the centre and the periphery, makes police states prone to violence. The absence of representation encourages political manipulation. In Algeria, clan warfare has been at the root of the major upheavals in the country, from the 1954 armed struggle to the prison mutinies of 2002, including the October riots and more recent events in Kabylia. However, the sponsors of such events are quickly overwhelmed.

In a context where the *hogra* is condemned by everyone, conflicts rapidly get out of hand, overtaking those who orchestrate them. The course of events is determined more by their own logic than by political manipulation. The public sphere soon becomes a battleground for all groups, both formal and informal.

The specificity of this protest movement lies in the fact that the security state is encroaching on the 'marginal zone' occupied by over 12 million Algerians. The new stakes of the bazaar economy are negotiated at the cost of further marginalization of the masses. Such a marginal zone is not only organized into armed groups, but into protest movements capable of sweeping off their path both the political elite and the entire country.

The social front and cultural movements could not join forces to give a new impetus to the fight against the crisis. The organic intellectual, an agent capable of federating both the collective and the personal and the public and private sphere into one dialectic unit, is profoundly resented in states that have marginalized the intelligentsia. Events capable of changing the course of history are politically manipulated and used as a pretext for all-out violence. Algeria has again missed its appointment with history and the third millennium. The long-expected radical change which should have ushered Algerians into modernity and social progress will have to wait for another generation of leaders and another political culture. The state sees this as yet another justification for extending the security redeployment nationwide. The intensification of such redeployment is supported as part of 'the war against terrorism' waged by the United States and European countries.

The exercise of state authority, far from declining, is developing and proceeding by delegation under the unprecedented influence of globalization and internal forces. Political power is no longer concentrated exclusively, as in the past, in the hands of a very small group of individuals referred to in the press as 'decision-makers' – not to say army generals. Contrary to the situation in the past, there is no single dominant group capable of imposing a political pact on other groups. Rather than developing into a political class that jealously guards its prerogatives and power, the Algerian political elite is made up of numerous clans, factions and cliques, none of which has been powerful enough to dominate the entire political system. The Algerian state has been captured by a set of power groups that have strong channels of influence within society through relations of patronage. These institutions and groups were not created with the purpose of allowing dissent against government policies, but rather a mechanism for the regime to co-opt any opposition and channel that does not threaten the status quo. Conflict thus becomes routine within a context in which state redeployment has succeeded in depoliticizing protests and social movements.

Real power, as opposed to formal power, is henceforth watered down by a hotch-potch of mechanisms, institutions and networks whose architects often propose more strategies for attaining personal or family power than national or regional power. Mobilization and demobilization strategies are deployed to accede to positions of authority. The ideological dimension becomes all the more secondary as politics is reduced to privatization of part of the state citadel. The stakes of the political transition are very high financially, economically and militarily. State forces and their collaborators use their privileged positions to take advantage of the informal market using old clandestine activities such as smuggling to go into business as import–export operators.

Although the Algerian state's room for manoeuvre has palpably shrunk, it remains a major agency in organizing the operations of power in the selective liberalized context and the bazaar economy. Those in power are apparently not ready to hand over the reins of power to another political class. No one is allowed to question fundamentally the origins of power in this game of influence.

The third wave of democratization which brutally toppled authoritarian regimes in Latin America and in Europe did not affect Arab and African countries. On the contrary, it somehow helped to consolidate the authoritarian system put in place soon after national independence. Changeover of political power is still by succession in Jordan, Morocco, Syria and the Persian Gulf states. Sham multi-party elections are organized in the other countries.

Shortly after independence, a strategy was adopted for building, not a constitutional state that would survive the whims and caprices of the prince, coups or palace revolutions, but a powerful state, in the repressive rather than the consensual sense of the term. The consolidation of such a state is not the product of internal pressure from the class struggle, as was the case in Europe (Tilly 1975). This state was built on the premise of a fragile and embattled balance of power which fluctuates with the ebb and flow of state revenue from the energy industry and other factors. The mobilization of state revenue has contributed significantly to building the security state. The state would not have survived popular pressures for long without the support of economic and military powers. Corrupt and discredited regimes have often succeeded in securing the protection and conniving assistance of such powers. They achieve this by purchasing huge stocks of arms at the expense of sustainable and harmonious development plans.

In spite of the market liberalization efforts of the last two decades, the nation-state crisis has not abated in this region. On the contrary, it has spread to all countries of the South and globalization has made it more intractable than before. Today, the crisis can no longer be contained at a local level. To defuse the crisis, a collective strategy involving all actors of the region must be put in place. Furthermore, the document on the New Partnership for African Development (NEPAD), adopted by African leaders in Abuja, Nigeria, in October 2001, confirms this option. However, it is difficult for elites who have brought the continent to the current situation[16] to produce a credible alternative capable of harnessing the region's abundant resources. The disrepute into which the elites have fallen is unparalleled in contemporary history. Only a new crop of leaders can produce a new vision that preserves human dignity. To overcome in the long term the new challenges that we are nowadays facing, social democracy that genuinely suits our ancestral values, cultures and traditions should be the option to procedural democracy and security redeployment. Otherwise the survival of our region is seriously at stake.

## Notes

1 The creation of three major multilateral agencies (the World Bank, the IMF and the GATT) the day after the Second World War not only produced non-democratic behaviour but the agencies also themselves function undemocratically. While there was high economic growth in the USA and Europe, 'democracy' was not on the agenda. Militarism, as a dominant ideology, has created an unstable situation in peripheral capitalism. Western powers and global financial institutions have rapidly supported it, partly to avoid radical nationalism or social revolution.

2 Irene Gendzier (1995) makes a very interesting radical critique of the abundant literature in her relevant and persuasive book, *Development against Democracy*. Unfortunately, it has not been translated for non-English readers.

3 But when democratic elections usher in new leaders who try radically to challenge the status quo, foreign powers try to destabilize the newly elected government. Recent events in Venezuela are a case in point. According to a *Newsweek* survey, the Bush administration, which did not hide its dislike of the newly elected president, had very close ties with the coup plotters.

4 The first war against terrorism was launched in Latin America. Washington's 'crusade for democracy', as it is called, was waged during the Reagan years. The democratic process was established together with neoliberal economic reforms.

5 The Algerian legislative elections of 30 May 2002 recorded the lowest voter turnout since independence.

6 The presidential elections held in Yemen in September 1999 were regarded as a major success for Arab democracy. The incumbent did not tolerate any adversary outside his party (Burgat 2000). Ironically, Zimbabwean President Robert Mugabe was recently 'democratically re-elected' for a six-year term.

7 The neoliberal Washington consensus is an array of market-oriented principles designed by the USA and the international financial institutions. The basic rules are: liberalize trade and finance, let the market set prices, end inflation and privatize.

8 This situation, which has reached a point of no return, compelled the international community to act. To this effect, the World Bank called on the rich countries in June 2002 to finance the first phase of its Education for All programme aimed at giving children in several countries access to primary education by 2015. At the G8 summit in Canada, G8 leaders agreed to increase their assistance to countries that show a real commitment to attaining the Education for All objectives.

9 If we take, for instance, the Eastern European countries whose democratic transition is considered a success story, the socio-economic situation has not improved for all social classes. In Poland, the showcase of neoliberals, liberal materialism has failed woefully. 'Each government – associated with both Solidarity and the post-communist leftwing – has been pursuing the same policy for the past eleven years. Coming to power is not synonymous with change of policy, but having access to the national cake,' wrote Bernard Margueritte in *Le Monde Diplomatique* (October 2002).

10 For a pertinent analysis of the nature of the relationship between procedural democracy and the international debt in Africa, see Lumumba-Kasongo (2002).

11 In the aftermath of the 1988 October riots, Algeria seemed to be embarked on a great experiment in democratization. This country was overnight the most pluralistic in the region. But the democratic spring ended abruptly when the FIS (Islamic Salvation Front) was on the verge of electoral victory in 1991.

12 More than 150,000 people were reportedly killed during the past decade, more than 15,000 persons were reported missing and material damage was estimated at more than 20 billion dollars.

13 In September 1992 a new elite corps, composed mainly of units of special forces, was set up. Initially consisting of 15,000 men, the corps' numeric strength stood at 60,000 in 1995. This corps played a very important role in the fight against Islamist groups.

14 In state corporations, civilians are appointed as ASPs. The ASPs' role is to act as indicators. They are neither paid wages nor catered for by the security services. However, officers are appointed as security advisers in ministries. University graduates were often hired at the end of national service. In addition to that, a special inquiry is conducted before co-opting a high executive in the government and diplomacy. Its results are reported in a *'fiche bleue'* (blue sheet) that Mouloud Hamrouche, when he was head of the government, attempted to stamp out.

15 This sum is associated with one year of oil revenues, which amount represents more than 97 per cent of state foreign revenues.

16 In 1980, there were 1.6 billion people in the countries of the South living on 2 dollars a day. That figure has risen to 2.4 billion people, 750 million of whom are in sub-Saharan Africa. Another significant finding is that primary

products represent 80 per cent of Africa's exports, whereas the percentage of primary products has fallen to 45 per cent for all countries of the South. There is a steady decline in public development assistance for the region. The international community is clearly dissociating itself from the situation in Africa.

## References

Benachenhou, A. (2001) 'L'avenir économique des pays méditerranéens du Sud et la refondation du processus de Barcelone', *El Watan*, 13 and 14 November.

Ben Yelles, R. (2002) 'Le boycott des élections: un devoir civique', *Le Matin*, 11 March.

Burgat, F. (2002) 'Les élections présidentielles de septembre 1999 au Yémen: du pluralisme armée au retour à la norme arabe', *Maghreb–Machrek, Monde Arabe*, no. 168 (April–June).

Burgat, F. and W. Dowell (1993) *The Islamic Movement in North Africa* (Austin, TX: Center for Middle Eastern Studies, University of Texas).

Callaghy, M. T. (1987) 'The State as Lame Leviathan: The Patrimonial Administrative State in Africa', in Z. Ergas (ed.), *The African State in Transition* (London: Macmillan), pp. 87–116.

Cassen, B. and F. F. Clairmont (2001) 'Au mépris des inégalités. Globalisation à marche forcée', *Le Monde Diplomatique*, December.

Chomsky, N. (1998) *Profit of War, Neo-liberalism and Global Order* (New York: Steven Press).

Clement, H. (2001) 'Bunker States', in H. Clement and R. Springboard, *Globalization and the Politics of Development in the Middle East* (Cambridge: Cambridge University Press).

Entelis, J. (2000) 'Democracy Denied: America's Authoritarian Approach Towards the Maghreb – Causes and Consequences', paper presented at the 18th World Congress of the International Association of Political Science, Quebec, Montreal, Canada, 1–5 August.

Gendzier, I. (1995) *Development against Democracy: Manipulating Political Change in the Third World* (Washington, DC: Thyrone Press).

Guilhot, N. (2001) *The Democracy Makers. Foreign Policy Activists and the Construction of an International Market for Political Virtue, 2001*. PhD dissertation, European University Institute, Florence, Italy.

Lumumba-Kasongo, T. (1998) *Rise of Multipartyism and Democracy in the Global Context: The Case of Africa* (Westport, CT: Praeger).

— 2002) 'Reflections on Liberal Democracy and International Debt Issues in Post-Cold War Africa', paper presented to the 10th General Assembly of CODESRIA, Kampala, Uganda, 8–12 December.

Mallet, R. (1996) *A Call from Algeria. Third Worldism, Revolution and the Turn to Islam* (Berkeley, CA: University of California Press).

Margueritte, B. (2002) 'Que reste-il des rêves de solidarité? La Pologne malade du libéralisme', *Le Monde Diplomatique*, October.

Oliver de Sardin (2000) 'L'espoir toujours repoussé d'une démocratie authentique', *Le Monde Diplomatique*, February.

Pierre, A. and W. B. Quandt (1996) *The Algerian Crisis. Policy Options for the West* (Washington, DC: Carnegie Endowment for International Peace).

Quandt, W. B. (1988) *Between Ballot and Bullet: Algeria's Transition from Authoritarianism* (Washington, DC: Brookings Institution).

Roberts, H. (2003) *The Battlefield. Algeria 1988–2002. Studies in a Broken Policy* (London: Verso).

Tilly, C. (1975) *The Formation of National States in Western Europe* (Princeton, NJ: Princeton University Press).

Tlemçani, R. (1986) *State and Revolution in Algeria* (Colorado: Westview Press).

— (1999) *Etat, Bazar et Globalisation. L'aventure de l'Infitah en Algérie* (Alger: Dar El Hikma).

— (2003) *Elections et Elites en Algérie. Paroles de candidats* (Alger: Chihab Editions).

# 3 | An explanation of electoral attitudes in Cameroon 1990–92: towards a new appraisal

JOSEPH-MARIE ZAMBO BELINGA

## Introduction: aspects of the problem and objectives

An analysis of electoral attitudes in the light of ethnicity draws its 'credibility' from a manipulated perception of ethnicity, an offshoot of colonialist anthropology that construed ethnicity as the unmistakable bedrock of determination of the social ethos in Africa. This perception of ethnicity as the prime basis for determining the African's identity, which has been espoused by politics, shapes and informs the way people think, feel and act (Durkheim 1986: 5) in many areas of social life in Africa. During the trusteeship period in Cameroon, 'the French government used the argument that Cameroonians could only be identified on the basis of particular ethnic groups – as opposed to an artificial "Cameroonian" nation' (Joseph 1986: 248) to thwart and discredit the clamour of the Union des Populations du Cameroun (UPC) for the reunification of the two territories. The official rhetoric that served as chief argument to support the institution of the single party was also based on this hypothesis. Such was the case, too, with the national unity ideology. Thus, the official restoration of political pluralism in Cameroon in 1990 provided yet another field for 'experimenting' on the primacy of ethnic considerations in social interaction in Africa in general and in Cameroon in particular. This has to do with choosing leaders through multiple-candidate elections. In Cameroon, the analysis of the results of the various elections adopts – following an approach which gives credit to the official results of the said elections – a method which explains political attitudes as largely enmeshed with ethnic considerations (Menthong 1998: 40, 42, 43, 44–50; Schilder 1993; Sindjoun 1994a: 406–413; 1997: 115–16).

This approach has two epistemological flaws. First, it flouts the methodological requirement of 'sociological objectification' (Bourdieu et al. 1983), that is, the need for the researcher to begin by establishing the subject of inquiry. The reasoning here proceeds from the validation of fundamentally empirical data. The official results as proclaimed by the authorities, who are often wanting in objectivity, and a certain '*doxa*' on ethnic sentiments fanned by people who manipulate identity, are endorsed by these researchers. Second, it betrays an all-too-obvious amateurism as it eclipses, consciously or unconsciously, the volumes of discourse on conceptualization and theorizing on the vote by political pundits as evidenced by the numerous works on this subject. These two shortcomings, which to our mind detract considerably from these works, spurred us on to carry out this inquiry, which basically seeks to answer the following question: Do electoral attitudes as portrayed by the few works on elections in Cameroon initiated in the 1990s and produced for the most part by political pundits capture this reality in Cameroon in all its dimensions? The answer to this question being no, this work seeks a dual epistemological objective.

After a critical review of the works produced by some political analysts on elections in Cameroon, the study concludes that these works offer a partial appraisal of Cameroonian voters' attitudes. Whereupon our inquiry undertakes to develop, through a review of the paradigms left out by these earlier works, an explanation of electoral attitudes that transcends ethnic identity and looks at this issue as a complete social phenomenon.

The approach we intend to adopt to explain electoral attitudes is based on a combination of two paradigms: the paradigm of historical trauma and that of rational choice, more specifically, one of its neo-utilitarian tenets, namely that of *retrospective voting*. Our study is underpinned by the contention that to grasp Cameroonian electoral attitudes in their entirety, we must adopt a pluralistic and complementary theoretical approach. Drawing theoretical sustenance partly from what can be considered as the main findings (Amselle and Mbokolo 1985: 39–41) of anthropological research on tribalism in Africa, namely, that 'it is always the sign of something else, the mask of social, political and economic conflicts',[1] we try to show that although the expression and distribution of votes in an election in Cameroon may bear the hallmarks of the ethnic identity dimension which is generally exploited by politicians, the reality actually transcends this immediate primary level ('navel-gazing')[2] of social links and, therefore, ethnic considerations, and becomes embedded in chains of existential claims and preoccupations which structure the social conditions for survival of each category or group of voters; these conditions themselves vary with history on the one hand, and with the electoral district on the other. This process brings in the historical events that shape and inform the political memory of the various areas participating in the political process (Tullock 1978) and the perception or representations people make of the act of voting in a specific social context. In other words, the way votes are cast in Cameroon reflects the type of social, political and economic preoccupations people have in each area, the collective memory forged through the answers brought by political powers to such preoccupations and the symbolic significance of the act of voting in the new context of democratization.

## Elections: a much-visited political subject

Reflection on theoretical models explaining voting is one of the most-trodden areas of political science. Accordingly, we are going to attempt a broad overview of the essential Anglo-Saxon and European schools of thought. The first paradigm of Anglo-Saxon tradition to explain voting is the one developed by researchers at the University of Columbia in the United States. The model developed in a study carried out by Paul Lazarsfeld, Bernard Berelson and Hazan Gaudet (1944) places social determinism at the centre of the analysis of electoral attitudes. The main conclusion these authors reach is as follows: 'As a person is socially, so does he/she think politically. Social habits determine political preferences' (Lazarsfeld et al. 1944: 27).

Accordingly, voting, though presented as an individual act, is portrayed as being embedded in the collective mores of the various groups to which people belong, for instance, at places of work or residence, where shared aspirations and experiences and common values enhance the sense of belonging. A French version of this model was developed from the works of Guy Michelat and Michel Simon (1977) following the left/right dichotomy.

The substance of the work of this school of thought was called into question by a team of researchers from the Survey Research Center of the University of Michigan who came up with the paradigm of partisan identification. This paradigm appeared following the publication of a collective work (Campbell et al. 1966) in which the authors presented the findings of their research on attitudes of American voters during the three presidential elections of the period 1948 to 1956. This work was followed by another (Butler and Stokes 1969). The foundations of the model actually appeared a decade before and were prefigured in two earlier works (Campbell and Kahn 1952; Campbell et al. 1954). According to the proponents of this model, to forecast voting trends all one needs to know is the trends and intensity of voters' attitudes with regard to the various political subjects. The main conclusion of this work was that voter choice was a result of the affirmation of an inherited sense of belonging manifesting a loyalty handed down essentially within the family (Campbell et al. 1966: 146–7, 148). This is a kind of primeval psychological attachment because it is developed from childhood and is handed down by the parents. It is known as 'partisan identification'. It takes the form of loyalty to a party that is personal, lasting and distinct from the short-term stakes of the election.[3]

Theoretical debate on electoral attitudes took yet another dimension following the introduction of the economic approach to the analysis of democracy. To understand this better, it is important to bear in mind that it finds its basis in the 'economic theory of democracy' as developed by

Anthony Downs (1957).[4] This theory is founded on the idea of the rational consumer posited by the neoclassical theory of the economy.[5] This idea is embedded in a broader, more complex framework relating to the rationality of social actors (Boudon 1997: 217).

The introduction of the analogy between the economic and the political markets in the study of political attitudes developed by the 'public choice' school led to the conceptualization of a new kind of vote. In his book cited above, Anthony Downs states his case: political actors are rational as they seek to adapt their means to the ends they pursue. Political parties are public enterprises seeking to maximize votes in their favour while voters vote for those who secure the greatest good or utility for them at the least cost. This analogy gave rise to the so-called rational voter, first defined as a voter who is informed, interested, competent and capable of weighing the stakes of an election and forming an articulate, consistent and stable judgement. The portrait of the voter depicted in this 'pure' version of the 'rational choice' theory as it is called, presents him/her as a calculating individual, a rational strategist acting on the promptings of individual utility but, at the same time, prompted by 'non-egoistic' utility.

This perception of the voter drew intense criticism with two views emerging. The first, realizing that all empirical attempts to verify the empirical validity of the above definition of the rational voter availed little, concluded that such a voter could not be found (Almond and Verba 1963: 474). This stance was corroborated by other works (Butler and Stokes 1969; Converse and Dupeux 1962). The second view started from the 'paradox of the voter'. The basic hypothesis of this view, which is the basis for the analysis of voting by proponents of neo-utilitarian theories, posits that the rationality that guides the individual voter lies in the expected utility of his/her act. Hence, the question: Of what use or benefit is participation in the election to the voter? Attempts at answering this question and others that came in the wake of this model ushered in the idea of economic rationality or, to be more precise, the economic relationship between voting trends and the economic situation (Kramer 1971: 131–43). These works were followed by a host of others, summarized by Lewis-Beck (1985: 1080–9) and André Bernard (1997: 245–64). These views forked into two fundamental directions. The first advanced the idea that citizens maximize their electoral utility function according to the perception they have of the economic performance of the outgoing team: this is *retrospective voting*. The second maintained that voters take a bet on the future, giving priority to electoral promises and programmes, and voting for candidates whose macro-economic priorities hold the optimum utility: this is *prospective voting*. These neo-utilitarian conceptual frameworks gave rise to two main varieties of models: the *pocket-book voting model* (Lewis-Beck 1997: 231–61) and the *political business cycles model*.

To complete this review of theoretical debate on electoral attitudes, let us add to this Anglo-Saxon catalogue one paradigm of French descent: the historical trauma model. This model was developed by the historian Paul Bois, whose work is based on a critique of the views of André Siegfried (1980).[6] Paul Bois finds the explanation of political attitudes developed by this author incomplete, and he brings out the cause: lack of historical perspective (Bois 1971: 10). Convinced that the traditions of the masses are rooted in the past (ibid., p. 29), Paul Bois thinks that current political cleavages have their origins in the past. His concern here is to discover the mother-events that gave birth to certain mental structures which subsequently reproduced for over a century, or to understand how 'in a few years, the fleeting event secreted the lasting attitude, the short time begot the long time' (Leroy-Ladurie 1973: 179).

### Elections: a superficially appreciated subject in Cameroon

As opposed to the depth of theoretical debate on the explanation of electoral attitudes as reflected in the above survey of the literature on the subject, the few works produced by political pundits on elections in Cameroon definitely fall short in terms of the theoretical framework. In substance, these works raise ethno-partisan identification into a univocal paradigm to explain the electoral attitudes of the population, thereby raising, by virtue of their conceptual convergence with the work of the Michigan school, the issue (that keeps coming up)[7] of validity and operational extent of works based on this model. However, whereas the Michigan school carried out intense fieldwork to validate their paradigm, the above-mentioned works betray a paucity of fieldwork.[8] The failure of these researchers to question the results is the shortcoming that destroys the heuristic validity of this paradigm of solidarity voting because it deprives them of a research tool that would have enabled them to cross-check these results in the field. Only such verification can generate strategies for prospecting and exploring other avenues in the search for a theoretical framework for explaining the electoral attitudes of Cameroonians.

*Shaky grounds of community or solidarity voting* Let us revisit the results of two of the elections that have been organized so far in Cameroon: the legislative election of March 1992 and the presidential election of October 1992.[9] In March 1992, President Paul Biya's Cameroon People's Democratic Movement (CPDM) won eighty-eight seats out of 180 at the National Assembly. Most of these eighty-eight seats came from what partisans of solidarity voting consider his 'main area of influence' (Menthong 1988: 42), namely, the Centre, South and East provinces. Bello Bouba Maïgari's National Union for Democracy and Progress (NUDP), for its part, won sixty-eight seats,[10] with a majority vote in the Adamawa and North provinces, but also the East and West provinces. The Union des Populations du Cameroun (UPC) scraped eighteen seats only in the Nyong-et-Kellé (Centre province) and Sanaga Maritime (Littoral province) divisions. Finally, Dakole Daïssala's Movement for the Defence of the Republic (MDR) won six seats in the Far North province.

The first observation that can be made about these results is that although the distribution of seats among the parties that took part in this election reflects a local following for each of the parties at the National Assembly for the 1992–97 legislature, this is not enough reason to conclude that voting was based solely on ethnic considerations. The results obtained by the political parties running covered areas that were quite culturally heterogeneous, inhabited as they are by several ethnic groups which do not always speak the same language and whose social relations – from one group to another – are generally scarred by negative stereotypes symptomatic of latent conflicts concealed by the semblance of cohesion which is often tagged to these entities hastily identified as ethnic groups. Let us look at vote distribution per candidate and per region of origin.

TABLE 3.1 Score obtained by each candidate in his region of origin, presidential election, of 11 October 1992

| Name of candidate | Name of party | Score in region of origin (%) |
| --- | --- | --- |
| Biya, Paul | CPDM | 94.82 |
| Bello Bouba Maïgari | NUDP | 50.42 |
| Ekindi, Jean-Jacques | Mouvement Progressiste (MP) | 0.679 |
| Fru Ndi, John | SDF | 86.3 |
| Ndam Njoya, Adamou | Cameroon Democratic Union (CDU) | 17.58 |
| Hygin Ema Ottou | Rassemblement des Forces Patriotiques (RFP) | 0.54 |

*Source*: Supreme Court Order I/PE/92–93 of 23 October 1992 to proclaim the results of the presidential election of 11 October 1992.

*Prima facie*, this table can actually make one endorse the ethnic voting hypothesis or, better still, ethno-regional voting. For each candidate performed best in the place presented as his area. But an analysis of these scores raises other questions which summon other 'windows' of analysis[11] when we realize that some candidates make incursions into areas considered as the 'electoral stronghold' of their opponents while 'sons of the soil' get 'ousted' from 'their' electoral village by candidates from 'elsewhere' fielded by parties whose headquarters are not in the area.

Candidates who went out of their 'stronghold' included John Fru Ndi, Paul Biya and Bello Bouba Maïgari.[12] The candidates whose 'strongholds' were 'grabbed' include Ema Ottou[13] in the Centre province, Jean Jacques Ekindi in the Littoral and, to a certain extent, Bello Bouba Maïgari, who came away only with half of 'his' electorate, and, finally, Adamou Ndam Njoya in the West province (although he had the majority vote in his native Noun division).

The incursion of some candidates into what can be considered as the 'private property' of their opponents cannot be dismissed as mere chance or happenstance. Even if that were the case, it would be worthwhile to explore the causes of such happenstance in order to elucidate any hidden meanings. For the case in point, this incursion offers two possible avenues for investigation, the common denominator being that they show how superficial the idea of ethnic voting is. To begin with, this incursion appears to be that of an embryonic national political culture which takes root more in the urban areas where the population shows an increasing desire to make its own contribution to the ongoing political process and to exercise some kind of surveillance over the political actors competing, with a view to ensuring that their choice is respected in a political environment where politicians are more prone to robbing citizens of their sovereignty. The external manifestation is, therefore, one of citizens who have won back their sovereignty. Conversely, seen differently, it appears as the desperate manifestation of this will of the population to express their opinions democratically. Thus, it is seen as part of the strategies for obstructing democracy, particularly elections, orchestrated by the elite who gerrymander results in order to give a national stature to candidates who sometimes were elected only thanks to their fraud and by ethnic groups just as artificial.

*Downscaling the importance of community voting*

SOCIOLOGICALLY ARTIFICIAL AND SHAM ETHNIC GROUPS We are going to proceed in three stages: deconstructing ethnic groups, showing that their present configuration results from wilful manipulation for utilitarian purposes, and highlighting the arbitrary nature of this approach as revealed by the electoral incivility in the construction of strongholds.

An examination of the concept of the ethnic group as expounded in anthropological works (Fortes 1945: 16; Nadel 1947: 13; 1971: 45; Mercier 1961: 65; Nicolas 1973: 103, 104, 107; Barth 1969: 10–11) shows that anthropologists, besides criteria such as territory, the same ancestry, language, customs and values, lay particular emphasis on another category of qualifier, namely, the common awareness the social actors have of belonging to the same entity. This collective awareness proceeds from established historical bearings acknowledged by all the members of the group and forming 'socially significant identification schemata' (Amselle and Mbokolo 1985: 21). Now, neither those who are called the Beti today nor the Anglo-Bamileke fulfil these criteria. The anthropological set-up of most of the ethnic groups that followers of solidarity voting have identified and on which they build their illustration of the validity of ethnic voting calls for a review of this hypothesis.

IS THERE A BETI ETHNIC GROUP? TOWARDS A CONSTRUCTIVIST CON-FUSION This question could be rephrased as follows: Do people who are subsumed under this ethnic group have a common collective mindset and an established historical memory? Such questioning may appear irrelevant in a context where political literature in the area of political pluralism in Cameroon answers everything in the affirmative, so obvious does the existence of this state of affairs seem to be in its analyses (Collectif 'Changer le Cameroun' 1992). And yet, looking at the peoples who constitute the group known as Beti, we can hardly validate the ethnic voting hypothesis. By breaking down the Beti ethnic group a little and examining the history of the peoples of the Centre and South provinces who are subsumed under this group, we quickly realize that it is simply an overstatement, a product of the imagination of people who exploit identity for their own ends.

If we take the Centre province, for instance, it comprises a host of ethnic groups including the Bene, Ewondo, Eton, Yambassa, Vute and Banen, to name a few. Each of these ethnic groups is made up of clans and lineages. In this part of the country, there are microcosms of peoples who think, feel and act differently. It is, therefore, difficult to talk about the Beti as if they were a homogeneous group. Even the languages spoken in this region will belie this hypothesis. Finally, a breakdown of the various peoples of the Centre province does not even identify a group of whatever size called Beti.

This appellation refers to the Bene, Ewondo and Enoa (Laburthe-Tolra 1977: 98) and readily extends to the Bulu (ibid., p. 91) who would rather stand on their own. In the same vein of exclusions/adoptions/naturalizations, the Beti refuse to be confused with the Fang (pp. 83, 91); the Ntumu follow suit (p. 100). In all, the confusion, generalization and assimilation which Laburthe (p. 421) criticizes as being present in works on peoples of the 'Pahouin' group which homogenize different entities, again, have not been corrected.[14] The socio-ethnic composition of the peoples of the South province, which is bounded by the republics of Gabon, Equatorial Guinea and Congo Brazzaville, is as follows: Bulu, Bene, Fang, Ntumu, Nwae, Ngumba, etc. In this province, too, are to be found differences between groups: differences in ancestry, in the existence of clans and lineages within the same group, the absence of a common history and differences in cultures we referred to with regard to the peoples of the Centre province. Hence, the question arises as to what would be the mainstay of the Beti ethnic group in a context where it does not exist and where some of the ethnic groups listed above, which are supposed to be part of this group, regard the other groups condescendingly (p. 92).[15]

Besides, an anthropological study of the notion of conviviality in this area reveals that the separatist and conflict instinct is always rearing its head among these populations. Deep down among the Bulu, Ewondo, Bene, Fang, etc., it is generally accepted that '*Nda ene djia, binon bine bibae*' (There are two beds in the same house). This proverb, which is often used when talking about polygamous families – to explain and, above all, justify the constant conflict between children of the same father but different mothers – should serve as a warning against any attempt at analysing the peoples concerned as a homogeneous group, and should call for a review of its bases. The friction that characterizes the life of these peoples can be compared to the atmosphere of constant subdued tension that reigns in polygamous families.

To grasp this better, all one needs to do is listen to the speeches of the leaders of these communities during electoral campaigns to discover the grievances they bear against those in power and, especially, the frailty of the group called Beti. These speeches reveal that the people complain that they are disregarded by those who come to them as their 'brothers' during elections. Such deceit has to do with the failure of the elite to keep promises made during past elections, to the extent that the population refuses to listen to them when they show up again or, at best, agree to attend rallies with the sole aim of ridiculing them or consuming their food, which is not very different from the attitude of the West Cameroon population with regard to the CPDM as described by Antoine Socpa (2000: 91–108).

THE 'ANGLO-BAMILEKE' ETHNIC GROUP The difficulty of establishing the sociological validity of the Beti ethnic group that we have demonstrated above would not have the same proportions here if we limit ourselves to some works (Warnier 1993). But even then, the homogenization tendency will also meet with some sociological divergences. According to works that posit the existence of this ethnic group, it includes the people of the West province and those of the North West province.[16] In general, the people of these two provinces come from part of the bigger group called Grassfields characterized, in terms of the traditional power structure, by powerful chiefdoms with centralized power. This is the land of the Fons, the sultan (Noun division) and the traditional chiefs in the rest of the West province.

Although areas of convergence, moorings and similarities have been sufficiently identified and listed by research on the way of life of the people of this geographical territory, the diversity of tribes we mentioned with regard to the big group called Beti is also present in the Grassfields.[17] We need only to look at the languages spoken by the people to understand this. In this regard, the West province, for instance, is a territory in which the language of communication changes from one village to the next, thus complicating the smooth flow of social intercourse.[18] These communication difficulties between inhabitants of neighbouring villages in the West and North West provinces and the persistence of social conflict in these regions are, from the standpoint of cultural anthropology, indicators of the disintegration of this Grassfields population and, consequently, a lack of common bearings or common history and memory on which cultural consensus could be built. This situation is further complicated by the expression of forms of collective mindset sometimes peculiar to each of the peoples of this province, mindsets equally tainted by the condescending attitudes of some ethnic groups towards others. This is the case with the low esteem suffered by the people of Dschang as a result of negative stereotypes used by their 'brothers' to poke fun at them and to show that they belong to a primitive age, while people of the Nde division enjoy a positive image by interpreting the three letters that constitute the spelling of their name as 'nobility, dignity, elegance'. These are the same observations we made with regard to the group called Beti.

## In the wake of the Muslim/Christian, North–South alliance/Bamileke hypotheses: a creative reversion to the ethnic-identity-based theories of the First Republic

The sociological analysis of the ethnic groups presented today as the electoral base of the CPDM on the one hand, and the SDF on the other hand, which we carried out above, reveals the existence of phony ethnic groups. The relatively recent character of the Beti 'ethnic group' is testimony to this.[19] It is with the reintroduction of political pluralism in 1990 that this 'ethnic group' as well as that known as 'Anglo-Bamileke' found their way into Cameroonian socio-political vocabulary. During the protracted single-party tenure of the Ahidjo regime, the formulae for explaining strategies behind the alliances formed by groups to win or keep power, on the one hand, and political confrontation, when it burst into the open, on the other hand, revolved round religion,[20] the North/South divide or the North–South alliance against the other groups, especially the Bamileke. The creation of the Beti and Anglo-Bamileke ethnic groups can be understood within the framework of this creative reversion to strategies for exacerbating or exploiting identity by 'professionals' of politics or their surrogates for purposes of winning or keeping power.

During the reign of Ahidjo, some circles developed a hypothesis of Foulbé power,[21] with the stronghold located in the North province (then made up of the present Adamawa, North and Far North provinces). What is interesting here is the uniform character attributed to the population of this vast and extremely heterogeneous group by subsuming the whole under the artificial ethnic group of 'Northerners', identified at the time as the group enjoying power.[22] It is this standardization that resurfaces here, this time, through arbitrary reference to the peoples of the Centre, South and East provinces.

From 1990, political confrontation once more crystallized around ethnic considerations. The power in Yaoundé being in the hands of a Bulu from the South province, political leaders creating parties to compete with the CPDM were quick to attribute a sociologically artificial – and, therefore, non-existent – ethnic base to this power. For their part, members of the ruling party, taking advantage of the silence of their national president over this issue, did everything to show that their main opponent (SDF) was nothing but the platform of an ethnic group which they too had previously created (the Anglo-Bamileke).[23] To operationalize this arbitrary conception of local bases for political parties, its supporters mostly used election results obtained after recourse to acts of electoral delinquency.

## Electoral delinquency and validation of the paradigm of solidarity voting

Electoral delinquency refers to all the forms of cheating initiated by political actors both upstream and downstream of the electoral process in a bid to frustrate their opponents while enhancing their victory during a poll. We are going to examine how bureaucratico–administrative and political classes in privileged positions exploit elections for their own ends.

The position of the voter in the early presidential election of 11 October 1992 in areas considered to be the strongholds of the CPDM or the SDF can be compared to that of the Supreme Court as analysed by Luc Sindjoun (1994b: 21–69). As the authority charged with the proclamation of election results, this institution was the focus of attention from the various forces on the electoral market and the target of repeated attacks from the main competing parties.[24] In both cases, the actors concerned were developing strategies to construct a monistic framework for presenting the results of the election in a manner favourable to them and were doing everything to legitimize this. These strategies were intended to reduce the autonomy of this legitimate body, thereby exploiting it for their own ends. The enterprise of taking the Supreme Court hostage, orchestrated by would-be conquerors of the supreme power and their allies, by trying to coerce the Court into proclaiming them winners of the ballot even if the actual results did not sanction such a victory, was simply a transfer, in the Republic, of the voting practices that obtained in the 'areas of influence' of the CPDM and the SDF during the election campaign and the poll proper, and which consisted of violating people's convictions with the aim of aligning them with some sort of electoral 'metasocial institutants' (Touraine 1973), that is, structures carrying voting behavioural content which lies beyond the electoral process itself.

An examination of the speeches of political actors touting for votes during the early presidential election of 11 October 1992 in the political parties under review shows permanent recourse to strategy designed to win over the voters. During political rallies organized as part of the election campaign and moderated by the 'elite',[25] the people, depending on whether they belonged to the one or the other zone deemed to belong to the SDF or the CPDM, were made aware of the urgent need to seize/take the power previously held by a 'lazy', 'hedonistic' ethnic group whose existence was reduced to the satisfaction of the pleasures of the 'stomach' and the 'lower abdomen' and which, consequently, was responsible for the economic crisis in the country, being themselves spendthrift and corrupt. This was the so-called Beti tribe (Collectif 'Changer le Cameroun' 1992; Nga Ndongo 1993). It is this image of the Beti that the opposition in general and the SDF in particular used as their main weapon in the quest for votes in their strongholds.

For its part, the CPDM advocated in its 'electoral village' the need to eschew all divisions and to form a homogeneous front to defend Beti power which was coming under increasing attack from the Anglo-Bamileke of the SDF whose bid for this 'trophy', which belonged by right (?) to the former, could only be driven by jealousy on the part of the latter. Their insistence on the holding of a sovereign national conference was merely a subterfuge. According to the point of view of the 'advocates' of Beti power,

57

in the collective mindset of the Anglo-Bamileke, the advent of political competition tolled the death-knell of 'Beti power'. It was these representations, underpinned by the generally private interests of the people in power and those of the classes aspiring thereto, that were served up to voters in the 'strongholds' of the CPDM and the SDF, making sure that they were attached to the whole population of each 'stronghold' so as to appear representative of the organic perceptions of the 11 October 1992 election. This was the basis of the ethnic voting hypothesis.

Yet this process was utilitarian in intent. By building up an artificial and fictitious electoral collective mindset based, as it was, on house-of-cards 'strongholds', 'advocates' of the two main political parties of Cameroon were laying the groundwork for the electoral manipulation and fraud that was going to align the results of the election with this previously constructed theoretical model. Nobody, or very few people, both in Cameroon and abroad, could question the credibility of the landslide victory of the CPDM in its so-called native Beti land or that of the SDF in the Anglo-Bamileke areas.[26]

After creating artificial identity focal points for each of these two main parties in the area of each national chairman who supported their cause, the finished plan thus established had to be translated into concrete form. This is what was done during the 11 October 1992 election through practices such as multiple[27] and guided voting, stuffing of ballot boxes, falsification of polling station reports, voter intimidation on the day of the poll, discriminatory voter registration and tampering with registers – all evidence of lack of civic responsibility in electoral behaviour (Deloye and Ihl 1993).[28]

With regard to CPDM,[29] the electoral districts where multiple voting was most rampant were the Centre, East and South provinces. To recruit their clients, the members of the privileged bureaucratico-administrative and political classes, who were charged with the conduct of the election campaign, turned to fragile social categories and those with uncertain futures. Most of these were students, young graduates on the labour market who were promised employment if they participated actively in the power preservation enterprise, unemployed persons or junior employees and those in insecure jobs whose fate depended on the whims of the 'boss'.[30] These persons were thus 'collected' by the latter who arranged to secure an environment for them in order to facilitate mobility in the field. Each member of this team was issued with additional identity cards and voters' cards and vehicles were placed at their disposal for transportation from one town to another or one neighbourhood to another.[31] In so doing, the promoters of this technique had one objective in mind: to vindicate the hypothesis of electoral 'strongholds' by relying on 'fortuitous' (?) votes picked up by the ruling party in the 'stronghold' of the SDF, for instance, and vice versa.

The analysis of the stuffing of ballot boxes and the falsification of polling station reports becomes very revealing when one tries to find out their causes (particularly the falsification of reports). This is a technique that is used after the voting. It takes shape at the moment when, after the poll and during the vote count, it is discovered that the people tried to exercise their sovereignty free of any external pressure. So, indulging in the falsification of polling station reports is tantamount to blaming the citizen for having strayed off the path intended by those who now appear, in the final analysis, to be the repositories of sovereignty in the district and, consequently, showing the citizen that he/she is a negligible entity in the choice of the supreme ruler. Thus, the election is stolen by the privileged classes.

The intimidation and calling to order of voters likely to catch the 'deviance' virus (in reality, those who feel like voting freely) in the 'strongholds' on polling day reflect this confiscation of the poll by privileged classes. In the southern part of the country, the discussions we had with officers of polling stations revealed that voters (mainly those in rural areas) had no choice at all. At the entrance to polling stations young people who had been brainwashed by elites defending their *'gari'* or *'tapioca'*[32] made sure that voters coming out of the polling booth presented the SDF ballot to them. Voters who refused to submit to this ritual had the CPDM ballot snatched from them and promptly put in the ballot box by these 'gendarmes' of the party. Alternatively, others were simply invited, by these same 'gendarmes', sometimes *manu militari*, to return to the ballot box and deposit their 'burden'. Furthermore, the fact that these intimidating practices prevailed in rural areas where the majority of the Cameroonian population still lives, proves that election results are still 'negotiated' outside a major portion of the electorate and against their will.

In areas declared SDF 'strongholds', unorthodox voter intimidation practices were equally reported. A sort of modern version of the 'sand-sand boys'[33] 'stormed' polling stations to make sure that the 'Lion man' was being devoured by the party that was restoring power (at last?) to the people and to nip in the bud anything that might prevent things from running smoothly. The manhunt that followed the official proclamation of the results of the 11 October 1992 election in Bamenda, during which Tita Fomukong, founder of the Cameroon National Party, was burned alive on the pretext that his party was actually an outgrowth of the CPDM, the ransacking of the houses of the majority of institutional notables of the

South West and North West,[34] and the confrontation between the indigenous and non-indigenous populations in two towns of the South (Ebolowa and Sangmelima), revealed the determination of the privileged classes to impose on the population, willy-nilly, a voting pattern favourable to themselves.[35]

The omnipresence of fraud[36] as part and parcel of the Cameroonian electoral process (Collectif 'Changer le Cameroun' 1993: 93–114), when compared with a paradigm that addresses the interpretation of electoral behaviour solely from the standpoint of primary identity, brings back this debate. The recourse to fraud in general and to violence, both physical and symbolic as manifested, in particular, through corruption, pressurizing and intimidation[37] of voters in the so-called 'strongholds', call for another approach to electoral behaviour that brings out the idea politicians have of the independence of voters or, at least, of a significant portion of them. If the choices of the people were irreversibly based on ethnic, ethno-regional or ethno-linguistic considerations, political leaders shopping for votes would not indulge in efforts to resensitize 'their' voters to the identity cause during political rallies. In other words, political leaders and their supporters would show more assurance in 'their' strongholds, steering clear of the numerous cases of violation of conscience they orchestrate among those they call their 'brothers'. By indulging in these identity 'reconstructions' in areas considered as their strongholds, political leaders betray a worry they harbour, namely, the fear of not succeeding in convincing people in their own areas and, consequently, being rejected by the very people who are supposed to carry them to power or keep them there, or who are supposed to persuade and rally other groups to achieve that end.

Thus, fraud appears as a form of technology invented to assuage the anguish of political failure in one's 'electoral village' and, above all, to mask the irrefutable evidence of the fragility of these leaders' political legitimacy in their own 'strongholds'. This fraud is present both upstream and downstream of the electoral process. Upstream, it is preventive. The leader who exploits voter registration, for example by over-registering voters who are his followers or are believed to be and by obstructing the registration of persons considered to be against him, seeks to give himself an ample margin of security to offset the unthinkable. Now, if the unthinkable becomes a preoccupation for a political leader in what is called his stronghold, it is clear that his electorate is not behind him.

The entrenchment of fraud categories, manipulation and violation of the consciences of the population in electoral districts by the party machine so that areas are won over beforehand (and irreversibly so) by that party, show that voters steer clear of identity-based patterns of voting. In other words, motivations, influences and experiences other than ones that are ethnic identity-based are at work when voters cast their ballots during elections in Cameroon.

## Ground-level voting in the Grassfields

The interpretation of the vote in the Grassfields is extremely biased in so far as it seeks to establish a close correlation between the ethno-regional origins of the SDF chairman and the following the party enjoys in this area to validate the ethnic voting hypothesis. The historical trauma hypothesis actually seems to be more relevant in explaining the electoral attitude of the Bamileke. Two groups of underlying events, one economic and the other political, can be considered as the origin of the historical trauma which swayed the people of the West to the left.

In the economic sphere, the people of this part of the country delved into the various economic activities at the beginning of the colonial period.[38] This immediately pitted them against the colonial authorities who tried to stop the economic expansion which they saw as a harbinger of a subsequent hegemonic enterprise, the evidence thereof being their rapid resettlement in all areas of the country. During the colonial period, the adversity these people suffered at the hands of the colonial authorities was underpinned by the competition their activities posed to the interests of the mother-country which wanted to maintain the economy of this territory as its exclusive preserve ( Joseph 1986).

Successive governments in Yaoundé since the country acquired international sovereignty have never been forgiven by economic operators from this part of the territory for perpetuating this state of affairs. The people of the West province have always complained that their businesses suffer from unfair competition perpetuated by these regimes. This competition goes as far as pitting them against Syro-Lebanese and French interests – that is, foreign interests – on the one hand, and the interests of national businessmen from the North or the Centre South (depending on the regime in power), on the other hand. Some of these businessmen, it is maintained, are supported by the regime with the sole aim of infiltrating the monopoly situation they have enjoyed in the wholesale and retail sectors since the departure of the Greeks.

The second traumatizing economic event that poisoned relations between this Grassfields region and the two successive regimes in Yaoundé concerns land tenure. Coming as they do from a province with a problem of space reflected in the very high rates of population density, and caught in a social system where the chief is the only recognized landowner, the peoples of the western high plateaus have, since independence, embarked

61

upon a migration process which has taken them to almost all parts of the country in search of less crowded living environments that can give them access to greener pastures for their economic activities. This adventuring process immediately brought them into conflict with people in the host regions creating, among other bones of contention, the land issue. In spite of the acquisition of land titles through leases on more or less considerable plots of land, and whatever the duration of occupancy of such plots, the emigrant population was always seen in the local collective mindset as strangers who were going to leave sooner or later. But it turned out that these people had invested a lot in these plots, and were determined to protect their investment. This situation soon elicited input from the population to the regime with respect to the land issue.

Basically, the people of the West province are expecting the authorities to issue a law on land tenure which will make it possible for them to be declared 'indigenes' and, consequently, owners of the land they have occupied for a certain duration instead of being treated as 'strangers in Cameroon'. The dilatory attitude of the government on this issue as well as its collusion with foreign and national interests have bred an atmosphere of traumatizing disappointment within the Bamileke population which can only translate into hostility against a regime which, according to the collective mindset, and to make matters worse, is an offshoot of French colonial interests, that is, their first tormentor. From this viewpoint, the vote of the Grassfields population for the SDF can be seen as sanctioning long-standing negative appraisals of the ruling government and as an expression of discontent at their living conditions. Henceforth, it ceases to be the reflection of ethno-regional identification of voters with a party that is ethno-regional, and becomes the external manifestation, in the political arena, of conflictual relations between a portion of the population and those in power on issues of social existence, driving home the veracity of a philosophical category: existential anguish.

The second group of events at the root of the trauma is political and comes from the socio-political history of this part of the country. The political history of the Bamileke people is tied to that of the radical wing of the nationalist movement which existed in Cameroon during the 1940s and whose political standard-bearer was the UPC (Joseph 1986). This party enjoyed immense support from the people of this region, a bastion of the said party. The fact that the *maquis* was deeply rooted here even after the UPC had been officially dissolved and had gone underground is testimony to this. Like other areas which were reluctant to put an end to political activities organized under the banner of this fallen party, at the level of the law, in all illegality, this province was the target of a rough 'pacification' mission initiated by the local authorities and enjoying the support of French troops, the ultimate aim of which was to efface from the minds of the population supporting the activities of the *maquisards* any reminiscences favourable to the party and its leaders as well as any other attempt, even occult, to collude with the opposition[39] by exposing them to scenes of horror.[40] The fact that the population was forced to witness these scenes bred in them unrelenting hatred for the regime. Although this population annexation enterprise seemed to achieve the desired effect during the long single-party period, this was mere make-believe. The people feared the former president, Ahidjo, more than they loved him (Bayart 1986). The advent of multi-partyism in December 1990, which discarded the enrolment approach in the recruitment strategies of political parties, gave citizens the freedom to express political convictions which for a long time had been stifled by a highly authoritarian regime. The vote for the opposition thus appears to be a vote from a people who have recovered, thirty years later, the freedom of choice of which they had been deprived, and who were taking advantage of this new-found freedom to express their feelings towards the government, feelings born of the period of the dismantling of the nationalist movement which carried all the hopes of the people of the region.

This is a kind of sanction. The people establish a link between the colonial power which was the source of their misfortune and those of the first (1 January 1960 to 4 November 1982) and second (6 November 1982 to date) republics which, according to them, are nothing but the perpetuation of the Aujoulat order in Cameroon. [41] The wrangles, and the obstructive clashes which Bamileke economic interests suffered in the face of the interests of metropolitan France, on the one hand, and those of business-men enjoying the blessing of the powers that be, on the other hand, the campaign of repression aimed at crushing the rebellion that followed the banning of the UPC, all contributed to build up among the natives of this province a radical and negative mindset *vis-à-vis* the regime and against any structure suspected or identified as colluding with anti-Bamileke ideology. It so happens that the successive governments that have come to power in Cameroon[42] are perceived in the predominant collective mindset of the people of this province as an unquestionable link in the perpetuation of this ideology. One just needs to refer to the frequent attacks on persons – as well as on their property – considered as part of the prevailing political order during periods of social tension fuelled by elections in this part of the country. In the same vein, the refusal of the electorate to observe voting instructions issued by traditional rulers considered as satellites of the Yaoundé regime appears as a dual exercise of recovery and reaffirmation of the autonomy of the people who have been victims of a dual traumatizing authoritarianism: local, at the level of the Grassfields society, and central, at the level of the whole society which is the state.

But the explanation of the electoral behaviour of this Grassfields region cannot be limited to this historical trauma. It needs to be supplemented by an exploration of the neo-utilitarian approach to voting. Although the cautious stance of Maurice Engueleguele (2002) on the total operationality of the explanation of voting in sub-Saharan African countries on the basis of the theory of economic rationality needs to be taken into account as we explore this avenue in an attempt to explain the electoral attitudes of the population, it must also be admitted that this approach does not always lead to dead-ends. The crisis that beset Cameroon in the second half of the 1980s, which was blamed on the government considered to be a bunch of shameless looters, influenced the vote of the Grassfields population.

One of the arguments often advanced by partisans of the rational voting hypothesis is that those in power are judged on their economic perform-ance and are exposed to sanctions from the governed at the next election where their performance may be deemed unsatisfactory. Followers of neo-utilitarian theories talk of 'retrospective voting'. This variable influenced voting trends during the elections of the 1990s. The population was wallow-ing in misery following a drop in their standards of living. Staff redundancy and dismissals in public and semi-public corporations, salary cuts for state employees, the plummeting of prices of raw materials, state withdrawal from social sectors imposed by the Bretton Woods institutions as part of structural adjustment programmes, all led to a drop in consumption that had a direct impact on the small business sector which is the monopoly of the population of the West. This situation was a threat to their survival as it impoverished their clientele. In our opinion, these effects of the economic crisis suffered by the small business sector hardened the position of the Bamileke towards the ruling government.

## Conclusion

The explanation of voting in one of the areas considered to be a strong-hold of the SDF, which we have addressed, has revealed the limited and, therefore, superficial nature of any attempt to analyse electoral attitudes by using a monistic framework and remaining confined within a single paradigm. As was brought out in the major collective work appraising the various explanations of voting trends in France (Gaxie 1985), several vari-ables come into play and criss-cross in the analysis of electoral attitudes, for it is impossible for a single paradigm to explain the voting phenomenon. An approach which draws from several theoretical models thus appears more operational. In our case, the combination of interpretations drawing from the historical trauma models of Paul Bois, the retrospective voting tenet of neo-utilitarianism, has brought home to us that the analysis of electoral attitudes in Cameroon is far from complete and the few works which have been produced so far have created more dead-ends than they have explained voting. Thus, the subject of elections calls for in-depth research.

The need to revisit this subject also arises from the volatility of attitudes, illustrated by the results of subsequent elections[43] when observed across time. This volatility takes the form of the veritable instability of electoral attitudes which translate, in turn, into permanent fluctuations at the level of voting constituencies, fluctuations resulting from break-ups and disintegration after each election in the supposed strongholds of the political parties.

This reality appeared on the Cameroonian electoral landscape once the results of the legislative elections of 17 and 18 May and those of the by-election of 3 August 1997[44] were proclaimed. At the close of that election, the NUDP lost most of what was considered its stronghold in 1992, the northern part of the country, in the main, and the Adamawa and North provinces where the CPDM won four seats out of the ten available and the absolute majority, that is, nine out of twelve, the rest going to the NUDP to which these seats were supposed to belong. During that election, the base of this party was significantly eroded.[45] These swings in the electoral attitudes of the population – who now choose more attractive political options – that first affected those parties which, following the results of the first competitive elections, qualified as smaller parties,[46] are increasingly evident in the way voters cast their ballots, thus bringing out the versatile nature of an electorate which has been over-hastily characterized as essentially lethargic. Such versatility equally affects the candidates whom political parties present to their electorate during elections for the renewal of members of the Cameroon parliament.

The two legislatures of the political pluralism era have shown that the number of mandates an MP can hope to hold in parliament has dropped to one term of five years. The versatility of Cameroonian voters, supported by an analysis of the results of the three sessions of elections already held in the country since the beginning of the 1990s, calls for a heterogeneous approach to the treatment of the electorate in research on political attitudes. The electorate should be treated, henceforth, as a heterogeneous reality with varying motivations from one electoral district to another, depending on local specificities. This approach has the advantage of generating region-based research work which can bring out the underlying motivations of each electorate, the specificities peculiar to each of the regions thus studied and, at national level, lead to cross-cutting reflections which can bring out areas of similarity and/or divergence.

## Notes

1 In the same vein, read: Paul Mercier (1961: 1044); Michael Gluckman (1960); Immannuel Wallerstein (1960); Jacques Lombard (1969); Robert Sklar (1981); Guy Nicolas (1972), other followers of this anthropological trend. This framework proved operative in a research project on what is known as 'ethnic conflicts' in Cameroon that we carried out as part of a multi-disciplinary team, the findings of which were published in a book (Mbock 2000). The results of the surveys we carried out in seven of the ten Cameroonian provinces – the provinces were selected on the basis of the existence of actual confrontation between different groups – show that these conflicts have social causes.

2 To borrow from the local lexicon.

3 The conclusions of the work based on this paradigm came under a lot of criticism (Key 1966; Nie et al. 1976) revolving, for the most part, round the phenomenon of electoral volatility.

4 The author describes his model as a study of political rationality from an economic standpoint. This theory maintains that each agent, be it an individual, a party or a private coalition, always acts in a rational manner (Downs 1957: 36), that is, it acts according to its goals, making maximum economy of its resources, and it indulges only in activities where marginal profit exceeds marginal cost. This view equally dominates the works of Gordon Tullock (1978). Read, for instance, chapters I, 'Economie et Politique', and II, 'Le Vote comme moyen de contrôle effectif'.

5 The neoclassical economic conception of rationality maintains that the social actor decides on the basis of a cost/benefit analysis of options at his/her disposal.

6 They range from the uncertainty and errors contained in the information gathered by Siegfried on the land tenure systems of the areas he studied to the tautology of the religious factor in explaining political choices. To Paul Bois, instead of being a factor in opinion, religious commitment is itself an opinion.

7 Read, in this regard, Daniel Gaxie (1982: 251–69); Annick Percheron in Daniel Gaxie (ed.) (1985: 244).

8 They use the official election results as source for most of their illustrations, without bothering to find out which strategies the electoral actors used to obtain the said results.

9 This choice is not arbitrary. These two elections brought about the debate on ethnic voting in Cameroon.

10 It should be noted that the results of the legislative elections of March 1992 were biased because of the refusal of John Fru Ndi's Social Democratic Front to participate. This decision of the SDF to boycott the election was advantageous to the NUDP and even to the CPDM as they gained votes from among its electorate.

11 In the case of Benin, where the ethnic voting hypothesis was also largely discussed, research is in progress, specifically a research project on the

theme 'Les élites politiques et leurs relations locales' (Political elites and their local relations), a project that covers the years 2003 to 2005, co-directed by a team of researchers from the Centre d'Etudes d'Afrique Noire of the Institut d'Etudes politiques de Bordeaux and the Abomey–Calavi University of the Republic of Benin, a project in which we participated. Although acknowledging the influence of identity in the voting trends of the population during the different elections held in the country, we abstained from pursuing analysis (considered superficial) in terms of ethnicity because it was noticed that the phenomenon of strongholds extended beyond the cultural bounds of some candidates and because some candidates – albeit of lesser importance – obtained votes throughout the national territory, with more concentration in urban areas which are more composite in population. These votes are seen as depending only on the candidate's personality and his plan of action. This is a new approach which has the advantage of eschewing the pitfall of remaining stuck to identity-based considerations and diversifying the approaches to the explanation of a phenomenon as complex as voting. But, in our opinion, the contribution of this research project is more at the level of the legitimization of the 'ethnic' strongholds to which it will lead. Since the return of political pluralism to Africa, politicians have regularly been criticized with regard to their village legitimacy. On the contrary, the project intends to take the opposite view to this 'fact' and to show that ethnicity can provide a sound basis for a lasting democracy.

12  The first won in the Littoral, the West and the South West. In the Centre, he obtained 39 per cent of the vote in the Mfoundi division (Eboko 1999: 107). The second, Paul Biya, obtained 52 per cent of the vote in Mfoundi (ibid.), 51 per cent in the Kaele district as against 33 per cent for Bello Bouba Maïgari, 35 per cent in the Lara district (Kees 1993: 121). On the whole, in this northern part of the country made up of the Adamawa, North and Far North provinces, which passes for the stronghold of the NUDP, the incumbent president beat the declared lord, in terms of score, in the last province. He obtained 47.6 per cent of the vote as against 42.5 per cent for the supposed leader. Moreover, in the North province (that is, the province of origin of the NUDP leader), the latter is virtually running neck and neck with the CPDM candidate, with scores of 50.4 per cent and 42.9 per cent respectively. The NUDP leader succeeded in beating the CPDM candidate clear only in the Adamawa province where he obtained 64 per cent of the vote compared with 26.1 per cent for the runner-up. In addition to these figures, the CPDM candidate came second in the Littoral, the South West with 21.4 per cent of the vote, the North West (9.6 per cent) and the West.

13  The stinging defeat of this candidate in his native Centre province proves that the population does not automatically choose 'one of theirs' and that cohesion does not necessarily exist among these peoples called Beti. This candidate was the brother of the late Emah Basile who was government delegate to the Yaoundé City Council. Also and above all, he was a CPDM bigwig. True to the ethnic voting approach, one would have expected these two brothers to unite to defend the party's cause among the Ewondo and the Bene who are described as base of the CPDM. Yet, it was not to be. Ema Ottou preferred to run under his own banner. Another case in point was the

67

announcement of the candidature of Ayissi Mvondo (another Ewondo from Mfou, 24km from the capital) at the 1997 presidential election. His candidature was peculiar in that he had been a CPDM militant for a long time. Besides, we have seen above that the SDF beat the CPDM in its native Mfoundi. Yet these indicators have not attracted the attention of the researchers who have worked in this domain.

14 According to Laburthe-Tolra, the generalizations and standardizations are the consequences of a methodological flaw. Some of the authors who have worked on this group do not specify where they carried out their surveys in order to present the results thereof as being representative of the entire group. To avoid falling into this trap, Laburthe-Tolra limits his field of research to Minlaaba and specifies that he worked on the Bene, the Ewondo and the Enoa (Laburthe-Tolra 1977: 98, 417).

15 To have a glimpse of the picture, we need to take a look at inter-ethnic social relations. Let us take the case of the Bulu Ewondo and Bene. Among the Bulu, it is believed that the Bene and Ewondo (whom the Bulu consider, strictly speaking, as Beti) are stupid from birth. The story is told in Bululand of how Charles Assale, then Prime Minister of independent East Cameroon and Bulu from Ebolowa, told the Bene-Ewondo that all it took was for a single letter (the letter T) to be added to the spelling of the word 'Beti' and their appellation would express exactly what they really are. In this case, the group would be called 'Betit', which is the Bulu plural for another word 'tit', meaning, 'animal'. For their part, the Ewondo and Bene have painted the portrait of the Bulu man in their community as being fundamentally untruthful. A well-known proverb in their society holds that a Beti man can be broke but can never be caught off guard in matters of rhetoric. Similar considerations characterize social relations between the Bulu and the Ntumu, for whom the former have always had little regard, and between the Bene and the Eton in the same manner.

16 Jean-Pierre Warnier (1993: 67) writes, in this regard, that if these peoples had not been separated in 1916, there is little doubt that the inhabitants of the North West province would have become 'Bamileke' as well.

17 With the former, it is possible to identify a cluster of groups that originally called themselves Beti, but such is not the case with the so-called Bamileke ethnic group. According to Stoll, the word Bamileke means 'a corrupt monster with as many faults as syllables. Only Dschang knows this name. It is completely unknown to all the other tribes. In Dschang, it is: Mbaliku.' So, this is the name that will be used to refer to the people of the West.

18 Another aspect of this social heterogeneity of people of the West is the persistent social conflicts, wrongly called ethnic conflicts, in this part of the country. The conflicts arise from border disputes between neighbouring ethnic groups or villages (Mbock 2000) and sometimes result in open confrontation with loss of life.

19 The political history of Cameroon from the first experience with political pluralism in the 1960–66 post-independence years to the protracted single-party period 1966–90 does not offer an analyst of the national political landscape any cases or reference points of political expression where this entity appears as a homogeneous group.

20  Then Christians were said to be opposed to Muslims; attempts at explaining the disagreement between Paul Biya and the former President of Cameroon in 1984 explored this hasty conclusion sufficiently.

21  It will appear that this 'ethnic group', in a bid to stop the Bamileke from taking power, joined the 'Southerners' and this 'alliance' brought about the alternation of power between the North and the South: hence, the North–South axis.

22  Whereas the sociological breakdown of the peoples of this vast northern part of Cameroon calls for two observations that deal a blow to this enterprise of confusion for utilitarian ends. First, the Foulbé are in the minority although they are fired with the stout determination to 'foulbeize' the region, that is, impose, with hegemonic aims, their culture on all the people of this part of the country. The Mémorandum des Kirdis (Kirdis' Memorandum) is eloquent testimony to this (Collectif 'Changer le Cameroun' 1992: 144, 153). Second, there are many other ethnic groups, including the Moundang, Toupouri, Mousgoum, Guiziga, Fali, Maya, Guidar, all animist or Christian who, although in the majority, were excluded from the exercise of this power which a Peul minority shared with their cronies (Mbembe 1993: 352; Collectif 'Changer le Cameroun' 1992: 140 et sub.).

23  This 'ethnic group' was later hastily identified with the 'Bosnians' during the most turbulent years (1991–92) of the 1990s in the collective mindset that was constructed around the exclusivist ideas of 'son-of-the-soil' politicians.

24  The CPDM to whom, according to the opposition, it was subservient, and the SDF who, spurred by this hypothesis, decided to proclaim its victory even before the body vested with the power to do so could come up with the official results.

25  It is not easy to tell who belongs to this category in Cameroon because it is very permeable. Even crooks who have made their wealth through practices that amount to organized crime are called elite and are treated as such. The most compelling example of this reality is the 'Feyman'. 'Fey' in Cameroonian slang is a verb that means to swindle, to extort something (generally goods) from somebody. A feyman is, therefore, someone who specializes in swindling, who extorts property from people. The collapse of the value system and the prevailing poverty have made things such that when the swindled property (money) is redistributed, the feyman is seen as a benevolent sponsor, an elite idolized by the society. With regard to feymen, see Banégas and Warnier (2001).

26  Thus, these parties succeeded in effecting a veritable electoral transposition of the Berlin Conference, during which Africa was partitioned in the absence of the Africans themselves. For this was, in reality, a distribution of political zones of influence in the absence of the voters, and sometimes against their convictions on this issue. This practice made the election look like an exercise in which the people were asked to 'vote without choosing' (Alade Fawole 2001). In other words, this is the reign of the 'election without choice' that Dominique Andolfatto (1993) talks about.

27  Multiple voting, in which the same person votes several times, in the

same poll, at different polling stations, with the intention of maximizing the chances of a candidate, was one of the most prized techniques used in 1992 by politicians of both the SDF and the CPDM.

28 In pointing out these practices, we do not by any means think that they are peculiar to Cameroon, or to Africa for that matter; there is a certain mentality that regards Africans as being 'uncivilized' and apparently predisposed to unpolished, uncouth or 'archaic' behaviour in their political dealings. Such practices have marked (and continue to mark, albeit to a lesser extent) the conduct of elections in countries considered democratic (Charnay 1962; Gaxie 1985; Huard 1991; Garrigou 1992; O'Gorman 1992).

29 Practices similar to those analysed below were orchestrated by the SDF. We analyse them in greater detail in another work (in progress) on voting conditions in the Mezam electoral district. We will, therefore, refer to them very briefly in this work.

30 A popular appellation in Cameroon for people who have succeeded socially or who employ others.

31 This information was obtained from interviews we had in 1994 with a group of students with bachelors' degrees – some enrolled for the postgraduate diploma (*Maîtrise*) – who took part in these operations. Most of them were promised admission into the Advanced Teachers' Training School (Ecole Normale Supérieure), but not all of them were granted this admission. The case of this institution needs to be explained. After the implementation of the SAP which forbade further recruitment into the civil service, it was virtually the only university institution where students, upon completion, could still enter the now narrow and, consequently, prized door to state employment. Accordingly, it became a means of bringing pressure to bear on university students and, *ipso facto*, an instrument of political profiteering for the ruling elite who used it either to compensate those loyal to them or to stifle any desire to differ with those in power.

32 This is the expression used in the collective mindset to refer to the benefits of all sorts to which members of the privileged bureaucratico-administrative and political classes in Cameroon are 'entitled' or which they enjoy.

33 This term dates back to 1945. It referred to the group of young unemployed persons, casual workers and sub-proletariat armed mostly with sticks who left the New-Bell neighbourhood in Douala to loot and attack black workers. This strike degenerated into bloody riots known in Cameroonian socio-political history as the September 1945 riots.

34 *Cameroon Tribune*, 5246, 26 October 1992 and 5249 of 29 October 1992.

35 In point of fact, in the areas considered as strongholds of these two parties, two practices contradictory in approach but clearly aimed at the same ultimate goal marked this phase of the elections: the two-way screening/full opening up of voter registration. Depending on whether the voting population was declared sympathetic to a political group by supporters of either of these parties, a range of strategies was deployed to maximize the chances of the party thus supported or to hamper the progress or reduce the success threshold of the rival party. In this atmosphere, registration officials withheld the registration of individuals identified as likely to vote for the opposing political class

while making certain that persons on their side were over-registered. All these practices aimed at paving the way for 'ethnic voting' were carried out without the knowledge of the voters. And yet, today, these same voters are described, in the light of community voting, as being attached to their native land.

36 Although some of the above-mentioned strategies are dying out as a result of amendments to the electoral process imposed by the outcry these fraudulent practices elicited from the national political class, it should be pointed out that fraud still exists in the national electoral process. The observation reports of the May 1997 and June 2002 elections produced by the Ecumenical Service for Peace (Service Œcuménique ... 1998), for the first election, and the Justice and Peace Commission of the National Episcopal Conference of Cameroon (Conférence Episcopale ... 2002), for the second, stress the existence of fraud, upstream, during voter registration where political parties, candidates and their allies swell the ranks of their militants arbitrarily, and downstream, on polling day, when the same actors try to influence the choice of voters, sometimes right into the polling station. The importance of fraud in the explanation of voting in Cameroon is such that we are currently carrying out comparative research on fraudulent practices in modern Cameroon and those in nineteenth-century France on the basis of the works of Raymond Huard (1991), Jean-Paul Charnay (1964) and Alain Garrigou (1992).

37 Read, for example, the reports of the special envoys of the CPDM in the Ocean electoral district (South Cameroon) during the campaign of the 1997 presidential election as reported by Maurice Engueleguele (2002: 5).

38 See Mongo Beti (1972); Dongmo (1978); Joseph (1986); Geschiere and Konings (eds) (1993); Warnier (1993).

39 This pacification enterprise through the use of repressive state machinery (army, police, gendarmerie, courts, etc.) was perpetuated during the first republic through another that did everything to render taboo, in the collective mindset of Cameroonians, any reference to the nationalist movement or to its various actors. The mere mention of the name of a leader such as Um Nyobe could be interpreted as an act of subversion. For more on this issue, see Achille Mbembe (1986).

40 The exhibiting, in villages, of the heads of *maquisards* freshly decapitated by the troops charged with the pacification.

41 The French doctor Louis-Paul Aujoulat is one of the personalities who shaped political life in a significant way in the part of Cameroon that was under French trusteeship. He created the Bloc Démocratique Camerounais (BDC), a moderate political party which espoused the views of the colonial administration with regard to the independence of the territory which, to the UPC nationalists, was an urgent need. The action of this party consisted, accordingly, in thwarting the rise of the radical nationalist movement epitomized by the UPC by encouraging the emergence of local, ready-made political leaders who, *ipso facto*, were loyal to the cause of the colonial administration which was their sponsor. It was the political leaders from this crop who came to power when the former French trusteeship territory of Cameroon achieved independence on 1 January 1960. For this reason, the Yaoundé government, to this day, is presented by partisans of 'pure' nationalism as an offshot or an outgrowth of

the Aujoulat era. This version gained ground after Christian-Tobie Kuoh (1991), former director of cabinet under President Ahidjo, published a book in which he relates the story of the recruitment of the current President of the Republic into that cabinet upon the recommendation of the same Aujoulat.

42 The moment one probes beyond the public declarations of some businessmen and traditional rulers of the West province whose calculated dealings with the ruling party are a subject of permanent suspicion.

43 Those following the first competitive elections of the era of the reintroduction of political pluralism in Africa in general, and Cameroon in particular.

44 This came immediately after the first competitive elections of 1992.

45 From sixty-eight MPs for the 1992–97 legislature, the NUDP dropped to thirteen MPs for the next legislature (1997–2002). During the legislative elections of 30 June 2002, only one candidate from this party succeeded in getting elected in the region considered as its natural stronghold, and this candidate was none other than the party's national president, Bello Bouba Maïgari. The SDF is not free from this base erosion phenomenon. Its representation at the National Assembly for the 1997–2002 legislature, forty-three seats out of the 180 seats of the Cameroonian parliament, came mainly from the Anglophone part of the country and the West province, with nineteen MPs out of twenty in the North West province and fifteen out of twenty-five in the West province. Although after the legislative elections of 30 June 2002 this party kept, by and large, its position as the second political force in the country and maintained its lead in the first province, it should be pointed out that, conversely, in the West province, which was also considered to be a stronghold of the same party, it suffered a major blow and lost the province.

46 This is the case with Augustin Frédérick Kodock's UPC and Dakole Daïssala's MDR. In the March 1992 legislative elections, these parties obtained in what was considered their strongholds at the time, Nyong-et- Kele division in the Centre province and the Sanaga Maritime division in the Littoral province (for the UPC) and the Far North province (for the MDR), eighteen and six seats respectively in parliament. In 1997, both parties succeeded in having only their national presidents elected. In 2002, the first consolidated its position in parliament slightly by obtaining five seats, but the second had its last MP thrown out by the electorate.

## References

Almond, G.and S. Verba (1963) *The Civic Culture* (Princeton, NJ: Princeton University Press).

Amselle, J.-L. and E. Mbokolo (1985) *Au coeur de l'ethnie. Ethnies, tribalisme et état en Afrique* (Paris: La Découverte).

Andolfatto, D. (1993) 'Les élections consulaires', *Politix*, no. 23.

Banégas, R. and J.-P. Warnier (2001) 'Les nouvelles figures de la réussite et du pouvoir', *Politique Africaine*, no. 82 ( June): 5–21.

Barth, F. (ed.) (1969) *Ethnic Groups and Boundaries. The Social Organization of Culture Difference* (London: Allen and Unwin).

Bayart, J.-F. (1986) 'La société politique camerounaise. 1982–1986', *Politique Africaine*, no. 22 (June).

Bernard, A. (1997) 'La conjoncture économique et le vote: une relation ambiguë', *Revue française de sociologie*, vol. XXXVIII: 245–64.

Bois, P. (1971) [1960] *Paysans de l'ouest* (Paris: Flammarion).

Boudon, R. (1997) 'Le "paradoxe du vote" et la théorie de la rationalité', *Revue française de sociologie*, no. 38: 217–27.

Bourdieu, P., J.-C. Chamboredon and J.-C. Passeron (1983) *Le métier de sociologue* [1968] (Paris: Mouton).

Butler, D. and D. Stokes (1969) *Political Change in Britain* (London: Macmillan).

Campbell, A. and D. Kahn (1952) *The People Elect a President* (New York: Wiley).

Campbell, A., G. Gurin and W. Miller (1954) *The Voter Decides* (Evanston, NJ: Row-Peterson).

Campbell, A., P. Converse, W. Miller and D. Stokes (1966) [1960] *The American Voter* (New York: Wiley).

Charnay, J.-P. (1964) *Les scrutins politiques en France: contestations et invalidations* (Paris: Armand Colin).

Collectif 'Changer le Cameroun' (1992) *Le Cameroun éclaté? Anthologie commentée des revendications ethniques* (Yaoundé: C3).

— (1993) *Le 11 octobre 1992. Autopsie d'une élection présidentielle controversée* (Yaoundé: C3).

Conférence Episcopale du Cameroun, Commission Justice et Paix (2002) *Rapport de la Conférence Episcopale Nationale du Cameroun sur l'Observation des Elections du 30 juin 2002* (Yaoundé).

Converse, P. E. and G. Dupeux (1962) 'Politicization of the Electorate in France and the United States', *Public Opinion Quarterly*, no. 26: 1–23.

Deloye, Y. and O. Ihl (1993) 'La civilité électorale: vote et forclusion de la violence en France', *Cultures et Conflits*, nos 9/10: 75–96.

Dongmo, J.-L. (1978) *Le dynamisme Bamiléké: essor démographique, expansion spatiale et réussite économique d'un peuple des hautes terres de l'Ouest-Cameroun* (2 vols). Doctoral thesis, University of Paris.

Downs, A. (1957) *An Economic Theory of Democracy* (New York: Harper and Row).

Durkheim, E. (1986) *Les règles de la méthode sociologique* (22nd edn) (Paris: PUF).

Eboko, F. (1999) 'Les élites politiques au Cameroun. Le renouvellement sans renouveau', in J.-P. Daloz (ed.), *Le (non-) renouvellement des élites en Afrique subsaharienne* (Bordeaux: CEAN).

Engueleguele, M. (2002) 'Le paradigme économique et l'analyse électoral africaniste: piste d'enrichissement ou source de nouvelles impasses?', paper presented at the conference 'Voter en Afrique: différentiations et comparisons', organized by the Association Française de Science Politique au Centre d'Etude d'Afrique Noir, Institut d'Etudes Politiques, Bourdeaux, 7–8 March.

Fawole, W. A. (2001) *Voting without Choosing*, paper presented at a session of the Institut sur la Gouvernance, CODESRIA, August.

Fortes (1945) *The Dynamics of Clanship among the Tallensi* (London: Oxford University Press).

Garrigou, A. (1992) *Le vote et la vertu; comment les français sont devenus électeurs* (Paris: Presses de la fondation nationale de science politique).

Gaxie, D. (1982) 'Mort et résurrection du paradigme de Michigan', *Revue française de science politique*, vol. 32, no. 1.

— (ed.) (1985) *Explication du vote. Un bilan des études électorales en France* (Paris: PFNSP).

Geschiere, P. and P. Konings (eds) (1993) *Itinéraires d'accumulation au Cameroun* (Paris: Karthala).

Gluckman, M. (1960) 'Tribalism in Modern British Central Africa', *Cahiers d'Etudes Africaines*, no. 1: 55–70.

Huard, R. (1991) *Le suffrage universel en France* (Paris: Aubier).

Joseph, R. (1986) *Le Mouvement nationaliste au Cameroun* (Paris: Karthala).

Kees, S. (1993) 'La démocratie aux champs: les présidentielles d'octobre 1992 au Nord-Cameroun', *Politique Africaine*, no. 50 (Paris: Karthala).

Key, V. (1966) *The Responsible Electorate* (Cambridge, MA: Harvard University Press).

Kramer, G. (1971) 'Short-term Fluctuations in US Voting Behavior: 1896–1964', *American Political Science Review*, no. 77: 131–43.

Kuoh, C.-T. (1991) *Mon témoignage. Tome 2: Une fresque du régime Ahidjo* (Paris: Karthala).

Laburthe-Tolra, P. (1977) *Minlaaba: histoire et société traditionnelle chez les Beti du Sud Cameroun*, 3 vols (Paris: Librairie Honoré Champion).

Lazarsfeld P., B. Berelson and H. Gaudet (1944) *The People's Choice* (New York: Columbia University Press).

Leroy-Ladurie, E. (1973) *Le territoire de l'historien* (Paris: Gallimard).

Lewis-Beck, M. (1977) 'Le vote du porte-monnaie en question' in D. Boy and N. Mayer (eds), *L'électeur a ses raisons* (Paris: Presses de la fondation nationale de science politique), pp. 239–61.

— (1985) 'Un modèle de prévision des élections législatives françaises avec une application pour 1986', *Revue française de science politique*, vol. 32, nos 4–5: 1080–9.

Lombard, J. (1969) 'Tribalisme et intégration nationale en Afrique noire', *L'Homme et la société*, no. 12: 69–86.

Mbembe, A. (1986) 'Pouvoir des morts et langage des vivants', *Politique Africaine*, no. 22 (June).

— (1993) 'Crise de l'Etat, restauration autoritaire et deliquescence de l'Etat', in P. Geshiere and P. Konings (eds), *Itinéraires d'accumulation au Cameroun* (Paris: Karthala), pp. 345–437.

Mbock, C.-G. (2000) *Les conflits ethniques au Cameroun. Quelles sources? Quelles solutions?* (Yaoundé: Editions du Service Œcuménique pour la Paix).

Menthong, H.-L. (1998) 'Vote et communautarisme au Cameroun: un vote de coeur, de sang et de raison', *Politique Africaine*, no. 69 (Paris: Karthala).

Mercier, P. (1961) 'Remarques sur la signification du "tribalisme" actuel en Afrique', *Cahiers internationaux de sociologie*, vol. XXI.

Michelat, G. and M. Simon (1977) *Classe, religion et comportement politique* (Paris: Presses de la fondation nationale des sciences politiques/Editions sociales).

Mongo, B. (1972) *Main basse sur le Cameroun* (Paris: Maspéro).

Moscovici, S. (1961) *La psychanalyse, son image et son public* (Paris: PUF).

Nadel, F. (1947) *The Nuba. An Anthropological Study of Hill Tribes in Kordofan* (London: Oxford University Press).

— (1971) [1942] *Bysance noire. Le royaume des Nupe du Nigeria* (Paris: Maspéro).

Nga Ndongo, V. (1993) *Les médias au Cameroun. Mythes et délires d'une société en crise* (Paris: L'Harmattan).

Nicolas, G. (1972) 'Fait ethnique et usages du concept d'ethnie', *Cahiers internationaux de sociologie*, vol. LIV: 95–126.

Nie, N., S. Verba and J. Petrocik (1976) *The Changing American Voter* (Boston, MA: Harvard University Press).

O'Gorman, F. (1992) 'Campaign Rituals and Ceremonies: The Social Meaning of Elections in England: 1780–1860', *Past and Present*, no. 135.

Schilder, K. (1993) 'La démocratie aux champs: les presidentielles d'octobre 1992 au Nord-Cameroun', *Politique africaine*, no. 50: 115–22.

Service Œcuménique pour la Paix et la Promotion Humaine (1998) *Les Elections camerounaises de 1997. Eléments du Rapport final d'Observation* (Yaoundé: Editions Service Humanus).

Siegfried, A. (1980) [1913] *Tableau politique de la France de l'Ouest sous la IIIe république* (Paris: Slatkine Reprints, A. Colin).

Sindjoun, L. (1994a) *Construction et déconstruction de l'ordre politique au Cameroun. La Socio-genèse de l'Etat*. Doctoral thesis, Universit of Yaoundé II.

— (1994b) 'La cour suprême, la compétition électorale et la continuité politique au Cameron: la construction de la démocratie passive', *Africa Development*, vol. XIX, no. 2 (Dakar: CODESRIA).

— (1997) 'Elections et politique au Cameroun: concurrence déloyale, coalitions de stabilité hégémonique et politique d'affection, *Revue africaine de science politique*, vol. 2, no. 1: 89–121.

Sklar, R. (1981) 'L'expérience démocratique de la seconde République au Nigéria', *Esprit*, nos 7–8: 116–19.

Socpa, A. (2000) 'Les dons dans le jeu électoral au Cameroun', *Cahiers d'Etudes Africaines*, no. 157 (XL-1): 91–108.

Touraine, A. (1973) *Production de la société* (Paris: Seuil).

Tullock, G. (1978) *Le marché politique. Analyse économique des processus politique* (Paris: Economica).

Wallerstein, I. (1960) 'Ethnicity and National Integration in West Africa', *Cahiers d'Etudes Africaines*, no. 3: 129–39.

Warnier, J.-P. (1993) *L'esprit d'entreprise au Cameroun* (Paris: Karthala).

# 4 | Factors influencing women's participation in democratization and electoral processes in Kenya: a case study of Gusii women 1992–97

BEATRICE N. ONSARIGO

## General issues

Democracy requires respect for individual and group rights and the establishment of institutions that enhance the enforcement of state legitimacy. People everywhere have basically the same needs; their aspirations for responsibility and self-determination are inherent. However, colonial rules or administrations were not interested in developing or nurturing democracy in Africa. The colonial state was essentially an authoritarian state, and did not groom future African leaders for democratic states in the post-independence era. Thus, in general, the independent states' rulers inherited non-democratic institutions which, as testified by the nature of the history of state formation in Africa, they have continued to perpetuate.

The main object of authoritarianism has been to exclude the people from the government and resources it controls. It should be indicated that most of the ruling oligarchies in Africa represent only a tiny fragment of their societies and a large majority of people are excluded from participating in the political process. At the political level, the development of authoritarianism was rooted in what Peter Anyang' Nyong'o (1988: 72) characterized as the disintegration of the national coalitions that brought African countries to independence. The incorporation of kith and kin into ruling oligarchies and the exclusion of other groups from enjoying the prerogatives of power generated problems of ethnicity, clanism, regionalism, religious bigotry and so on. Elaborate programmes of exclusion were implemented and the vast majority of Africans lost their individual and collective rights to full participation in the political, civil and economic lives of their countries. The most affected groups have been women, youth, ethnic and religious minorities. In this regard, Claude Ake correctly noted that, under authoritarian regimes, the human being, the instrument and object of development itself, has been abused excessively:

> Repression has led to an enormous waste of human resources, the very
> engine of development. At the level of the community, people have been
> sub-objected to such arbitrariness and harassment that even their tradi-
> tional capacity to cope has been undermined and for the most part, many of

them are in different sages of confusion, withdrawal despair or silent revolt. (Ake 1990: 2–3)

In short, it should be emphasized that post-independence Africa has been characterized by undemocratic regimes, rampant abuses of fundamental human rights, military coups and governments, economic and social decay and a state of hopelessness (Kanyinga 1998: 41).

Although Kenya became independent in 1963 under a multi-party system of governance, it was under single-party leadership until 1992, when section 2(a) of the Kenyan constitution was amended. With the repeal of section 2(a) in 1992 and the consequent multi-party politics, more Kenyan women have been expressing their desire to participate in active political leadership. It was also during this period of multi-party politics that the general election of 1997 had for the first time in Kenyan history two female candidates vying for presidency (Charity K. Ngilu and Wangari Maathai). It is also important at this stage to note that the 1997–2002 Kenyan parliament had nine female MPs. The failure of either of the two women candidates to capture the presidency and the election of only a very few women into parliament is clear evidence of lack of support for women in leadership (AA WORD 1998: 97). Although many leaders argue that democracy is a western concept, it cannot be disputed that its goals are functionally appropriate and relevant for citizens and are therefore universal. Although democracy in different environments may have some variations in terms of practical application, it cannot fail to focus on the interests of the men and women it seeks to govern and protect.

It is argued, therefore, that denying Kenyan women these rights is to rob them of their identity. The principle of equality of men and women is enshrined in the UN Convention of 1948. However, with or without the UN Convention, it is clear that full and effective participation of women at all levels is a basic human right. Also, effective solutions to social problems can best be achieved when all citizens exercise equal rights in participating fully in the decision-making processes. Indeed, it is imperative that any society that claims to be just, democratic and progressive ensures women's significant presence and participation in the highest levels of the decision-making process.

In the arena of political decision-making, women in Kenya have been under-represented since independence, as shown in Table 4.1.

The exclusion of women from the key political and decision-making levels in Kenya as seen in Table 4.1 clearly reflects the country's level of political development. As argued in this chapter, the issue is not to privilege women but rather to take account of the specificity of their situation. It is

TABLE 4.1 Distribution of women representatives in Kenya's National Assembly (1963–97)

| Elections and appointment | Seats | Men | Women | (%) of women |
|---|---|---|---|---|
| 1963 | 170 | 170 | 0 | 0 |
| 1969 | 172 | 170 | 2 | 1.2 |
| 1974 | 172 | 166 | 6 | 3.5 |
| 1979 | 172 | 167 | 5 | 2.9 |
| 1983 | 172 | 169 | 3 | 1.7 |
| 1988 | 188 | 186 | 2 | 1.1 |
| 1992 | 202 | 196 | 6 | 3.0 |
| 1997 | 222 | 214 | 9 | 3.6 |

*Source*: *The East African*, 4–10 September 1997, p. 15.

necessary to do so constantly within the society as a whole and not make 'women' a separate category.

Indeed, the fundamental principle of democracy is equity (equality), that of integrating all or various components of the population in order to avoid exclusion or discrimination; women should be informed of the opportunities they have to make their voices heard and to express their choices according to different feminist views, first at the local, regional level then at the international level. If they are informed voters and represented in the highest decision-making organs, then there is hope that their problems will be taken into account and not viewed as private issues.

It is stated that women should be involved in consultative structures that will strengthen their participation in the economic, social and cultural realms of society. In so doing, women will develop their leadership capacities for tackling national issues. Therefore, informing and sensitizing both the male and female populations in readiness for a change in attitudes would make it possible for men to accept women's presence and participation in decision-making and for women to understand that politics is not a 'man's affair' but involves all citizens.

### Problem statement

Most decisions affecting society are made at the political leadership level. Representation of all interests in this decision-making level is therefore very important. Unfortunately, Kenyan women are not well represented at the political leadership level, where decisions affecting many areas of their lives are made. With only nine women (3.6 per cent) in a parliament of 222 members during the period the study was conducted, it is clear that women's issues have not been taken seriously. There is therefore an urgent need to understand the factors limiting women's access to political leadership in Kenya, and Gusii in particular.

## Objectives of the study

The general objective of this project is to analyse factors influencing the participation of women in the democratization and electoral processes in Kenya.

The main objectives of the study are:

- To determine how political party organization impacts on women's participation in democracy and electoral processes.
- To establish how the politics of money impacts on women's participation in democracy and electoral processes.
- To investigate how the culture of political violence impacts on women's participation in democratization and electoral processes in Kenya.

## Justification of the study

Political participation of women in Kenya is of course not limited to parliamentary representation. However, the percentage of women in parliament in the last regime was a clear indication of the level of participation by Kenyan women. Once women are marginalized politically, it is very unlikely that gender-sensitive policies will emerge from government.

In Kenya, women contribute 80 per cent of agricultural labour and therefore play a very important role in the economy. My position is that when people are ruled by righteous and selfless leaders, they are free and are able to contribute to national development. In view of this, denying women their political rights reduces society's quality of life. The study is important because it unveils the major factors affecting women's participation in democracy and electoral processes in Kenya. It establishes the different relationships that exists between bad governance, weak political organization, political violence, and women's participation.

There are serious misconceptions regarding what constitutes free and fair elections. It is a dangerous notion to claim that free and fair elections take place only during the days of voting. But this is untrue since elections are in fact a process culminating in voting, which takes place at a later stage. All the stages (i.e. selection of candidates by political parties, allocation of funds for campaigns, free movement and freedom of assembly, etc.) must have elements of freedom and fairness. Therefore, to determine the elections as free and fair on the basis of the voting day is itself unfair, and entrenches dictatorial rule in society.

## Theoretical framework

It is a fact that women the world over exhibit some kind of apathy towards contemporary politics and political activities. This apparent lack of interest in pursuing nation-state or political leadership roles is not necessarily because women are less ambitious; rather, it is a function of socialization, the nature of the political system, and that of political philosophy, which ascribes responsibilities according to sex. Given that Kenyan women do not feature much in the political realm, that they lack the economic resources of men, that the options for changing the situation are very limited, how then do scholars seek to explain and remedy such situations?

The work of classical political theorists and feminists will be analysed to show how relevant they are in answering the questions of women's low participation in Kenyan politics. Classical political theorists such as Plato, Aristotle and Rousseau in the West constructed women and their interests as being irrelevant to political discourse. The major concepts of classical political thought were built on the acceptance of the idea that the public is fundamentally distinct from the private and the personal. This distinction between the public and private made women and their political interests invisible. The conceptual distinction between public and private realms reflects the classical understanding of the private realms of the household (reproduction) and the economy (production) as realms of necessity.

The activities of the private sphere provide the material and physical necessities of life. However, they are categorically different from political action in the public realm, since this is characterized by 'rationality' and 'autonomy'. Since women are associated by and through nature with the private sphere, they are excluded functionally from the practices of freedom that define political life (Paterman 1983: 285).

Consequently, based on the above assumption, women's exclusion from public life is based on their natural inability to transcend their biological and economic subordination in the household. Politics, by definition, encompasses both the rulers and the ruled. Because women have been associated with the private realm, public life is not only without women, but against women.

Feminists, predominantly those in the West, have argued that women are kept out of politics by a series of powerful conventions that distinguish sharply between the public and private. This separation has seriously prevented women from participating in public life because of the way their private lives are run. Feminist theorists, especially the liberal ones, therefore argue that if democracy matters in the state, it matters just as much at the workplace and within the family. This approach stresses the importance of democracy. Women need and want to be involved in decisions that directly affect their lives. Democratic practices are learnt in the supposedly 'private' world of family, school and work; because of this, it is absurd to achieve democracy at the level of the state when there is subordination elsewhere. For example, in many developing countries women are still the main sources of agricultural work as they retain their primary responsibilities for childcare and household. Pressure of time will keep most women out of any of the processes of decision-making on offer. This means that if women have no experience of affecting decision-making at home, then there is nothing much they can do in public. This is because the private sphere underpins the public world of politics; what happens in one sphere of life shapes or constrains what is likely to occur in the others (Paterman 1983: 285).

Therefore, according to Green (1985: 179), social equality is a precondition for significant political democracy. A lifetime's access to education and training, shared parenting, combined with greater social support to those with young children, are the crucial additions that will get women included in politics. Each individual must be genuinely not just formally free to change his or her position in life, and only with this substantive job mobility can society begin to talk of citizens being equal. Social equality thus means that society will never say of anyone that he or she is statistically unlikely ever to exercise public responsibility merely because of the possession of some social attribute such as being poor or a member of an ethnic sub-culture or female (Philips 1991: 99).

### Introduction to the study area

Gusii districts (i.e Kisii, Gucha and Nyamira) are found in Nyanza province of Western Kenya. These districts are occupied by the Gusii people, who are Bantu speakers. The three districts are bordered by Trans-mara to the south, Bomet to the east, Rachuonyo to the north and Homa bay to the west.

There are a total of ten constituencies in the three districts, namely, Bonchari, Kitutu Chache, Kitutu Masaba, Nyaribari Chache, Nyaribari Masaba, Bobasi, Bomachoge, North Mugirango, South Mugirango, West Mugirango, with several local authority wards in each constituency.

The three Gusii districts had a combined population of 1.03 million in the year 2001 with 534,794 females and 496,079 males with a ratio of 100:108. In general, females outnumbered the males from the age of fifteen to seventy-four years. Despite this fact, the Gusii community has been very conservative in electing women into political positions. Since Kenyan independence, no constituency in Gusii has ever elected a woman to parliament. The highest electoral position was held by Clare Omanga as mayor of Kisii municipality for two years during the 1992–97 electoral period. Although the number of women seeking political positions in Gusii districts increased tremendously during the 1997 general elections for both parliamentary and civic positions, the number of women elected for civic seats was marginal. This is despite the fact that women constitute over 60 per cent of the registered voters. Women in the Gusii community have therefore minimal representation in decision-making bodies as compared to their numerical strength. This includes local authorities, land boards, school boards, and private and public employment (Kisii Development Plan 1997–2001: 7).

## Definitions of the key concepts

*Democracy* It is important to clarify the meanings of the key concepts as used in this research project. This also helps appreciate my theoretical assumptions. Within the context of liberal political thought, democracy means free and periodic elections, a multi-party system, a free press and judiciary, the rule of law, other liberal democratic rights and freedoms. Another related concept is empowerment, which is the ability of individuals, communities, associations, interest groups and other organizations to participate in and influence the decisions that affect their lives, as well as the creation of an environment that facilitates such outcomes.

As used in this study, empowerment is more oriented to micro-, community and marginal groups (e.g. women) and emphasizes the group (rather than the individual) and direct (rather than indirect) participation. Empowerment is important for self-governance, as it enables Kenyan people to lead themselves and contribute to development using the available local resources. Empowerment also implies redistributing power and transforming institutions so that people can take direct control of their affairs.

*Political violence* As generally accepted in the literature of political science and human rights organization, political violence refers to any act or series of acts that result or are likely to result in harm (physical or psychological) to an individual or group for the purpose of influencing the manner in which the power to run a country's public affairs is distributed and acquired. In the Kenyan context, political violence includes:

- political thuggery that targets an opponent and his/her supporters (often such action is paid for)
- political zoning
- attacks on property

- bribing of voters and opposition candidates
- individual beatings/attacks/assassinations
- biased media coverage
- ethnic clashes
- kidnapping and detention of candidates

All the above instil fear in individuals and groups likely to challenge those holding political power.

*Electoral violence* This concept refers to any act or series of acts that result or are likely to result in harm, whether physical or psychological, to an individual or group of people for the purpose of influencing electoral choice and outcomes. Electoral violence in the Kenyan context involves the use of gangsters such as 'Jeshi la Mzee', *masai moran* or *chinkororo* to intimidate voters, destroy property or displace those individuals or communities that are part of the opposition. 'Jeshi la Mzee' has been involved in disrupting political rallies organized by opposition parties countrywide, and particularly in the areas claimed to be Kenya African National Union (KANU) zones. This type of violence is not specifically geared towards women candidates. However, its impact tends to affect women candidates more than their male counterparts who are likely to counter violence with violence. This type of violence instils fear in the voters, resulting in election outcomes that may not reflect the wishes of the people.

*Democratization* Finally, the process of building or developing democracy is called democratization. It is a struggle for greater democracy by the various institutions, individuals and social groups within society. It may be slow or difficult to build or it may be quick and easy to achieve, depending on how sensitive or complicated the political interactions are in society.

## Review literature, hypotheses and a research methodology

*Literature review* It is important to localize the hypotheses and arguments developed in this empirical study in Kenya within a broader theoretical and historical context. Throughout history, women leaders have emerged. In modern times such powerful female political figures and personalities include: Margaret Thatcher, Indira Gandhi, Benazir Bhutto and Corazon Aquino. Although there have been very few women in international politics, they are increasingly participating in national and local politics. As of 2000, on average, women comprised only 10 per cent of national legislatures and 7 per cent of executive cabinet ministers worldwide. Women were best represented in the Nordic countries of Europe, with an average of 36.7 per cent, compared to 11.4 per cent in sub-Saharan Africa and 3.5 per cent in Arab states. In sub-Saharan Africa, political liberalization meant constitutional change within the framework of the state. The introduction of multi-party politics by itself does not constitute a process of democratization, as has been demonstrated by Kenya. It is only when there exists open multi-party competition that democracy becomes real (UNIFEM 2000 Report).

It can be generalized that discrimination against women is rooted in most of the traditional social structures and institutions in Kenya. The continued existence of many of these institutions has meant continued discrimination against women. For example, few laws passed in our country address the issues that discriminate against women. This indicates that although Kenyan society has been undergoing thorough social, economic and political change, there exist some social structures that limit women's participation in society and more particularly in policy-making (*Daily Nation*, 8 March 2001, p. 13).

In the post-independence period, women have continued their political activism. The United Nations first Decade for Women (1975–1985) and the end of the Decade for Women conference, held in Nairobi in 1985, were particularly tortuous for Kenyan women in that they provided a political platform for these women to articulate goals and strategies that could be used in their relations with the state, in order to improve their position in society *vis-à-vis* that of men. However, data from the 1997–2002 parliament clearly indicate that a number of barriers still exist with regard to women's access to political power.

One way to measure the impact of democratization would be to assess the extent to which women have been able to penetrate the formal political realm in terms of their participation in key decision-making institutions and their ability to exercise power over final policy outcomes; unfortunately, thus far women's gains in these crucial areas have been marginal. Although a few women have been elected to serve in key political institutions at the local and national levels of politics (i.e mayoral positions, local branch offices at party levels, parliament and the ministries), their overall participation has been marginal (Nzomo 1987: 1–3).

Therefore, according to Nzomo, women's marginal participation in some of the informal political institutions in society suggest that the mere presence of multi-party democracy alone may not necessarily be a solution to all of the problems that continue to plague Kenyan women. Other areas of society must be dealt with to enforce principles of gender equity and fairness.

Kenyan women's involvement in the political realm is not a new phenomenon; on the contrary, their participation in politics can be traced back to the colonial period. Although they have rarely been analysed in any of the major studies of Kenyan nationalist movements, women played extremely important roles in both the organization of anti-colonial strategies and the dissemination of political ideas. Kikuyu women were, for example, actively involved in all aspects of the nationalist movement and served as members of gangs in the forest (Presley 1986: 54–69).

Women developed political power through both formal and informal processes. On the informal level, women utilized avenues through which their vocal protests could be heard. Women sang protest songs about chiefs, government policies and retainers who forcibly used their labour. On the formal level, women split from the male-dominated Kikuyu Central Association and formed their own political organization, the Mumbi Central Association.

Democracy involves the transformation of economic, political and social structures. Therefore, the democratization of society cannot be successful where the political structures and institutions alone are transformed. In fact, the democratization of political structures and institutions alone cannot be meaningful and cannot be borne by the current economic structures.

The democratization of African societies, therefore, means that the African people must master their economies as well as their political and social structures. The question that must be raised here is to determine how the African people can control this process so as to make its content meaningful. However, for this to happen, democratization must be effectively translated into participation in economic, political and socio-cultural power.

According to the World Bank (1991) and Huntington (1968), despite the lack of consensus of their views, good governance is vital for economic development because it complements sound rules and economic policies. Governance implies the exercise of political, economic and administrative authority in the management of the country's affairs at all levels. The legitimacy and the transparent nature of any such government will determine how good it is. The Kenyan government has not been transparent and accountable to its citizens and this has paved way for abuses of power. The failure of the Kenyan government to be transparent and accountable to its citizens is centred more on the interests of the rulers than on the ruled. The words of Abraham Lincoln in the United States have not sunk deep into the heads of Kenyan leaders, 'government of the people by the people' (Kapur 1984: 222).

Democracy is not a concept reserved for a particular section of Kenyan society. Even if we concede that there is a special African concept of democracy, it can be deduced from the past that the system of government practised by our forefathers was accountable and did not discriminate against women, since women's affairs were also considered important in society's affairs. On indigenous African contributions to democracy in Africa, Nelson Mandela wrote:

> Then our people lived peacefully, under the democratic rule of their kings. There were no classes, no rich or poor and no exploitation of man by man. All men were free and equal and this was the foundation of government. The council of elders was completely democratic in that all members of the tribe could participate in its deliberations: chiefs, subjects, warriors and medicine men all took part in decisions. (ong 2000: 20–21)

If we are advocating the recognition and defence of democracy in Kenya, we are not advocating anything new. All that we ask is for a government that is participatory in nature and accountable. Those in power must be educated to accept the fact that they are the people's representatives and must stay in power for that purpose only. If the democratic institutions are fully functional with free and fair elections on a regular basis, then the government can be held responsible. In a situation where the ruling party knows that there is no way in which it can be forced to change, then it breeds corruption, arrogance and non-accountability. As demonstrated by Martha Koome (1992), women fought alongside men in the struggles for independence, though they were sidelined from positions of national leadership and policy-making at independence. However, Koome does not discuss the factors that influenced the low participation of women at high levels.

The post-independence marginalization of women in Kenya is difficult to explain. According to Kimani (1998), in the liberation struggles both men and women fought together and won as partners. One would have expected the women to be on the same footing as their male counterparts. Unfortunately, Kenyan women are the ones who have borne the brunt of economic mismanagement and conflicts. There are so many traditional practices as well as legal barriers that still disadvantage women. To redress the inequalities between the sexes in Kenyan politics, as already stated, this study seeks to establish which cultural practices and laws discriminate against women's civil and economic rights and how these laws and traditions can be reformed to ensure women's access to power.

Maendeleo ya Wanawake Organization (MYWO) was Kenya's first formal women's organization. Its goal was to improve the lives of women by equipping them with modern skills for housekeeping and healthcare. They were not to engage in politics but were to be devoted to social justice and humanity. The independence era, from the 1960s to the 1990s and beyond, has seen the women's movement attempt to shun political feminism. This apoliticism was mostly translated into conformist politics. The conformity saw the MYWO affiliate itself with KANU, the party that has been in power since independence in 1964. This meant that male politicians in the ruling party KANU would define the agenda of MYWO, and consequently that of the entire women's movement, as MYWO is an umbrella body. Generally, MYWO has been under male leadership, as demonstrated by its frequent interference in the affairs of women. For a long time, elections to MYWO have been controlled by the government with the president or minister setting the dates of elections, putting them off and even preferring candidates. The officials who win must be acceptable to the male leadership of the country. Usually it is the wives of status politicians who win the elections (Kibwana 2001: 197).

In 1999, the Minister for Culture and Social Services (the ministry registers women's groups) is reported to have denounced the Kenya Women's Political Caucus (KWPC) and noted that the ministry recognized only MYWO. This was prompted by the KWPC's stated goal to have women participate meaningfully in the constitutional review process, a process that the country's leadership has frustrated to date.

In the content of the women's rights discourse, the male leadership in Kenya attempted to delegitimize the movement by casting it as a sexual liberation movement led by elite women. While reacting to the reforms packaged by the International Federation of Women Lawyers Kenya (FIDA-Kenya), the president reduced it to a campaign for the legalization of lesbianism and abortion in Kenyan society. It should be emphasized that the two are taboo subjects for both the leadership of the state and the religious sector (*Daily Nation*, 19 March 1999).

Kenya's leadership have not allowed the women's movement to flourish, despite the fact that in 1985 Nairobi hosted the UN end of the Decade for Women conference. There has not been any significant internationalization or regionalization of the women's movement. The state has resisted such a trend because, if rigorously pursued, it would free the women's movement from the clutches of the political leadership. Despite the multiple setbacks MYWO has suffered, especially in its affiliation to KANU, it has survived and should use its numerous strengths to advance women's issues at all levels. In order to achieve this, MYWO must clearly identify itself with the political happenings in the country. This is a painful process, but without it MYWO is not likely to achieve its primary objective of improving women's welfare in Kenyan society.

Political parties are, according to Nzomo (1993), the indispensable links between the people and the representative machinery of government. Their role is more obvious when elections are in prospect, but they need continually to involve both men and women in their internal organization. It is only when political parties are democratic in nature that we can expect to have more women participating in politics. The Kenyan experience has shown that very few political parties are supportive to their female candidates both financially and psychologically. Democracy, according to Kapur (1984), does not recognize class, race or gender distinctions. It is only in a society of equals that harmony can be secured. By equality we mean of course equality of opportunity, a fair and open field for all. This kind of equality ensures social justice, which is the very life blood of democracy. When there exist vast inequalities on the basis of wealth and gender, social justice cannot be obtained. A wide gap between the rich and the poor (54 per cent of the Kenyan population is living in poverty) makes it impossible for the poor, and particularly the women, to exercise their political rights independently and freely. For example, election campaigns in Kenya tend to concentrate on giving handouts (e.g. food, blankets, money) to the electorate, setting up projects and contributing to harambees rather than spelling out party policies and strategies for development. Therefore, it is clear that where there is no equality there can be no liberty or fraternity or rationality. Democracy is, however, the product of liberty, equality and fraternity, and these three all make for rationality. This study therefore seeks to establish the links between poverty impacts and women's participation in democracy and the electoral processes in Kenya.

Van Kessel (2000) states that in a democratic society there should be adequate provision of opportunities for the individual to develop his/her personality. This can be realized when everyone has access to knowledge, security against unemployment and a minimum wage. Democracy here invades the economic realm. It has become a common demand that economic democracy, particularly for women, must precede political democracy. In a society where wealth is distributed unevenly on the basis of gender and where one group of people is out to exploit the other, democracy cannot survive. A democratic society is a partnership among equals. The democratic ideal cannot therefore be realized until women's access to the economy is democratized and the inequalities that exist in the distribution of national wealth are reduced to the minimum.

Another important aspect that cannot be ignored is the issue of literacy and how it is related to participation in democracy and electoral processes. According to Carceles (1994), Africa has the highest illiteracy rate in the world: 40 per cent, as compared with Asia (31.5 per cent) and the industrialized countries (1.5 per cent). But the most disturbing fact is that the largest proportion of the adult non-literates are women. Africa's adult illiteracy by gender in the year 2000 was 50 per cent of women and 29.8 per cent of men. This disparity raises two basic questions. How are women expected to fit into and take full advantage of development activities? And how can women (civil society) be strong enough to make any meaningful contribution to the building of a democratic society, if more than 50 per cent of them are illiterate? Since literacy has an empowering value, it becomes therefore important to understand how illiteracy affects women's political participation.

Kassam (1994) has indicated that it is evident that the question of literacy is fundamentally political and one of political will. Widespread adult literacy affects existing power relations and power structures and the distribution of wealth and resources at the international, national and local levels in general; it can be argued that those who demand literacy are interested in social justice and egalitarian development, and those who deny widespread adult literacy have a vested interest, either deliberately or unwittingly, in maintaining their political and economic control and the privileges derived therefrom. Therefore, if the Kenyan government is keen to promote women's participation in politics, it must be committed to improving their literacy rates. Otherwise, without proper education women are handicapped and forced to live at the periphery of society, where they do not benefit and are unable to contribute to its welfare, improvement and transformation.

*Hypotheses of the study*
1. There exists a significant relationship between society's cultural practices and women's participation in democracy and electoral processes in Kenya.
2. There exists a significant relationship between the country's political institutions and women's participation in democracy and electoral processes in Kenya.
3. There exists a significant relationship between economic democracy for women and their participation in democracy and electoral processes.

*Research methodology* Data used in this study were obtained through research conducted in Gusii districts, with the aim of assessing factors impacting on women's political participation in democracy and electoral processes in Kenya. The field research involved interviewing participants using a structured questionnaire.

From the list of all the Gusii districts' political participants in the 1992 and 1997 electoral periods, a shortlist was made of all women candidates. From the shortlisted sample of sixty women, a simple random sampling technique was used to determine thirty-eight respondents for civic seats, while two other respondents were selected as being the only ones who had stood for parliamentary positions. The study had therefore a total sample of forty respondents. Due to constraints of time and money, forty respondents were considered sufficient, since they were representative of all the women aspiring for political office in the districts, i.e. both civic and parliamentary.

The main source of data in this research was primary data obtained by way of interviews. The interviews were conducted by use of questionnaires. The questionnaires were designed to collect information on factors influencing women's participation in democratization and electoral processes in Kenya and Gusii in particular. The researcher was also able to obtain official records from political parties, government documents, publications and so on, concerning the women candidates. This information was important, since it acted as a database for the researcher.

Finally, the data were analysed using percentages, frequencies and ratio where applicable.

## Data analysis

*Presentation of the data collected and general characteristics of the respondents* This section describes the respondents and the data collected. Here the author analyses these data as well.

TABLE 4.2 Age of the respondents

| Age range | No. of respondents | Percentage |
| --- | --- | --- |
| 30–39 | 15 | 37.5 |
| 40–49 | 20 | 50 |
| 50–59 | 4 | 10 |
| Over 60 | 1 | 2.5 |
| Total | 40 | 100 |

According to Table 4.2, 50 per cent of the respondents in the study were aged between forty and forty-nine years of age. This is because at this age group most women are no longer tied down by family responsibilities and are therefore more likely to join public and political life in particular.

From Table 4.3 it can be observed that 75 per cent of women seeking political leadership in Gusii districts are married, 15 per cent are single, and 10 per cent of the respondents did not give their marital status. This is contrary to the common view that most women seeking political posi-

TABLE 4.3 Marital status of the respondents

| Status | No. of respondents | Percentage |
|---|---|---|
| Married | 30 | 75 |
| Single | 6 | 15 |
| No response | 4 | 10 |
| Total | 40 | 100 |

TABLE 4.4 Level of education of respondents

| Status | No. of respondents | Percentage |
|---|---|---|
| Primary level | 15 | 37.5 |
| Secondary level | 20 | 50 |
| University | 2 | 5 |
| No response | 3 | 7.5 |
| Total | 40 | 100 |

tions in Kenya are either single or divorced and are therefore regarded as 'social misfits' in society.

Table 4.4 indicates that 50 per cent of respondents have secondary education. However, it is important to note that about 37.5 per cent of the respondents of the sample have only primary education and can be termed as being semi-literate or illiterate. Therefore, for this group of women to be effective leaders in society, they must be trained in leadership skills.

TABLE 4.5 Involvement of respondents in leadership positions

| No. of years | No. of respondents | Percentage |
|---|---|---|
| 1–5 | 20 | 50 |
| 5–10 | 10 | 25 |
| 10–15 | 5 | 12.5 |
| over 15 | 5 | 12.5 |
| Total | 40 | 100 |

Table 4.5 shows that the majority of the respondents have been involved in one way or another in leadership positions in women's groups, community organizations, at church or at party level. Despite such leadership capacities at the grassroots level, most respondents felt that they had been

handling local issues and were not well equipped with skills for national issues. This clearly shows that women lack the necessary leadership skills needed to deal with national issues.

TABLE 4.6 Number of respondents who contested positions

| Position | No. of respondents | Percentage |
| --- | --- | --- |
| Civic (local authority) | 38 | 95 |
| Parliamentary | 2 | 5 |
| Total | 40 | 100 |

Most of the women (95 per cent) in the study contested civic positions in local government, that is as councillors, while only 5 per cent contested parliamentary seats. The study therefore clearly shows that very few (i.e. two out of forty) women contest parliamentary posts. However, although political participation is not limited to parliamentary representation, the percentage of women seeking parliamentary positions is one index of the state of participation of Gusii women. Since women constitute roughly half the population, they are entitled to comparable numerical representation at decision-making levels. Women's exclusion or under-representation in political activities, therefore, mean that women's interests and needs are poorly represented.

TABLE 4.7 Party affiliation of respondents

| Party | No. of respondents | Percentage |
| --- | --- | --- |
| KANU | 10 | 25 |
| DP | 15 | 37.5 |
| SDP | 8 | 20 |
| FORD | 4 | 10 |
| Others | 3 | 7.5 |
| Total | 40 | 100 |

Table 4.7 shows that the majority of respondents contested positions in the DP (37.5 per cent) compared with 25 per cent in the ruling party KANU. The study also showed that women are represented in all major political parties, although only KANU had two female aspirants for parliamentary seats. The other political parties supported women mainly for local authority positions as councillors. This clearly showed that although the

TABLE 4.8 Amount of money used for campaigns

| Amount in Ksh. (1$ = 75) | No. of respondents | Percentage |
| --- | --- | --- |
| 50,000–100,00 | 30 | 75 |
| 100,000–150,000 | 5 | 12.5 |
| 150,000–200,000 | 3 | 7.5 |
| Above 200,000 | 2 | 5 |
| Total | 40 | 100 |

opposition parties supported women's participation, in electoral processes they were limited to local representation.

*Economic empowerment and political participation*  In order to establish whether there exists any relationship between women's economic status and their participation in democracy and electoral processes in Kenya, the respondents were asked for information on the amount of money used for the campaigns, the sources of the funds and whether there existed any gender differences between men and women in accessing finances.

Table 4.8 shows that about 75 per cent of the respondents used Ksh. 50,000–100,000. This amount of money may seem small compared with the amount spent in developed countries during election campaigns. However, it must be noted that in a country such as Kenya with over 56 per cent of its population living on less than 1 dollar per day, money is a resource that is used to influence election outcomes. The fact that the majority of the respondents used relatively little money for their campaigns is a clear indication that they had little chance of winning the elections on financial grounds.

Table 4.9 shows that about 50 per cent of the respondents funded their own campaigns, while 37.5 per cent received support from their political parties and only 12.5 per cent of the respondents did fundraising for their campaigns.

TABLE 4.9  Sources of funding of respondents

| Source | No. of respondents | Percentage |
| --- | --- | --- |
| Self | 20 | 50 |
| Party support | 15 | 37.5 |
| Fundraising | 5 | 12.5 |
| Others | – | – |
| Total | 40 | 100 |

TABLE 4.10 Respondents' response to economic constraints

| Response | No. of respondents | Percentage |
|---|---|---|
| Strongly agree | 20 | 50 |
| Agree | 12 | 30 |
| Disagree | 6 | 15 |
| Strongly disagree | 2 | 5 |
| Total | 40 | 100 |

The information in Table 4.10 shows that most respondents felt that women candidates were faced with more economic constraints during the campaigns as compared with their male counterparts. This is because socio-economic factors limit women's access to property and high-income jobs. Therefore, for women to participate effectively in Kenyan politics they must be integrated into the main socio-economic spheres of the country.

*Political participation and electoral violence*  Kenya has been experiencing electoral violence since the introduction of multi-party politics. While there is a commitment to prevent violence throughout the country, the study is particularly concerned about the impact of such violence on human rights, freedom of assembly and electoral outcomes. To get more information on the impact of electoral violence on women in Kenya, the respondents were asked whether electoral violence affected women more than men.

Seventy per cent of the respondents strongly agreed that election violence affected women more than male candidates, while only 25 per cent strongly disagreed. Violence has become a tool of the trade in the political arena and those parties and individuals that are able to utilize it do better in elections. As a consequence, the electorate has been conditioned to view

TABLE 4.11 Respondents' response to electoral violence

| Response | No. of respondents | Percentage |
|---|---|---|
| Strongly agree | 20 | 50 |
| Agree | 8 | 20 |
| Disagree | 6 | 15 |
| Strongly disagree | 4 | 10 |
| No response | 2 | 5 |
| Total | 40 | 100 |

violence as inevitable during electioneering; politicians and the government exploit this attitude to discourage certain political parties and individuals, particularly women, from participating in electoral processes. This has resulted in voter apathy, and thus the expected outcomes of the elections do not represent the wishes of the people.

## Conclusion and generalizations

*Concluding remarks*  Findings of the study indicate that women are poorly represented in high decision-making levels in Kenya. Since the introduction of multi-party politics in the country in 1991, the level of women's participation in democracy and electoral processes has not improved. Instead, the country has witnessed a decline in the number of women in positions of leadership both at national and local levels. Since democracy relies on the principle of full participation of all citizens in government activities, the poor participation of women (3.6 per cent) is a clear indication that Kenya is not a democratic society. Democracy is able to survive only in a democratic society where the principles of liberty and equality are applied. These principles hold that all persons fit to perform the duties of citizens should have a share in the direction of the state so that each man and woman may have an identical opportunity to grow and expand to the best of his/her capacity and no group should exploit the weakness of others.

Therefore, for women in Kenya to be actively involved in political participation, the social and economic inequalities that exist between men and women must be addressed. The study revealed that low educational attainment is a major constraint limiting women's participation in democracy and electoral processes in Kenya and Africa as a whole. Education is critical because it enhances women's political participation. To a significant extent, it is the key to economic and social empowerment. So long as 52 per cent of the Kenyan population do not exercise their political leadership in Kenya, women will continue to remain outside the political leadership in Kenya unless their educational levels are improved to equal those of men.

The effect of income in determining women's participation in politics was considered by inquiring how much money was used in the campaign and the sources of funding. Table 4.8 shows that 75 per cent of the respondents spent between Ksh. 50,000 and Ksh. 100,000 on the campaign. This is relatively little money compared with the amount of money used elsewhere in Kenyan campaigns.

Contemporary Kenyan politics requires high financing and with only 37.5 per cent of the women being supported by the party, it is clear that the financial status of women politicians directly influences their participation in politics. However, it is important to note that women in Kenya do not have access to productive resources such as land. Economic resources available to women are very limited and even these limited resources are still subject to the whims of men. Few women have well-paid work; they occupy low cadre jobs, because the majority of them have not had higher education. Women are therefore hardly suited to high-paying jobs that require highly skilled personnel.

Yet the study revealed that in Kenya economic empowerment is a pre-requisite to political participation and leadership. An important aspect to note here is that without economic empowerment, women's participation in democracy and electoral processes in Kenya/Africa is limited and will always work against the majority. This is because the few women favoured by the system will not work for the benefit of their fellow women and society at large but must be accountable to those who appointed or supported them.

The effect of the above is a predominant class of economically dependent women. Economically dependent and low-income status women show little or no interest in the exercise of their right to influence decision-making by government. This study therefore revealed that women's political participation in Kenya today depends on their economic power. Since 54 per cent of the population lives below the poverty level, it is very unlikely that most people (citizens) will exercise their political rights (to vote) without being manipulated.

The importance of group identification in politics cannot be overemphasized. And the ability to organize oneself differs from group to group. The involvement of women in party affairs determines their level of political awareness and commitment to political participation. At times, political parties can even engineer their members into partisan politics by sponsorship in a bid to represent their interests. Thus the idea of group identification increases people's involvement in the social, economic or political affairs of their communities. However, the study showed through party sponsorship that only a few women (37.5 per cent) are integrated into party affairs.

It could therefore be explained that women who identify themselves with political parties are politically active because women's organizations are often politically gender sensitive and even take an openly political stance. Such a stance has the effect of mobilizing members, thereby increasing levels of political awareness and interest.

The number of Kenyan women belonging to political parties is, however, very small. Most Kenyan women do not concern themselves with political issues and this may account for why most women are also found to be apathetic towards politics. They can therefore not articulate their interests or represent themselves in government. So even though Kenyan women belong to some political parties, these organizations have not equipped them with the necessary political skills, knowledge and financial support needed for present-day politics.

Finally, on the issue of traditional and cultural practices that may limit women's access to politics, most respondents expressed the view that women's multiple roles in the family and the way they are socialized makes it difficult for them to seek leadership positions. However, most respondents also lamented the inheritance rights existing in Kenya. Most respondents cited economic challenges as the major constraint to political participation, as family wealth is controlled by men even when women are its major sources.

*Recommendations* In view of the findings and conclusion from the study, the following recommendations may be made.

1. The political environment in Kenya must be levelled to give both men and women equal chances of political leadership. This may be achieved through affirmative action as in South Africa and Tanzania where women are 30 per cent of the parliamentarians or by involving women in development issues.

2. There is a need to educate the public on their political rights and particularly on their responsibility to support women seeking political leadership. Democracy is all about justice, equality and fairness. Once fairness and justice have been done, the status and dignity of women are likely to improve and this will lead to sustainable development for all in a democratic society.

3. There is a need for election monitoring programmes that are able to address the issue of violence before, during and after elections so as to determine whether or not the elections were free and fair. To do this based on the events of the election day is unsatisfactory and may encourage corruption and poor governance.

## References

AA WORD (Association of African Women for Research and Development) (1998) *Women's Political Leadership in Kenya: Involvement, Challenges and the Way Forward* (Nairobi: AA WORD).

Ake, C. (1990) *The Case for Democracy: African Governance in the 1990s*, Emory University: The Carter Center.

Carceles, G. (1994) 'Is Literacy for All by the Year 2000 a Feasible Target?', in Z. Morsy (ed.), *The Challenges of Literacy: From Reflection to Action* (London: Garland).

Frompong, K. (2000) 'Contemporary Africa and the struggle for Democratic and Fundamental Right', a paper presented at the African Institute of South Africa (AISA) 40th Anniversary Conference 30 May–2 June Pretoria, S. Africa.

Green, P. (1985) *Retrieving Democracy: In Search of Civic Equality* (London: Methuen).

Huntington, S. P. (1968) *Political Order in Changing Societies* (New Haven, CT: Yale University Press).

Kanyinga, K. (1998) 'Contestation Over Political Space: The State and the Demobilization of Opposition Politics in Kenya', in A. O. Olukoshi (ed.), *The Politics of Opposition in Contemporary Africa* (Stockholm: Elanders Gotab).

Kapur, A. C. (1984) *The Principle of Political Sciences* (New Delhi: S. Chad & Co.).

Kassam, Y. (1994) 'Who Benefits from Illiteracy? Literacy and Empowerment', in Z. Morsy (ed.), *The Challenge of Illiteracy. From Reflection to Action* (London: Garland).

Kibwana, K. (2001) 'Women Politics and Gender Politiking: Questions from Kenya', in J. Oloka-Onyango (ed.) *Constitutionalism in Africa; Creating Opportunities, Facing Challenges* (Kampala: Fountain Publishers).

Kimani, E. (1998) 'Gender and Class in the Struggle for Democracy', paper presented to the DPMF Democracy Conference II; Democracy, Civil Society and Governance in Africa, Addis Ababa, Ethiopia, 7–10 December.

Kisii Development Plan (1997–2001) *Kisii Development Plan* (Nairobi: Ministry of Planning and National Development Government Press).

Koome, M. (1992) *Women and Democracy* (Nairobi).

Nyong'o, P. A. (1988) 'Political Instability and the Prospects for Democracy in Africa', *Africa Development*, vol. XIII, no. 3: 72–87.

Nzomo, M. (1987) 'Women, Democracy and Development in Africa,' in W. Oyugi and A. Gitonga (eds), *Democratic Theory and Practice in Africa* (Nairobi: Heinemann).

— (1993) 'Empowering Kenyan Women: A Report of a Seminar on Post Election Women's Agenda: Forward Looking Strategies to 1997 and Beyond', in W. M. Kabira, J. A. Oduol and M. Nzomo (eds) Democratic Change in Africa: Women Perspective (Nairobi).

Paterman, C. (1983) 'Feminism and Democracy', in D. Graeme (ed.), *Democratic Theory and Practice* (Cambridge: Cambridge University Press).

Philips, A. (1991) *Engendering Democracy* (Pittsburgh, PA: Pennsylvania State University Press).

Presley, C. A. (1986) 'Kikuyu Women, Women in the Mau Mau Rebellion', in G. Y. Okihiro (ed.), *In Resistance: Studies in Africa, Caribbean and Afro-American History* (Boston, MA: University of Massachusetts Press).

United Nations Development Fund for Women (UNIFEM) (2000) *The World Women Report 2000* (New York: UN).

Van Kessel, I. (2000) 'Is Democracy Good for Women?', paper presented at AISA 40th anniversary conference, Pretoria, 30 May–2 June.

World Bank (1991) *Managing Development: The Governance Decision* (Washington, DC: World Bank).

# 5 | Alliances in the political and electoral process in the Republic of Congo 1991–97

JOACHIM EMMANUEL GOMA-THETHET

## Introduction: issues and objectives

For political scientists, sociologists, historians and other researchers, the democratization process initiated in the last decade of the twentieth century was a goldmine for further research on Congo's immediate political past. The period in question was marked by the eruption of political violence whose outcome has not yet been fully assessed. Recurrent violence plunged the country into a 'deep-seated crisis unparalleled since the era of kingdoms and chiefdoms' (Baniafouna 2001: 17). That crisis yielded abundant literature which should, nevertheless, be taken with a pinch of salt, given the bias of some authors who were actors in the events they describe. Such literature was also produced by Congolese researchers (e.g. Ossébi, Tonda, Yengo, Baniafouna, Kissita, Soni-Benga, Bazenguissa-Ganga, Nkouka-Menga, Nsafou); by recent protagonists in Congo's political life following the National Conference (Mokoko 1995; Dabira 1998; Obenga 1998 and 2001; Makouta-Mboukou 1999; Menga 1993; Ikounga 2000; Moukouéké 2000); as well as external researchers, especially those of the Bordeaux school known as the Centre for Black African Studies.[1]

Such literature reveals that the post-National Conference period was marked by a slow phasing out of institutions. This led to a privatization of violence (Ossébi 1998), the transformation of the state party into party militias (Quantin 1997), and a partitioning of the national capital and the entire country by various parties; each party or group of parties grabbed a given portion and administered it with its own militia (Dorier-Apprill 1997). But how did the country get into such a situation of state destruction and the breakdown of the democratization process? The immediate cause was the refusal by Pascal Lissouba's Union Panafricaine pour la Démocratie Sociale (Pan-African Union for Social Democracy, UPADS) to honour the alliance it had signed with Dénis Sassou-Nguesso's Parti Congolais du Travail (Congolese Labour Party, PCT). The collapse of the Lissouba–Sassou alliance, on the one hand, and the marriage and then divorce between Sassou and Kolélas, on the other, resulted in political instability and civil wars fought on the altar of ethno-regionalism (Baniafouna 1995; Ossébi 1995; Quantin 1994). However, the intervention of the Angolan army on the side of Dénis Sassou-Nguesso's militiamen in 1997[2] not only internationalized the civil war so that it became a 'North–South' conflict, but also revealed, in particular, dubious vested interests and relations with certain foreign business circles, mainly French (Verschaves 2000).

This chapter raises the central issue of the significance of political alliances in the electoral process or government formation mechanism. Does this question alone enable us to understand why the Congolese political scene, apparently peaceful for close to three decades (1963–92), and without any large-scale outbursts of violence between the various ethno-regional communities, should suddenly erupt in such a severe socio-political crisis on the advent of democratization and, what is more, shortly after an electoral process that was considered regular (Quantin 1994)? This chapter investigates why and how Congolese political parties contracted alliances during the period from the advent of democratization in the country to the 1997 civil war; it also discusses the consequences of such alliances. The said alliances will be studied, first, at the time of the holding of the National Conference and under the transition, and then during the Pascal Lissouba government from 1992 to 1997.

### Alliances during the National Conference and transition

*Political protagonists, mission and scope of the conference* After about thirty years of one-party politics (1963–90), Congo joined the democratization movement sweeping through Africa in the early 1990s, with the advent of multi-party politics. The new parties and numerous non-governmental organizations called on the government to organize a national conference. The said conference, held in June 1991, laid down the institutional framework for Congo's future political life. Prospects of replacing the old single party in the state apparatus prompted political groupings and personalities to form alliances. Such alliances became, in that historical phase, an important tool for conquering and/or retaining power. What form did the first alliances of the post-one-party era take? A study of the protagonists present at the conference and the conduct of proceedings should shed light both on the process whereby alliances were contracted and on the setting up of the institutions that left their imprint on the transition.

The conference opened on 25 February 1991 and was presided over by Prime Minister Louis Sylvain Goma. It was attended by about 1,100 delegates representing various political and social groupings (political parties, associations, religious denominations, NGOs, trade unions, etc.). According to *La Semaine Africaine*, some seventy political parties, established in a *de facto* manner on the basis of the 1901 French Law, were represented at the conference.[3] The founders of those parties were either renegades from the old one-party regime or young Turks in quest of a status in the new political arena. The said parties, many with astonishing names, such as Parti unique de Dieu (One and Only Party of God), in most cases consisted only of a leader and his relatives or friends. And if they included militants, the latter joined not on grounds of ideology or a political programme but rather because they identified with the founders of the parties.

With the executive committee in place, delegates had urgently to define the framework of the conference, specifying its mandate and area of jurisdiction. These were laid down in the conference's rules of procedure adopted on 11 March 1991.

The mandate of the conference was stated in the preamble to the rules of procedure: 'to redefine the fundamental values of the nation; and to put in place conditions congenial to a national consensus with a view to establishing the rule of law and multi-party democracy, which conditions are necessary for the development of our country'.

Article I of the rules of procedure lent the conference a sovereign character. Thus, all decisions taken would be enforceable and binding. From the very outset, there was a legal battle between supporters of the PCT hostile to the adoption of that article and those keen to overturn the one-party system.

Article II defined the conference's area of jurisdiction: all issues relating to the country's political, economic and socio-cultural life, on the basis of an analysis of the past and current situation. Such an analysis was intended to enable the country to, *inter alia*, organize the transition, develop new ideas for the drafting of a new constitution, define the broad outlines of the electoral law, the press law, the law on public and individual freedoms, the law on political parties and the law on non-governmental organizations and foundations.

The National Conference was therefore viewed by all participants as the framework for inventing a new public order by consensus. How did the National Conference unfold in practical terms?

*Conduct of the forum* Participants at the conference fell into two camps. On one side were the renegades of the PCT associated with the new political protagonists searching for status in the new emerging political scene. On the other side were the political actors who remained faithful to the old PCT one-party regime. The former wanted to seize power and take control. The latter wanted to rescue the PCT and its leader from the political disaster to which it had been condemned by the former.

The invention of the new political scene set at loggerheads the two camps that had come up with the eight commissions: a commission in charge of institutions and freedoms; a commission in charge of political defence and security; an economy and finance commission; a health, social affairs and environment commission; an education, cultural affairs, arts, science and technology commission; an ad hoc commission on killings; an ad hoc commission on ill-gotten property; an ad hoc commission on the repatriation of funds.

The conference played a triple role: that of executive organ, legislative organ and people's court. It monopolized most of the powers of the political organs and state institutions. No important decision could henceforth be taken without its approval. That reduced the state to a mere errand boy. The president of the republic was divested of all his powers. Measures agreed on by the various commissions and which had to be immediately implemented became the resolutions of the conference. In the legislative domain, the chairman of the National Conference signed about 300 resolutions. However, it was the conference's character as the people's court that fascinated the public. In this regard, the conference indicted all the Congolese regimes from 1963 to 1991. It exposed the misdemeanours committed by their political leaders during that period and reviewed the major politically-motivated killings with which the political history of the country is riddled. Thus, the unpublished report of the Commission on Politics, Defence and Security (1992) stated: 'both collectively and individually, the main political leaders of that era who, having placed the entire state apparatus under their thumb, went about protecting their positions and eliminating those they considered as a threat to their ambitions, are presumed responsible for those barbaric crimes'. The report of the ad hoc Commission on Killings recommended that 'all necessary measures be taken to make sure no Congolese citizen ever again perishes on political grounds or as part of the settling of scores'.[4]

The issue of politically motivated killings was debated at length, on the one hand, by opponents of Pascal Lissouba who sought to weaken him politically ahead of the election of the prime minister, by blaming him for the 1965 assassinations of Pouabou (the then president of the Supreme Court), Matsokota (State Prosecutor) and Massouémé (director of the Agence Congolaise de l'Information [Congolese Information Agency, ACI]). On the other hand, that issue was also going to work against Dénis Sassou-Nguesso by eliminating him from the race for the presidency, but a draft resolution to disqualify all those accused of crimes and killings was dropped. Nevertheless, discussions on the question of power, particularly the role of the future transitional institutions, led to an alteration of the physiognomy of both camps. These camps were transformed into two ethno-regions: the north and the south. The northern camp is identified as the geographical region that monopolized power from 1969 to 1991. It is represented here by the PCT and its satellite associations. The south, united circumstantially to foster political change at the head of the executive, was numerically stronger and was represented by Bernard Kolélas' Mouvement Congolais pour la Démocratie et le Développement Intégral (MCDDI) and its numerous associations.

What political institutions did conference delegates finally adopt to govern the transition?

*Adopted political institutions* At the end of conference deliberations, the Fundamental Law proposed by the commission in charge of institutions and freedoms was adopted. During the transitional period, this law served as the Congolese constitution. Its main feature was the existence of three institutions responsible for guiding the political process during the twelve-month transitional period: the Presidency of the Republic, the Transitional Government and the Conseil Supérieur de la République (Supreme State Council, CSR), the legislative organ. The Presidency of the Republic was maintained after intense debate. Dénis Sassou-Nguesso therefore continued to be president during the transition, although he was divested of most of his powers which were devolved to the prime minister. The presidency was no longer the real centre of power. The president reigned without ruling. The Fundamental Act emphatically stated that he incarnated the nation but, in practice, he had no means of incarnating the unity of the nation; management of external relations and the accreditation of ambassadors were devolved to the prime minister. The enactment of laws voted by the Conseil Supérieur de la République fell under his jurisdiction. However, those laws automatically went into effect if they were not enacted within the time-frame specified by the Fundamental Act.

This Act made the Transitional Government the real centre of power. Having been elected by the National Conference, executive power was concentrated in the hands of the prime minister, the head of government. The president's traditional prerogatives were entrusted to him (appointment and accreditation of ambassadors, appointment of senior civil servants and military officers, etc.). Fearing a *coup d'état* that would jeopardize the ongoing democratization process, conference participants made the prime minister the Supreme Commander of the armed forces. He was accountable to the CSP and not to the president to whom he had no constitutional obligation.

The CSP, the transitional parliament, had 153 members designated by conference participants. It was also responsible for mediating between the transitional institutions. The Bureau of the Conseil consisted of nine members. Conference participants made the CSR a powerful institution. It could dismiss both the president of the republic and the Transitional Government by a vote of no confidence in the event of any serious public misconduct on their part. The president of the republic and prime minister could not take any legal action against the CSR.

The Fundamental Act produced a Conseil Supérieur de la Magistrature (Higher Council of Magistracy) and a Haut Conseil de la Communication (Higher Communication Council). Unfortunately, neither institution was set up. It should be recalled that before the end of the National Conference, the country was renamed 'Republic of Congo'; the national emblem of the First Republic, the green-yellow-red tricolor, and the national anthem '*La Congolaise*' were reinstated.

As the president of the republic was maintained in office, the National Conference had to elect the two other institutional officials, that is, the president of the Conseil Supérieur de la République and the prime minister, before breaking up. The election of president of the CSR did not pose any problems. Conference participants unanimously elected Mgr Kombo on 5 June 1991. However, the election of the prime minister on 8 June gave rise to political wrangling, which split the southern bloc into two distinct blocs: Pool (with which Kouilou was associated), on the one hand, and Niari or Grand Niari (Greater Niari), on the other. Pool and Kouilou supported the candidacy of André Milongo while Grand Niari sided with Pascal Lissouba. As the National Conference had underlined the need to have a prime minister during the transitional period who had a mastery of the workings of the global economy and who had connections in the area of international politics, the MCDDI rallied behind André Milongo, a former World Bank administrator in retirement, who was unknown on the national political scene.

Fearing that Bernard Kolélas' supporters were going to take legal action against its militants, Sassou-Nguesso's PCT chose to ally with Lissouba's supporters who were now without a party. This former PCT militant, now an international employee of UNESCO, was considered by the PCT as a moderate and experienced politician. Being a member of a minority ethnic group in Congo, the Nzabi, he was not suspected of harbouring any retaliatory sentiments against anyone, or power aspirations in favour of Bernard Kolélas. After four rounds of elections, André Milongo was elected prime minister by 454 votes against 419 for Pascal Lissouba. The Pool–Kouilou alliance (with which some northern elements hostile to Sassou-Nguesso were associated) thus triumphed over the Grand Niari northern alliance. That election was viewed in the southern neighbourhoods of Brazzaville, a majority of whose inhabitants were from the Pool ethnic groups, as a victory for Pool.

Will the three transitional institutions tailored to strategies and partisan ambitions make good bedfellows during future elections? Will they be able to manage the deeply rooted heritage of the one-party system and, in particular, the vengeful sentiments of certain political protagonists ushered in by the conference?

## Alliances and electoral processes under the transition

*Alliances within the National Conference: the Forces du Changement et du Progrès (FCP) and the Alliance Nationale pour la Démocratie (AND)* The National Conference revolved round two major stakes. On the one hand, supporters of the PCT strove to avoid the trial and imprisonment of their officials, particularly the president of the republic, and, on the other hand, those opposed to the one-party regime wanted to come to power, first at the National Conference and subsequently through transitional elections. The election of André Milongo as prime minister therefore marked a turning point in this partisan struggle which would gather momentum under the transition. During the transition, that struggle would configure the political scene into two alliances: that of supporters of the prime minister, and that of supporters of Sassou-Nguesso and Pascal Lissouba, on the other.

The thirty or so parties and associations that supported André Milongo's election as prime minister during the National Conference formed an alliance to support the transitional government. That alliance whose most important party was Bernard Kolélas' MCDDI was named the Forces du Changement et du Progrès (Forces of Change and Progress). As had been the case at the National Conference, the target of that alliance was the president of the republic and his party. The Forces du Changement et du Progrès was considered as the alliance of people of Pool origin. Given the rigidity of its leaders on certain national issues, it was dubbed an extremist alliance.

The AND braced itself to confront the FCP. At the National Conference, these sixty-odd parties, the biggest of which was Pascal Lissouba's Union Panafricaine pour la Démocratie Sociale (UPADS), had joined the PCT in supporting Pascal Lissouba's candidacy for the post of prime minister. This alliance regrouped personalities considered moderates who were more lucid and less extremist than the rival alliance. Unlike the Forces du Changement, the AND immediately chose its candidate for the presidential election, in the person of Pascal Lissouba, thereby acting coherently right up to the immediate aftermath of the presidential election. How did these coalitions fare during the transition?

*Fanning of ethno-regional sentiments* In the transitional parliament, the two alliances ruthlessly locked horns. The Forces du changement supported the government tooth and nail, while the AND rose up against the government. The situation paralysed the parliament, particularly during the crisis of January 1992. As a matter of fact, keen to put an end to the concentration of military power in the hands of officers from the north, the transitional government appointed a Secretary of State for Defence who effected changes at the helm of the armed forces. This triggered a strong reaction from the General Staff of the army, which occupied the national radio and television stations on 15 January 1992. In a statement issued on that day, it demanded the resignation of the new Secretary of State and rejected the new appointments. A trial of strength ensued between the army and the government.

The parliament, instead of proposing solutions that would take the country out of the economic quagmire, continued with its internecine divisions and the trading of accusations among its members.

Following several rounds of negotiations, the crisis was finally diffused. The prime minister reshuffled his government; the contested Secretary of State resigned and was replaced by General Ngollo, a former PCT dignitary appointed Minister of Defence.

The episode of the barricades erected by supporters of the government constituted a precedent in the democratization process. From then on, political groupings opposed to the execution of certain government decisions had recourse not to the law but to violence. Pascal Lissouba's refusal, in 1992, to appoint a prime minister from the URD–PCT coalition caused a resurgence in violence and barricades.

Interference of the army in the democratization process, particularly by causing the dismissal of the Secretary of State for Defence, revealed two factors: first, the weight of the army as a pressure group capable of swinging the political process in one direction or the other; second, most important, subjecting the armed forces to civilian authority was not yet a reality; the constitution of March 1992, in its thirteenth chapter devoted to the armed forces, sought to remedy this situation which was likely to be prejudicial to democracy. That text actually stated that 'the armed forces are apolitical'.

Shortly after that crisis, a new coalition was formed. This alliance, which regrouped more than sixty parties including the AND, was named the Front pour la Défense de la Démocratie (Front for the Defence of Democracy, FDD). No sooner had it been formed than it demanded the resignation of the Ministers of Interior, Justice and Communication whom the parliamentary investigation commission had found to have been involved in the recent politico-military crisis. They were accused of having set up barricades but, in reality, behind those accusations, lurked the spectre of future elections. The fanning of partisan, ethno-regionalist sentiments would constitute the backdrop for all elections provided for by the National Conference. The said elections brought to the fore the issues of identity and, in particular, unveiled once and for all the ethno-regional entity referred to during the National Conference: Nibolek.

*Elections and identity realities: data analysis* The series of elections envisaged by the National Conference started in March 1992 with the constitutional referendum and ended in August of the same year with the presidential election.

This referendum was trouble-free because none of the political groupings called for a boycott. That was the only election not contested by anyone. The high turnout (70 per cent) in all regions and the Yes vote (96.2 per cent) according to the Agence Congolaise d'Information, showed the extent to which the Congolese people wanted change. The whole country was therefore unanimously in favour of the adoption of a new constitution. The issues relating to its interpretation that arose shortly after the election of the president were a reflection of partisan power struggles. What political lessons can be learnt from those elections? Can they shed light on the problems of Congo's new-born democracy?

At the end of local, senatorial and legislative elections, power-sharing revolved round five major political groupings: Pascal Lissouba's UPADS, Bernard Kolélas' MCDDI, Dénis Sassou-Nguesso's PCT, Jacques Joachim Yhomby Opango's Rassemblement pour la Démocratie et le Développement (RDD) and Jean-Pierre Thystère Tchicaya's Rassemblement pour la Démocratie et le Progrès Social (RDPS).

The big winner of all the elections was the UPADS. With 468 seats won during local and regional elections, this party was 224 seats ahead of the MCDDI which won a total of 224 seats. The PCT came third with 191 seats, followed by the RDD with 122 seats and the RDPS with eighty-nine seats. The 125 seats in the future Assembly were distributed as follows: UPADS: thirty-nine; MCDDI: twenty-nine; PCT: thirteen; RDPS: nine; and RDD: five. Of the sixty senatorial seats, the UPADS won twenty-three seats against fourteen for the MCDDI; eight for the RDD; five for the RDPS; and three for the PCT.

In both chambers, the UPADS did not win the majority seats necessary to constitute a stable parliamentary group. It was therefore the determination to form a stable group that led to the signing of alliances.

What is the new electoral sociology of Congo that emerged from those elections? To answer this question, it is necessary to analyse, for instance, the results of the regional elections, particularly those of the five main political parties.

In Brazzaville, out of thirty-one seats, the MCDDI scooped fifteen seats; the PCT: four; the AND: four; the RDD: three; and the RDPS: 1. The UPADS did not present a list. Its militants voted for the AND. The MCDDI backslid into Pool where they snapped up a total of twenty-six out of the thirty-five seats, the Forces du Changement et du Progrès managed to win two seats. The PCT and four small political groupings each won one seat; the UPADS was absent. The MCDI's results in the other regions were insignificant: one seat respectively in the Cuvette, Lékoumou and Plateaux regions; Bouenza: two seats; and Niari: three seats. It was the third party in the Kouilou regional council with seven seats behind the AND which won twelve seats and the RDPS which had eleven seats.

The UPADS grabbed 76.19 per cent of the 105 seats in the regional councils in the whole geographical zone called the Grand Niari, with eighty seats. Those seats were distributed as follows: twenty-six out of thirty-five seats in Lékoumou; twenty-five out of thirty-five seats in Bouenza; and twenty-nine out of thirty-five seats in Niari.

The RDD and the PCT were neck and neck in the north, particularly in Cuvette (RDD: fifteen seats, PCT: thirteen seats) and in Likouala (PCT: sixteen, RDD: twelve). The PCT was ahead of the RDD in the Plateaux region with thirteen seats against one for the RDD.

The above results elicit the following analysis:

- Three parties share the southern electorate: the UPADS in the Grand Niari, MCDDI in Pool and Brazzaville, and the RDPS in Kouilou. The northern electorate, particularly that of Cuvette, is shared between the PCT and the RDD.
- These five parties got the most votes in the regions where their militants are based, that is, in ethnic groups or regions corresponding to those of their party leaders. Those regions, as we have already stated, have become electoral strongholds. The country is henceforth partitioned: all other parties are considered *non grata* in the regions reserved to the party supported by the predominant ethnic group. Analysing the results of local and regional elections, Congolese sociologist Côme Manckassa (1992: 7), asserted: 'the single party has made a powerful come-back. This time, it is regional.'
- Two lessons can be quickly learnt from such electoral partitioning of the country. In Grand Niari, Pool and Brazzaville, the ethno-parties are sure of managing single-handedly or by majority the regional councils of Niari, Bouenza and Lékoumou for the UPADS; while those of Pool

and Brazzaville are managed by the MCDDI. Elsewhere, the parties are condemned to negotiate or form political alliances. In Kouilou, the RDPS and the MCDDI are thus condemned to join forces to bar the door to the AND.

- The elections revealed the true electoral weight of the PCT, the former single party which had claimed to be a national party. Like its peers, it was reduced to its true regional size: that of its chairman. Its scores were not so low in the north: Brazzaville (four seats), Lékoumou, Niari and Kouilou (two seats, respectively), and Pool (one seat).

- AND is an alliance that played the game. In Brazzaville, in Pointe-Noire and *Kouilou* where it presented lists of candidates, its scores were better than those of its rival, the Forces du Changement et du Progrès – Brazzaville: four seats (FCP: two); Kouilou: twelve seats (FCP: one) and Pointe-Noire: nine seats (FCP: one).

- The elections were, in the final analysis, not political but ethnic. People did not vote on the basis of a political programme but by reference to the leader with whom they identified. The UPADS and the MCDDI succeeded in mobilizing the electorate not only in their respective strongholds, but also in their ethno-regional diaspora. This latter element accounts for the fact that the UPADS won some seats in Pointe-Noire and Brazzaville, mainly in neighbourhoods inhabited by people from the Grand Niari ethno-region.

- The UPADS, by placing personalities of northern origin openly opposed to the PCT in certain northern electoral constituencies, succeeded in winning some seats. There again, the people did not vote for the UPADS programme but for sons of the soil. It was a proximity vote rather than one premised on political considerations.

- The elections therefore gave rise to a very subtle process of negotiations and alliances based on ethnicity. Understanding such a process is crucial to appreciating the entire future political course of the country. It needs to be taken into account in order to understand the nature of the alliance making.

### Alliances and counter-alliances at the end of the transition to the 1997 civil war

*The UPADS–PCT alliance: reasons for the entente and split* The local, legislative and senatorial elections held in 1992 certainly brought five parties into the political limelight but, in reality, the political situation would revolve round the first three and their respective leaders: Pascal Lissouba, Bernard Kolélas and Dénis Sassou-Nguesso. In a context where none of the three dominant parties had the parliamentary majority required to form a government, the system of alliances was henceforth open. Generally, parties form alliances solely with a view to taking power or participating in a government whose political programme has not been previously formulated and discussed. After the alliance comes to power, failure on the part of the majority party to meet the expectations of the minority ally frustrates the latter, giving it good reason to pull out of the alliance and look for a more 'understanding' partner. The immediate consequence of such an action is that the former ally is politically weakened. The withdrawal of the PCT from the presidential majority to join the opposition is the most patent illustration of this phenomenon in the Congolese democratization process.

The results of the first round of the 2 August 1992 presidential election announced on 8 August by the Minister of Interior were as follows:

Pascal Lissouba (UPADS): 282,020 votes (35.89 per cent)
Bernard Kolélas (MCDDI): 159,682 votes (20.32 per cent)
Dénis Sassou-Nguesso (PCT): 131,346 votes (16.87 per cent)

On 11 August, that is, three days after the above results were announced, Christophe Moukouéké, Secretary-General of the UPADS, and Maurice Stéphane Bongho-Nouarra, National Coordinator of the AND, on the one hand, and Ambroise Noumazalay, Secretary-General of the PCT, on the other, signed an agreement subsequently called the UPADS–PCT Alliance. That agreement was based on three decisions: to lay down the foundation of a stable parliamentary majority; to sign a government agreement at the end of the presidential election, whatever the outcome of said election; and to participate jointly and in a complementary manner in the campaign for the election of a single candidate representing both parties at the second round of the presidential election. That alliance was confirmed on 14 August by the political bureau of the PCT whose spokesperson stated that 'Pascal Lissouba is capable of rallying the Congolese people and strengthening national unity which was seriously undermined during the transition' (Baniafouna 1995: 101).

This terse statement was silent on the number of ministries and ministerial departments that would be given to the PCT, and also on the sharing of civilian and military posts. The hidden agenda in the agreement was subsequently understood only thanks to documents published after the collapse of the alliance.

In December 1992, PCT published a *Mémorandum sur la rupture de l'alliance UPADS–PCT* (Memorandum on the Collapse of the UPADS–PCT Alliance). In February 1993, the UPADS in turn published *Les dessous des accords UPADS/PCT–URD/PCT* (Hidden Agenda of the UPADS/PCT–URD/ PCT Agreements).

The immediate cause of the split is related to the second point in the agreement, that is, the sharing of ministries. As a matter of fact, in the Bongho-Nouarra government announced on 8 September, the PCT had three ministries assigned to young executive officers, much to the disappointment of the barons of the party. The PCT old guard considered the sharing disproportionate. Invoking its electoral weight (twenty MPs out of the seventy who now constituted the presidential majority), PCT demanded a third of the portfolios, that is, seven ministries in a government of twenty-two ministries. It further demanded a say and a fair share in appointments to civilian and military posts.

The reasons for the split were interpreted differently. Charles Bowao (1995: 17) saw the UPADS' refusal to share power with the PCT on a fair basis proportionately to the electoral weight of each party as the root cause of the split. Patrick Quantin was of the opinion that, for Sassou-Nguesso, the 11 August 1992 agreement 'was an opportunity to stage a powerful return to power by reinstating the former barons of his regime to key government posts and to emerge as the clear winner of the so-called "democratic" transition tug-of-war' (Quantin 1997: 165). This interpretation was shared by the UPADS which believed that the PCT wanted to use the UPADS both as a shield and as a stepping stone from which to hoist itself to the top of the political ladder (UPADS 1993: 23).

## The URD–PCT alliance and its socio-political consequences

THE UNION POUR LE RENOUVEAU ET LA DÉMOCRATIE (URD): OFFICIAL OPPOSITION TO LISSOUBA'S POWER What is this group with which PCT allied after leaving the ruling alliance? What are the terms of the new alliance and what will be the consequences for the National Assembly and the entire country?

On 27 August 1992, the seven parties that supported the candidacy of Bernard Kolélas during the second round of the presidential election, and which had won forty out of 125 seats in the National Assembly, decided to establish an opposition front known as the Union pour le Renouveau Démocratique (Union for Democratic Renewal).

The two heavyweights in this front were the MCDDI, with twenty-nine MPs, and the RDPS with nine MPs. Except for Yvon Norbert Gambeg (Parti National, PANA), Gongarad-Koua (Union Patriotique pour la Démocratie et le Progrès, UPDP) and Clément Miérassa (Parti Social Démocratique Congolais, PSDC), all the other leaders of the front were from the south of the country, specifically the Pool region, apart from Thystère Tchicaya who was from Kouilou. From the sociological standpoint, that alliance regrouped southern leaders belonging to the Kongo ethnic group, broadly

speaking. The URD consolidated the alliance formed at the National Conference at the time of the election of the prime minister, thereby reviving
an older alliance that was contracted at the time of independence between
Fulbert Youlou, political leader of the Pool and Brazzaville (which Bernard
Kolélas was purportedly affiliated to) and Stéphane Tchitchelle, the Kouilou
leader. Both personalities respectively became, on the ticket of the Union
de Défense des Intérêts des Africains (UDDIA), mayors of Brazzaville and
Pointe-Noire.

*Terms of the URD–PCT agreement* The PCT, which had just withdrawn
from its alliance with UPADS, wanted to come to power at all costs. It did
not hesitate to join even the politician who had hitherto been viewed as
its enemy: Bernard Kolélas and the front he was leading. On 30 September
1992, PCT therefore signed a government agreement with URD.

Unlike the UPADS–PCT agreement, the new one bore the signatures of
the two highest officers of both parties and seemed to be better drafted.
For URD, the text was signed by its president, Bernard Kolélas, and vice-
president, while party president and secretary-general, respectively Dénis
Sassou-Nguesso and Ambroise Noumazalay, signed for PCT. Although the
UPADS–PCT alliance seems to have been contracted hastily, in a context
where the presidential candidate, Pascal Lissouba, was the favourite in
the polls, the new alliance was more considered and clearly addressed the
concerns of the PCT. The text contained a preamble and nine articles.

The preamble stated the reasons which had led URD and PCT to sign the
government agreement. These reasons included the fight against regional
and ethnic strangleholds on power. That was the main grievance voiced by
PCT throughout the crisis with its former ally. The first article states that
'both parties undertake to constitute a stable majority in order to govern
together on the basis of a government platform'. Such a government will
be formed, 'taking into account the electoral weight of the two contracting parties, in a split of political balance' (Article 2).[5] In this article, the
PCT pre-empted the experience of the Bongho-Nouarra government. The
fair power-sharing was also extended to the National Assembly (Article 3).
Article 4, which was certainly the initiative of the PCT, underscored the main
concern the PCT had voiced throughout the transition and which had been
the subject of debate under item 018 of the agenda of the National Conference: amnesty for political leaders of the one-party era. In that article, both
parties agreed to 'promote the initiative of the President of the Republic
relating to the amnesty'. The same article integrated the proposals made
by President Lissouba in his inaugural address with regard to the status
of the leader of the opposition and that of the three institutional officials

of the transition: Sassou-Nguesso, President of the Republic, Mgr Ernest Kombo, President of the Conseil Supérieur de la République (Supreme State Council, the Transitional Assembly), and prime minister André Milongo.

By that agreement, the PCT sought to attain two objectives. First, to provide for the security of its officials threatened with legal action on the basis of the findings of the National Conference with regard to embezzlement and gross economic mismanagement during the one-party period. Second, to regain power. The PCT did not wait until 30 September to start preparing strategies for destabilizing its former partner and acceding to power. When it was still flirting with the URD, the PCT had succeeded even before the signing of the alliance, and with the support of URD MPs, to secure the election, on 24 September, of one of its members to the post of Speaker of the National Assembly: André Mouélé.[6] The 30 September agreement therefore only formalized a *de facto* situation in the National Assembly. The change of alliance was mirrored by the emergence of a new parliamentary majority; the URD–PCT alliance henceforth had a total of sixty-six out of 125 seats (URD: forty; PCT and affiliated political groupings: twenty-six).

This agreement nullified the previous one; PCT and its new ally decided to change gear to the active phase of their strategy to gain power. The first action of the new political majority was to demand the post of prime minister.

*Consequences of the URD–PCT alliance in the assembly and in the country*
Pursuant to Article 75 of the 15 March 1992 constitution which stipulates that the prime minister, the head of government, must be appointed from the parliamentary majority group, the URD–PCT alliance demanded the post of prime minister. Not wishing to find himself in a situation of cohabitation less than two months after his election, President Lissouba refused to concede to the demands of the new alliance.

Following this refusal, the URD–PCT caused a vote of no confidence against Maurice Stéphane Bongho-Nouarra's government. The vote was by a show of hands and it was held in the absence of the fifty-nine MPs of the presidential group. On 11 November, the prime minister was forced to resign. His resignation, however, did not allay political contestation by URD–PCT members, for instead of appointing the leader of the new alliance, Bernard Kolélas, to the post of prime minister, President Lissouba opted to dissolve the National Assembly and to call for the organization of new legislative elections, by virtue of his constitutional powers (Article 80). The URD–PCT reacted by erecting barricades in the south of Brazzaville, specifically in the Bacongo and Makélékélé neighbourhoods, as of the night of 12 November.

On 17 November, the URD–PCT called for civil disobedience. Acts of violence became rampant and intensified in neighbourhoods controlled by the opposition, not against state symbols but against citizens from Niari, Bouenza and Lékoumou regions considered to be strongholds of Pascal Lis-souba. This led to an escalation of all forms of violence in Brazzaville.

Faced with escalating violence and the breakdown in law and order, the army, under orders from its supreme commander, decided to intervene between the various political protagonists. After negotiations conducted under the auspices of the army, the two major political groupings (URD–PCT and the president's alliance) signed an agreement on 3 December 1992. According to the agreement, they consented to form a government of national unity in which the URD–PCT coalition and affiliates had 60 per cent of the posts while the presidential alliance gained 40 per cent. In addition to its traditional duties, that government decided to organize legislative elections and set up a Commission Nationale d'Organisation et de Supervision des Elections Législatives (National Commission in Charge of Organizing and Supervising Legislative Elections, CONOSEL). The chair-man of this commission came from the URD–PCT and affiliates while the vice-chairman came from the president's alliance. Claude Antoine Da Costa (minister under the Massambat-Débat regime from 1965 to 1966) was appointed on 5 December 1992 to form and head a coalition government with the opposition.

The agreement provided, *inter alia*, for the liberation of prisoners and the dismantling of roadblocks. For the first time it implicitly acknowledged that, for political reasons, the Congolese had suffered mental and bodily harm, that political parties and groupings had set up militias, that private prisons had been built in defiance of the supposedly humanist traditions of the Bantus, the laws of the land and international protocols relating to human rights. One of the provisions of the agreement emphasized that it would be binding on the signatory parties until the new Assembly was put in place.

Confronted by their first political crisis, the protagonists discarded con-stitutional solutions and resorted to extra-constitutional ones. Two other crises soon arose; these were related to the results of the early legislative elections.

The first round of the early elections was held on 1 May 1993. As early as 9 May, the URD–PCT alliance and its affiliated political groups issued a statement demanding the annulment of the first round of the legislative elections. It alleged that the elections were marred by flagrant irregularities in five northern constituencies and in one south-western constituency. The opposition accused the president's alliance of electoral fraud. The accusations of one camp and denials of the other were echoed by the CONOSEL Bureau. The cacophony and pernicious manoeuvres that set in within the Bureau stalled the announcement of the election results for some time. The impasse within the CONOSEL prompted the Minister of Interior, Colonel Ayayen, to announce the following results on 20 May: President's alliance: fifty seats; the URD–PCT and affiliates: forty-nine seats; André Milongo's Union pour la Démocratie et la République (UDR-Mwînda): two seats;[7] UPRN: one seat.

On 23 May, the URD–PCT alliance issued a new statement calling for a boycott of the second round of the elections and a rerun of the elections in constituencies where there had allegedly been irregularities. The second round, boycotted by the opposition, was held on 6 June in a tense atmosphere. Two days later, the opposition called for civil disobedience, and from 12 June barricades resurfaced in neighbourhoods in Brazzaville controlled by the opposition. The political and social climate deteriorated with the issue by the Supreme Court of Decisions nos 8 and 9 relating to the elections. The Supreme Court had in fact been seized on 10 June by the Minister of Industrial Development, a member of the URD–PCT alliance, on the one hand, and on 11 June by the President of the Republic, on the other. The Court ruled on both cases on 28 June (Decision no. 8 in the first matter, and Decision no. 9 in the second).

By those decisions, the Court had, on the one hand, added grist to the mill of the opposition which was vehemently clamouring for a rerun of the elections, and had given the president's alliance the green light to reinstate the National Assembly. This confusing situation exacerbated disturbances in neighbourhoods held by the opposition. This was the turbulent backdrop against which Jacques Joachim Yhomby Opango (former President of the Republic from 1977 to 1979 and chairman of the RDD and the president's alliance) replaced Claude Antoine Da Costa as prime minister. He wanted peace to be restored at all costs. In spite of the curfew imposed in Brazzaville on 16 July and the state of emergency nationwide, urban violence intensified, leaving dozens dead.

The Chief of Staff was dismissed, accused of laxity, while the Minister of Defence was appointed national mediator.[8] The latter, on 26 July, managed to broker a joint communiqué by the URD–PCT and its affiliates and the president's alliance calling for calm. This important step led the various protagonists to Libreville, Gabon, where they met under the mediation of Gabonese President Omar Bongo from 29 July to 4 August 1993. That meeting closed with the signing of the Libreville agreement to refer the electoral dispute to international arbitrators. That agreement established the results of the first round of elections as follows: 114 elected MPs (sixty-two for the president's alliance; forty-nine for URD–PCT and its affiliates; two for UDR–Mwînda; one for UPRN), and eleven requiring a second ballot.

On 3 and 4 October, the international committee in charge of organizing and supervising early legislative elections conducted a second round of elections under the watchful eyes of all parties in the eleven constituencies involved. These elections were presided over by Mamadou Bah. On 10 October 1993, the committee proclaimed the results: the president's party won three seats and the URD–PCT alliance and its affiliates won eight. At the end of both rounds, the configuration of the Assembly was as follows: the President's party: sixty-five seats; URD–PCT and affiliates: fifty-eight seats. André Milongo, chairman of the UDR-Mwînda and former prime minister, became Speaker of the National Assembly. The election of André Milongo to that prestigious post was an indication of Pascal Lissouba's determination to defuse the tension between the Pool and the Niari region so as to contract new alliances to consolidate peace and tighten his hold on power.

*Towards a south–south alliance: the inter-regional committee of MPs of Grand Niari and Pool* On 16 December 1993, the National Assembly sitting in plenary adopted a statement on the restoration of peace in Congo. That statement marked the starting point for peace nationwide. It paved the way for the setting up of an ad hoc parliamentary commission to monitor and control measures and directives adopted by parliamentarians with regard to the restoration of peace. Victor Tamba Tamba of UPADS was appointed chairman of that commission while Bernard Tchibambéléla of MCDDI was designated vice-chairman. On 28, 29 and 30 January 1994, at the invitation of the ad hoc Parliamentary Commission for Peace, MPs from the Pool and Niari regions met to seek solutions to the armed violence rife in their respective constituencies.

The three days of reflection resulted in the setting up of a sub-commission of the ad hoc Parliamentary Commission for Peace. This sub-commission was named Comité inter régional des députés du Pool et des pays du Niari (Inter-regional Committee of MPs from Pool and Niari regions). On 30 June 1994, this committee published a statement setting out seven practical measures for restoring peace to the country.

Thanks to the work of the ad hoc commission, the government negotiated a ceasefire, free movement in the turbulent neighbourhoods of Brazzaville, and the resumption of railway traffic between Brazzaville and Pointe-Noire. On 2 December, the Inter-regional Committee issued a new statement by which its members pledged henceforth to vote together. The actions of the committee therefore gradually diffused the political tension in the country although they also started to raise concerns among certain observers who saw therein the shadow of a new alliance aimed at isolating the PCT: the south–south alliance. In this climate of peace restored thanks to the MPs, the Congolese government could then organize, with the support of UNESCO, the national forum for the culture of peace. Shortly after the forum, a new government, including MCDDI representatives, was formed. The MCDDI representatives were entrusted with important ministries such as the Ministry of Interior, Ministry of Budget, and Ministry of Humanitarian Action.

*New alliances and political manoeuvres shortly before future presidential elections* One year before the end of the president's term of office, the major Congolese political groupings were confronted by either cleavages or attempts to redefine the balance between the existing forces. Behind the feuds between personalities or supposed political leanings, there emerged new political alliances keen to position themselves in the political scene. Neither of the two political alliances could escape the cleavages.

The president's party was rocked by two secessionist movements led by two important UPADS officials: Benjamin Bounkoulou and Maloula Nzambi. Immediately after the National Forum for the Culture of Peace, Pascal Lissouba appointed Joachim Yhomby Opango prime minister. The latter set up a broad-based government which included MCDDI ministers. Benjamin Bounkoulou, Minister of Foreign Affairs from 1992 to 1994 and a native of Bouenza, was replaced at that post by Arsène Tsaty Boungou, a young lawyer of Niari origin. Benjamin Bounkoulou and his ethnic community (the Dondo, the Kamba and the Sundi) felt the alienation from government as a form of marginalization of Northern Bouenza within the president's party. They attributed this situation to the Bembé, another community of Bouenza (Southern Bouenza) some of whose members were close and influential associates of the president. After futile attempts at reconciliation, twelve parliamentarians from the president's alliance, all natives of Northern Bouenza, resigned from the UPADS to join Benjamin Bounkoulou in forming a new party: the Union pour la République (Union for the Republic, UR).

The revolt within that political alliance affected Niari, Pascal Lissouba's region of origin. MP Maloula Nzambi, acting as spokesman for members of the alliance who were of Niari origin, reproached Lissouba for giving in to the 'gang of four', that is, Christophe Moukouéké (secretary-general of the UPADS), Moungounga Kombo Nguila (Minister of Finance), Mbéri Martin (Minister of State in charge of decentralization) and Claudine Munari (Minister/Director of the President's Cabinet). Like militants from Northern

117

Bouenza, those from Niari were not satisfied with the daily management of state affairs. UPADS militants from Niari, Lékoumou and Northern Bouenza had the general feeling that an ethnic lobby had taken over the presidency and power. Against this backdrop of discord within the UPADS, shortly before the party congress Maloula Nzambi formed a movement called the Courant des démocrates rénovateurs (Movement of Reformist Democrats, CDR). To avoid a situation whereby the movement would be transformed into a party, the UPADS Congress, in the purely one-party tradition, co-opted the leader of this movement into the UPADS National Council.

In addition to the two secessionist movements, there was a third movement within the president's party. This movement demanded the resignation of Prime Minister Yhomby Opango. Supporters of this movement put on the mantle of ethnicity; on behalf of the Téké ethnic group (about 35 per cent of the population spread out over seven administrative regions), they demanded that post which the Bongho-Nouarra ethnic group had held less than one month after Lissoubas' election. Lissouba, himself a Téké, not wanting to alienate the Mbochi-Kouyou electorate of the north, dragged his feet. Faced with growing pressure from the Téké lobby, Pascal Lissouba was forced to part with his prime minister and appoint David Charles Ganao to replace him on 27 August 1996. In appointing this Téké notable and career diplomat of northern origin to the post of prime minister, Lissouba reassured not only the Téké but also people of northern origin by maintaining the geo-political balance: a president from the south with a prime minister from the north.

Bernard Kolélas' MCDDI was not spared by the secessionist movement. It had to concede the departure of Jean Blaise Kololo, former Minister of Foreign Affairs during the transition. The latter formed his own party: the Alliance Congolaise pour l'Unité et les Libertés du Peuple (Congolese Alliance for Unity and People's Freedoms, ACULP). This party earned him a post in the broad-based government as High Commissioner for Human Rights. Only the PCT seemed unruffled by the divisive movements. The remaining militants of the party seemed faithful to Sassou-Nguesso. Political manoeuvres were stepped up ahead of the upcoming presidential election.

In November 1996, a new political alliance emerged: the Mouvement pour l'Unité et la Reconstruction (Movement for Unity and Reconstruction, MUR). The MUR consisted of Bounkoulou's UR, Thystère Tchicaya's RDPS and Paul Kaya's MDS (Mouvement pour la Démocratie et la Solidarité). This new alliance brought under the same umbrella UPADS renegades, one of the leading lights of the URD and a so-called centre party (the MDS). In the agreement, these three parties declared their common will 'to unite their efforts in view of the 1997 presidential election', while remaining free to present separate candidates. What were the underpinnings of the new alliance? It was not founded on ideological grounds. In contracting this alliance, the leaders of those parties were positioning themselves ahead of the 1997 presidential election. Their intention was to form a strong movement capable of outweighing the three major heavyweights in the political arena, namely, Lissouba, Sassou-Nguesso and Kolélas. MUR therefore appeared as the alliance of small parties keen to outweigh the major parties.

Certain generals in the army also chose to enter the political arena to support the election. These were Generals Michel Mokoko and Raymond Damase Ngollo. The first, a former chief of staff of the Congolese armed forces, founded the Mouvement Congolais pour la réconciliation (Congolese Movement for Reconciliation, MRC). He relied on the wealth of confidence won from the people for upholding the army's neutrality during the National Conference as well as the signing of the 3 December 1992 agreement between the president's party and the URD–PCT and affiliates. The second general, who was the former Minister of Defence during the transition and the first months of President Lissouba's term of office, founded the Rassemblement pour la Démocratie et la République (Rally for Democracy and the Republic, RDR). Far from having the electoral weight that could be used as a bargaining chip on the political scene, the two generals, both from the north, were instead asserting the presence of the army. That was a strong signal to politicians: the army is an important and unavoidable stakeholder in the political process, particularly at that stage of the democratization process.

On 5 June 1997, just when the Congolese least expected it, Brazzaville was hit by another socio-political crisis that rapidly degenerated into a violent civil war.[9] The war was supposedly triggered by the deployment of government troops around Dénis Sassou-Nguesso's residence in a bid to arrest persons wanted by the law who had sought refuge there. The war resulted in the victory of Sassou-Nguesso's forces, supported by the Angolan army, the eviction of Pascal Lissouba from the presidency, and the abolition of the previous institutions.

The war tore apart the URD–PCT alliance and pitted two new political alliances against one another: the Espace Républicain pour la Démocratie et l'Unité Nationale (Republican Forum for Democracy and National Unity, ERDUN) around Pascal Lissouba and Bernard Kolélas, on the one hand, and the Forces Démocratiques Unies (United Democratic Forces, FDU) around Dénis Sassou-Nguesso. In having Bernard Kolélas replace David Charles Ganao as prime minister, Pascal Lissouba broke with the tradition of geo-political power-sharing which had been observed since 1966. As a matter of fact, since the appointment of Ambroise Noumazalay as prime minister in 1966, the political system had made sure the head of state and prime minister did not come from the same region. That was particularly the case when Dénis Sassou-Nguesso was president (1979–91). In opting to join Pascal Lissouba's camp, in spite of his status as national mediator, Bernard Kolélas confirmed what PCT and other political protagonists had been suspecting since the setting up of the Comité inter régional des députés du Pool et du Niari: the establishment of a south–south alliance with a view to isolating PCT ahead of future elections.

## Conclusion

The National Conference and the transitional period were the place and time where and when the ethno-regional coalitions emerged and were organized by the various political protagonists with a view to gaining power. The Congolese had expected the forum to adopt consensually the legal instruments setting out common rules for better governance so as to contain political intolerance, thereby creating an enabling environment for resolving the nation's problems more effectively and guaranteeing a more peaceful and democratic transition. The political challenges and, in particular, prospects of gaining power and, by extrapolation, control over state financial resources led leaders of 'ethno-parties' to revive ethnic sentiments and use them as a source of energy for their approach and strategy to gain power. This was self-evident right from the National Conference, in the fierce criticism levelled against the Parti Congolais du Travail and its chairman, Dénis Sassou-Nguesso.

A split then occurred between the latter's supporters and opponents. The election of the prime minister gave rise to a reconfiguration of the political scene as at the close of the conference in the Niari (Nibolek) and northern regions, on the one hand, and Pool (specifically in Kouilou), on the other. The entire transitional period revolved round the two opposing alliances. The Niari and northern regions fought against regional 'extremism' in Pool (holder of executive power). Within both alliances, each ethno-regional bloc played its own ethnic identity card. Thus, Nibolek, which was more densely populated but had not yet given the country a president, believed it was its turn to enjoy the presidency. By allying with the north, it hoped to attain that objective. The north, handicapped by two decades of power condemned at the National Conference, hoped that by forming an alliance with Nibolek it would return not to power but to spheres of political decision-making. The Pool region, which succeeded in controlling the National Conference and monopolizing most of the political and administrative posts, believed that its return to the power was guaranteed. The ethno-regional identity of each of the protagonists was the backdrop against which all elections, from local to presidential, were played out.

Analysis of the election results has shown the monolithic presence of 'ethno-parties' in the ethnic groups or regions, transformed into electoral strongholds, sometimes through intimidation. In such a context, democratic liberalization was bound to be reduced to ethno-partisan pluralism (Bowao 1995: 17).

There is a need for reflection on political parties, with regard to problems of democracy and ethnicity. Such reflection, by tapping into the experience of South Africa, Botswana and Mauritius (the latter two countries have inserted in the law clauses designed to prevent ethnic contradictions from paralysing the functioning of multi-partyism), would definitely contribute in better defining the legal framework of parties in Congo and buttressing democracy. To solve the problem effectively, it will be necessary to transcend ethno-regional consciousness and embrace nationhood. Such a long-winded and arduous enterprise calls for a radical change of attitudes on all sides. To effect change, people need to be educated and trained. Education and training should therefore play a primary role. In this regard, the Congolese educational system and, in particular, the universities, should be endowed with the wherewithal to transform it into a privileged forum not only for the development and dissemination of knowledge, but, more important, for the nurturing of a democratic culture that is freely acquired, such that it would yield a new crop of citizens with a new attitude – citizens capable of rejecting the easy way out, the law of the jungle and recourse to violence.

## Notes

1 Various references relating to the democratization process in Congo-Brazzaville are listed in the References at the end of this chapter.

2 To understand the alliances and stakes at sub-regional level which led to the intervention of Angolan troops in Congo-Brazzaville, see Mabéko Tali (1997: 153–64); Vallée (1997: 165–81).

3 *La Semaine Africaine*, nos 1873–4, 10–16 January 1991, p. 5.

4 Conférence nationale souveraine. *Rapport de la commission ad hoc sur les assassinats* (Brazzaville, 1992), p. 54 (unpublished document).

5 *Accord de gouvernement URD–PCT du 30 septembre 1992* (unpublished document).

6 André Mouélé, member of the PCT Political Bureau, was elected with the support of URD MPs by sixty-six votes against fifty-two for the UPADS candidate, Ange Edouard Poungui, with seven blank votes. The erstwhile informal alliance between PCT and URD enabled MCDDI to gain the post of

vice-president of the National Assembly Bureau, while UPADS made do with the post of second vice-president.

7 Shortly after the presidential election, André Milongo formed his own party, the Union pour la Démocratie et la République whose symbol was a hurricane lamp (*Mwînda* in Kongo language). The party's grassroots was constituted mainly by the Kongo (*stricto sensu*). He had actually been elected MP in the Boko district in the Pool, his region of origin.

8 For more on that turbulent period in the political life of Congo and the reasons behind the dismissal of the Chief of Staff, see Mokoko (1995).

9 It is worth noting that on 31 May 1997 leaders of parties in the president's alliance and those of the opposition signed a Code of Good Conduct in Brazzaville. In the said code, the signatories (Bernard Kolélas of the MCDDI, Dénis Sassou-Nguesso of the FDU, Jean Pierre Thystère Tchicaya of the RDPS, Saturnin Okabé of the president's alliance and Pascal Tsaty Mabiala of the UPADS) committed themselves to a refusal to resort to arms to resolve political conflicts. The agreement was never put into effect because of the partisan interests of all sides.

## References

Baniafouna, C. (1995) *Congo Démocratie. Vol. 1: Les déboires de l'apprentissage*; *Vol. 2: Des références* (Paris: L'Harmattan).

— (2001) *Congo Démocratie. Vol. 4: Devoir de mémoire. Congo-Brazzaville (15 octobre 1997–31 décembre 1999)* (Paris: L'Harmattan).

Bowao, C. (1995) 'Congo. Conférence Nationale Souveraine – Ethnopartisme et démocratie: le ruse historique?', *Démocratie Africaines* (November–December): 12–18.

Dabira, N. (1998) *Brazzaville à feu et à sang. 5 juin–15 octobre 1997* (Paris: L'Harmattan).

Dorier-Apprill, E. (1997) 'Guerre des milices et fragmentation urbaine à Brazzaville' *Hérodote*, nos 86–7: 182–221.

Ikounga, M. P. (2000) *Devoir de parole* (Paris: NM 7).

Kissita, A. (1993) *Congo: Trois décennies pour une démocratie introuvable* (Brazzaville, Ed. SED).

Koula, Y. (1999) *La démocratie congolaise 'brûlée' au pétrole* (Paris: L'Harmattan).

Mabéko Tali, J.-M. (1997) 'Quelques dessous diplomatiques de l'intervention angolaise dans le conflit de 1997', in *Rupture-Solidarité nouvelle série no. 2 Afrique Centrale. Les Congos dans la tourmente* (Paris: Karthala).

Makouta-Mboukou, J.-P. (1999) *La destruction de Brazzaville ou la démocratie guillotinée* (Paris: L'Harmattan).

Manckassa, C., (1992) 'De l'Etat-parti à l'Etat-ethno-régional', *La Semaine Africaine*, no. 1927 (6–12 August): 7.

Menga, G. (1993) *Congo: la transition escamotée* (Paris: L'Harmattan).

Mokoko, J. M. M. (1995) *Congo: le temps du pouvoir* (Paris: L'Harmattan).

Moukouéké, C. (2000) *Congo-Brazzaville, 30 ans de révolution pour rien: la fin d'une illusion* (Abidjan: Editions Condor).

Nkouka-Menga, J. M. (1997) *Chronique politique congolaise du Mani-Kongo à la guerre civile* (Paris: L'Harmattan).

Nsafou, G. (1996) *Congo: de la démocratie à la démocrature* (Paris: L'Harmattan).

Obenga, T. (1998) *L'histoire sanglante du Congo-Brazza (1959–1997). Diagnostic d'une mentalité politique africaine* (Paris: Présence africaine).

— (2001) *Pour le Congo-Brazzaville: réflexions et propositions* (Paris: L'Harmattan).

Ossébi, H. (1992) *Production démocratique et transition post-totalitaire au Congo: portée et limites d'une expérience* (Dakar: CODESRIA).

— (1995) *Ethnicité, logiques partisanes et crises transitionnelles en Afrique: le cas du Congo* (Dakar: CODESRIA).

— (1998) 'De la galère à la guerre: jeunes et "cobra" dans les quartiers nord de Brazzaville', *Politique Africaine*, no. 72 (December): 17–33.

Quantin, P. (1994) 'Congo: les origines politiques de la décomposition d'un processus de libéralisation (août 1992–décembre 1993)', *L'Afrique politique 1994* (Paris: Karthala), pp. 167–90.

— (1997) 'Congo: transition démocratique et conjoncture critique', in J. P. Daloz and P. Quantin, *Transitions et démocraties africaines* (Paris: Karthala), pp. 139–91.

Rupture-Solidarité (1999) *Congo-Brazzaville: dérives politiques, catastrophes humanitaires, désirs de paix* (Paris: Karthala).

— (2000) *Le Congo dans la tourmente* (Paris: Karthala).

Soni-Benga, P. (2001) *La guerre inachevée du Congo-Brazzaville (15 octobre 1997–18 décembre 1998) noir(s) délire(s)* (Paris: L'Harmattan).

UPADS (1993) *Les dessous des accords UPADS–PCT, URD–PCT* (S. L.: Ed. UPADS).

Vallée, O. (1997) 'Congo-Brazzaville, Angola: camarades et amigos', in Rupture-Solidarité, Nouvelle série, no. 2, *Afrique céntrale, Le Congo dans la tourmente* (Paris: Karthala), pp. 165–81.

Verschaves, F. X. (2000) *Noir silence. Qui arrêtera la Françafrique?* (Paris: Ed. les Arsènes).

## Other sources consulted

Règlement intérieur de la Conférence nationale: 10 March 1991

Acte 018 de la Conférence nationale, portant amnistie: 18 June 1991

Constitution: 15 March 1992

Accord électoral UPADS–PCT: 11 August 1992

Discours d'investiture de Pascal Lissouba: 31 August 1992.

Accord de gouvernement URD–PCT: 30 September 1992

Mémorandum sur la rupture de l'alliance UPADS–PCT: December 1992

Mémorandum URD–PCT: 4 October 1992 (relatif à l'application de l'accord conclu entre l'URD d'une part et le PCT d'autre part)

Communiqué conjoint URD–PCT–Apparentés: 3 December 1992

Déclaration URD–PCT–Apparentés sur le boycott du deuxième tour des élections anticipées: 23 October 1993

Accord de Libreville: 4 August 1993

Déclaration URD–PCT–Apparentés sur l'application de l'accord de Libreville: 10 August 1993

Pacte pour la paix: 24 December 1995

Code de bonne conduite en vue des élections futures: 31 May 1997

# 6 | The electoral process and the 2000 general elections in Ghana

EMMANUEL DEBRAH

## Introduction: objectives and issues

This chapter examines the Ghanaian electoral process and the conduct of the 2000 general elections. I begin by exploring some concepts and theoretical perspectives on elections and democratization using the less-than-democratic regime model to explain the pattern of electioneering in Ghana's 2000 elections. Thereafter, I examine the 2000 electoral playing field, including the campaigns, and expose the unfair competition between the incumbent party and the opposition parties in the struggle for electoral victory. While some scholars have concluded that the elections were free and fair based on their assessment of the elections' outcome, a thorough scrutiny of the electoral process reveals otherwise. I therefore proceed on the assumption that the use of manipulative strategies by incumbents in elections does not necessarily guarantee victory for their parties. The opposition victory in the 2000 elections was therefore a 'protest vote' against the ruling party rather than a competitive electoral contest fought on a level playing field.

Until very recently it was observed that despite the fact that there were many elections in Africa, not one brought about a change of government (Young 1993: 299). Only Botswana, the Gambia, Senegal and Mauritius had a tradition of continuous multi-party politics, and it was only in Mauritius that power alternated through the ballot box. Following the 'third wave of efforts to inaugurate democracy in Africa' (Diamond 1999: ix), however, elections in Africa have begun to assume their proper functions of changing governments and legitimizing the assignments of elected representatives to political offices. Thus, in the early 1990s, many hitherto impregnable African rulers, often 'fathers' of their nations, suffered electoral defeat at the hands of their opposition. In South Africa, the apartheid government finally succumbed to both domestic and foreign pressures to release Nelson Mandela from prison, lifted the ban on the African National Congress (ANC), and called for multi-party elections, which culminated in the transfer of power to majority black rule. Similarly, in Mali, as in Cape Verde, Niger and Zambia *inter alia*, results of multi-party elections stunned the world when incumbents lost and oppositions won astonishing victories (Diamond 1999; Lumumba-Kasongo 1998).

This remarkable trend in African politics has continued to produce significant outcomes in second and third round elections as evidenced in the 2000 Senegal and Ghanaian elections respectively. Indeed, the Ghanaian 2000 elections and the subsequent smooth handover of the baton of governance from J. J. Rawlings (who completed his two terms of four years each as an elected president) to J. A. Kuofor (the opposition candidate) – a rare phenomenon in African politics – were both epochal and memorable in the annals of the history of Ghana's electoral politics.

In spite of these developments, it is becoming increasingly clear that the rush for competitive elections by the military autocrats, who traded their uniforms for civilian clothes, was a political gimmick intended to save their regimes and eroding legitimacy from total collapse. Holding elections was to ensure their continuous stay in power and not to change their regimes. Said Adejumobi captured vividly this bizarre phenomenon that is becoming the norm in the conduct of elections in Africa:

> Recent developments suggest that elections appear to be only an expedient political exercise for ruling regimes, partly because of its economic implications in terms of external aid flows and economic assistance and also partly because of its public relations advantage, in propping up the political profile of the regimes in the international arena. The dominant practice is that most rulers organize electoral 'coup d'etat' which ensures their selection in the name of popular electoral process. (Adejumobi 1998: 50)

Michael Bratton (1999) further noted the pervasive narrowness of the political arena, the subtle means by which the press is intimidated and subdued, and the variety of tactics incumbents use to manipulate the electoral process and delegitimize the opposition. For instance, constitutional engineering to alter the laws, including the insertion of new nationality laws designed to disqualify opponents from participating in competitive elections, have been vigorously pursued by Gambia's Yaya Jammeh, Zambia's Chiluba and Kona Bedie's Côte d'Ivoire, among others. Interestingly, however, it is becoming fashionable for western donors and governments hastily to credit regimes that vacate their seats after competitive elections with high democratic scores without scrutinizing their handling of the electoral process and circumstances leading to their defeat and exit from power. The thrust of this chapter, therefore, is to examine the electioneering process and its ramifications for the outcome of the 2000 Ghanaian elections.

## Defining the problem

Ghana, the first sub-Saharan African country to offload colonial domination in 1957, had not fared well in the liberal democratic project, for during the forty-seven years of its existence as a sovereign nation there had been about twenty years of military rule rather than civilian administration. The negative consequences of this military adventurism interrupting the democratization process are, to say the least, disastrous. Not only have human rights abuses created social and ethnic cleavages, but the military are also responsible for the nascent electoral politics with its narrow focus on personality rather than issues.

Political contests in Ghana represent wealth accumulation and the building of neo-patrimonial relationships. In Africa generally, and Ghana in particular, elections have been the vehicle through which power is used to reward political insiders; this encourages fraud or theft of state money (Sandbrook and Oelbaum 1999). Elections are now preceded by a process of political and constitutional engineering under the pretext of establishing the requisite institutions and structures for democratic rule. Seldom have elections been a process whereby contending forces negotiate for the political viability of an even playing field. Incumbents have been preoccupied with the need to organize the electoral system in their favour as the surest way to maintain their stranglehold on political power.

Consequently, in the past, an incumbent's victory was not understood to be the result of his popularity among the masses, but rather as something 'stolen' from the opposition. The corollary of this development was the challenging of election results through boycotts, court battles and protests on the grounds that the poll had been rigged. The fear of losing elections inspires incumbents to resort to all manner of ploys to ensure their return to power. It is, however, important to emphasize that in the face of popular disillusion with a regime, the deployment of manipulative strategies does not necessarily guarantee victory for the incumbent.

## Concepts and their usage

*Neopatrimonialism* This term is derived from Max Weber's concept of patrimonial authority and describes authority in some small and traditional societies. According to Weber, the patrimonial ruler governs by dint of personal prestige and power and subordinates are extensions of 'the big man's' household, with no rights or privileges other than those bestowed on them by the ruler (Weber 1968; Theobold 1982). Unlike the legal–rational authority where laws define the conduct of the ruler, a patrimonial ruler governs according to his whims and caprices.

The term 'neopatrimonialism' is thus used to describe political systems of emerging societies that exhibit both patrimonial and legal–rational tendencies in their mode of governance. In a bureaucracy, for instance, the powers of officials are formally defined but they exercise those powers, as far as they can, as a form not of public service but of private property (Clapham 1985: 48). In this case, authority is personalized and shaped by the rulers' preferences rather than the existing laws in the polity.

The idea of patron–client relationships and clientelism are subsumed under this broader discussion of neopatrimonialism which Clapham, Sandbrook and Oelbaum agree are characteristics of African politics and governance. The concept is used to describe Rawlings' style of governance and the relationship between himself and the rest of his party members which is a variation on the relationship between vassal and lord or between patron and client. Existing rules and regulations carried no weight in the National Democratic Congress (NDC). Rawlings' personal authority and distribution of benefits depended on having a relationship with Rawlings and his party.

*Ethnicity* This refers to a pattern of cultural characteristics that are collectively held and passed on from one generation to another. It has been defined as a named human population with myths of common ancestry, shared historical norms, one or more elements of culture, a link with a homeland, and a sense of solidarity among its members (Hutchinson and Smith 1996: 6). Ethnicity describes a group of people who have cultural distinctiveness, a common history and origin that separate them from others (Horowitz 1985: 3). The importance of ethnicity resides in the fact that it provides an existential answer to the question of one's identity, creates meaning, serving as the epistemological foundation or reference point of an individual and group cognitive structure (Hayward 1987: 45). Ethnicity is, however, fluid and may be contradictory over time. When it is politicized, it becomes a powerful political force that may ultimately enhance or hinder the political integration of states, legitimize or nullify their political systems, and stabilize or undermine their governments (Rothchild 1981). The link between ethnicity and multi-party democracy is ambiguous. While, on one hand, a multi-party system is seen as a favourable context for the management of ethnicity, especially in Africa because of its plurality, in reality multi-party politics rather reinforces divisions in society.

In this chapter, 'ethnicity' connotes a group of people having common heritage, ancestry and language. In politics, ethnic groups and their organizations may emphasize the need to vote for parties and candidates that will promote and protect the interest of members of their groups. The chapter makes reference to such groups with a common identity, and to politicians and political parties that identified themselves with a group and appealed to people for their votes during the 2000 elections to advance the cause or interests of the group.

*Electoral process* 'Electoral process' refers to the chain or stages of activities and procedures that define the conduct of elections. Different perspectives have been expressed regarding the shape of the electoral process. According to Jorgen Elklit, the electoral process should be seen as unfolding in a number of chronological systematic procedures/steps, beginning with the calling of an election and ending with the final decision about the winning candidates. Some of these steps are simultaneous and some overlap throughout (Elklit 1999: 39).

Robert Dahl (1956) asserted that two election stages are discernible from a developed electoral process in a polyarchy. These are the election and inter-election stages which in turn consist of at least three periods, namely, the voting, pre-voting and post-voting periods. According to Dahl, each of these election periods also consists of several stages and sub-stages. The pre-election procedure begins with constituency demarcation and voter education. The election period consists of voter registration and distribution of voter identity cards, party and candidates' registration processes, campaigns and balloting. In post-election procedures, Dahl identifies three sub-stages, namely, counting and reporting, electoral decision and solution of electoral disputes (Dahl 1956: 67).

Post-Dahl electoral processes analysis provides an array of procedures that are geared towards improving the quality of elections management. In his presentation of the problems related to voter registration, Bill Kimberling (1991) identified a ten-stage structure of the electoral process. J. Elklit provided an additional two stages to give Kimberling's model a slightly more complete coverage of the entire electoral process.[1] The twelve-step standard electoral process thus provides a logical and systematic sequence of events that should be followed in an orderly manner. Good quality elections, therefore, are those where full respect for and procurement of basic preconditions are accompanied by an election preparation process more or less like the one outlined, with ample time allowed for all the different phases (Elklit 1999: 39).

The model thus emphasizes a high level of inclusiveness and participation of all actors in the process, as well as transparency and compliance with the rules of the game. Scholars are also unanimous in their opinion that the electoral process in a democratic polity operates as an independent entity, and the functional roles of the electoral actors should be defined in unambiguous terms long before the electoral game commences (Choe 1997: 20). This chapter uses the term 'electoral process' to refer to electioneering (campaigns) and polling processes to draw attention to the behaviour of political actors.

## Overview of election studies in Ghana

Studies of electoral politics in Ghana to date have displayed common preoccupations. While there is a paucity of material on opposition politics in Ghana, studies of the electoral process have dominated scholarly analyses. Early post-independence Ghanaian studies tended to focus more on the political processes than on the mechanics of the elections. Issues discussed include political mobilization and competition among parties and candidates (personalities) in electoral contests. The spotlight is more on the role of the two dominant political parties and traditions in Ghana, namely, the Convention People's Party (CPP) and the United Gold Coast Convention (UGCC)/United Party (UP) in securing the mandate of the people (Apter 1963; Austin 1964). There is a heavy concentration of later studies on analyses of election outcomes rather than on the electoral process. Such discussions have tended to focus on political engineering intended to influence voters in the elections (Hayward 1987; Chazan 1987). Electoral studies that use election results to analyse aggregate change in electoral politics also feature prominently in the literature. Here, scholarly analyses concentrate on explanations of who wins elections, rather than on the processes themselves. Only sporadic references to the electoral process appear in the analyses (Twumasi 1975; Chazan 1983).

Two trends are discernible from post-1990 studies: first, studies that discuss attempts to hold credible elections with little emphasis on the mechanics of campaigns and electioneering (Debrah 1998 and 2001; Ayee 1998; Oquaye 1995; Jeffries 1998; Gyimah-Boadi 2001; Nugent 1996). Second, studies that analyse empirical data about voting patterns and voter behaviour as well as the role of Rawlings as incumbent in electoral contests (Ayee 1998 and 2001; Gyimah-Boadi 2001; Shillington 1992; Nugent 1996). The opposition–incumbent conflict over political mobilization, campaigns and the electoral manoeuvrings of the latter, which explain the political dynamics between the incumbent and opposition in those elections, are conspicuously absent from the analyses. As stated earlier, this study closely examines the electoral process and competition for electoral success in the 2000 elections to fill important lacunae in our understanding of electoral politics in Ghana.

## Methodological and theoretical perspectives

*Sources of data and information* The study draws heavily on primary and secondary materials/data to analyse the electoral 'behaviour' of the incumbent *vis-à-vis* the opposition in the Ghanaian 2000 elections. It combines opinion randomly sampled through face-to-face interviews, focus group discussions with key actors in the electoral process as well as existing scholarly views on various subjects of elections. I also engaged in indirect discussions with voters, election administrators, journalists and retired political activists.

Each of these methods sheds light on the unfair competition between the incumbent and opposition in the 2000 electoral contest. A process-oriented approach posits democratization as an actor-driven political process, one involving conflicts, struggles and power relations among pro- and anti-democratization groups (Franco 2001: xxxiii). The study examines these interactions, struggles and relations and the key actors involved in them.

*Elections and democratization – exploring the less-than-democratic regime model* Democratization is a difficult process involving struggles within society and the state to extend effective access to democratic governance to the entire citizenry. These struggles are part of the ongoing two-way battle between a pseudo-democratic (Joseph 1999b) incumbent and a democratic opposition for control of the political and electoral processes and their outcomes. For an election to qualify as democratic it must provide for fair competition and guarantees of basic freedoms for an equal contest such as a level playing field and an equitable distribution of resources. Developments in recent elections in newly democratic regimes, especially in Africa, suggest that the process of democratization is gradually returning to 'authoritarian' rule (Franco 2001; Diamond 1999; Joseph 1999b, Lumumba-Kasongo 1998), partly due to unfair competition in election contests.

Admittedly, the theoretical literature on democratization offers a wide array of competing explanations for regime change/transition without any analytical categories about 'predictive power concerning what happens after the first democratically elected government has been installed' (O'Donnell 1993). Thus, to explain the aftermath of the transition from centralized authoritarian rule to democratic constitution requires 'finer shades of models that explain the classical polar opposites of authoritarianism and democracy' (Pye 1990: 13). This model highlights the problems of electoral politics specific to the next transition (Franco 2001: 6).

The model posits that the putative transition to democracy fails to eliminate electoral fraud, elections-related violence and other forms of electoral manipulation practised under previous authoritarian regimes. Some protagonists of this model contend that, as political regimes move from 'founding elections' to consolidation elections, the electoral game and process are supposed to break from the authoritarian past but, as Franco (2001) asserts, elections are held under repressive conditions that provide a thin veil for 'authoritarian' elites' efforts to reinforce undemocratic power relations in the state after the transition to elected rule (ibid., p. xxx). Competition, the driving force behind democratic elections, often yields to the spectre of political rancour, acrimony, controversies and violence, usually directed against radical reform oppositionists by state forces during national elections.

While the political and electoral system encourage moderate rates of political participation in multi-candidate competitive elections, the regime pursues strategies that tend to adulterate elections with populist mobilization through either a deregulated or 'controlled' elections to secure nominal legitimacy for the incumbent (Mozaffar 2002: 89). The institutional hallmarks of regimes that hold less-than-democratic elections is neopatrimonialism – a system of governance based on the monopoly of state power and resources as well as the integration of certain groups and interests as representational monopolies closely tied to the ruling party (ibid.).

Ethno-political cleavages remain the salient determinant of political interests and mobilization because of their comparative advantage to the political survival of the regime. Although an electoral contest is characterized by competition, continuous harassment and threats to opposition parties as well as physical attacks with brute force remain the currency of the regime's political control (Joseph 1999a: 5). In order to exert some modicum of monopoly over the electoral process, incumbents may weaken opposition by informal practices such as bribing the leaders of old and new opposition parties until a split occurs or key members defect to the ruling party (Barkan and Ng'ethe 1998: 33).

While the model helps us to understand electoral politics by explaining the context of the 'menu of manipulation' (Schedler 2002: 104) used by incumbents in new democracies to strip the electoral process of its democratic practices, critics draw attention to inherent weaknesses in the model. It is the contention of some scholars that even if incumbents try to steal elections, weaken opposition parties, create artificial cleavages and establish unfair rules and conditions of competition, citizens may still vote against them (Schedler 2002; Franco 2001). This is because citizens are rational beings who frequently make informed choices and cannot be manipulated. Consequently, the less-than-democratic regime model tends to fall into a grey area of institutional ambivalence that lies between the poles of partial authoritarian control and full democratic uncertainty. A democratic opposition contesting elections to institutionalize democratic uncertainties will also refuse to play to the gallery of the incumbent's game when it falls below the thresholds of democratic quality.

## Intra-party democracy and the candidate selection process

The measurement of fairness of elections is particularly important with reference to the mode of the selection of party candidates. The conventional liberal democratic standard for the selection of candidates to contest elections on the ticket of a political party, either at the state/constituency or national level, is by a contest of all the prospective candidates at a primary election by delegates chosen from branches of the party. While the modern practice allows for 'dredging up' a presentable candidate, party organizers are encouraged to foster competition among all contestants without discrimination (Katz and Kolodny 1992; Ranney 1981).

The selection process of the National Democratic Congress's (NDC) presidential and parliamentary candidates flouts the acceptable democratic norm described above. The selection procedure for NDC parliamentary candidates started as a process of electoral and political engineering to intimidate some of the aspirants whose loyalty to the founder and leader of the party (Rawlings) was perceived to be weak. For instance, persons in the party who were less critical of the opposition were not backed by the leadership during the primaries. Instead, Rawlings and his group of party stalwarts initiated several intra-party manoeuvrings that ensured that candidates they favoured but who were not likely to be endorsed by party delegates were returned unopposed. As some of these candidates intimated, the ruse was to prevent their most serious opponents from winning the primaries by replacing them with straw men who later withdrew from the contest leaving the candidate to be nominated unopposed [*interview with NDC candidates*]. With promises of big jobs and other favours to awe opponents, the party leadership managed to impose their own candidates without input from grassroots delegates. For instance, in Keta constituency, the then Foreign Minister, Victor Gbeho, the favourite of the NDC leadership, was chosen over Squadron Leader Sowu, the incumbent MP – a person known for candidly expressing his opinions on many national issues and appearing to corroborate the opposition's perspectives.

Similarly, Rawlings blocked the democratic channel of competition and fair play in the selection of the presidential candidate in his party by singlehandedly announcing his successor at a rally at Agona Swedru, to the consternation of everyone present. When it became apparent that Rawlings was stepping down in the 2000 presidential race, many contenders within the NDC started politicking to fill the Rawlings vacuum. By early 2000, the ambitions of long-serving loyalists of the party, such as Dr Obed Asamoah and Augustus (Goosie) Tanoh among others, had begun to manifest themselves. Opinion within the party suggested that these loyalists were interested in the contest [*interview with NDC National Executive members*].

The authoritarian selection process, however, denied most potential candidates the opportunity of being selected by the rank-and-file of the party. The same undemocratic practices were followed by Professor Evans Atta Mills in the choice of a running-mate. Thus, contrary to popular wishes, he chose Martin Amidu, the then deputy attorney-general, instead of Dr Obed Asamoah, the attorney-general.

The consequence of these actions led to a schism in the NDC, as those who resented such undemocratic procedures revolted and vowed to destroy the NDC's empire. Many of the rejected parliamentary aspirants stood as independent candidates and Goosie Tanoh led a faction to form the National Reform Party (NRP) on 27 July 1999. The NRP, an offshoot of the NDC, is made up of some of the cadres who had previously supported Rawlings in his election-rigging strategies[2] [*opinion of some groups interviewed*]. They had been fighting for changes in the party to reflect democratic principles, especially after the 1996 elections, with little success. The party therefore indicated its commitment to working to advance the course of intra-party democracy. Contrary to the NDC capitalist prescription, the NRP appeared to be nostalgic for the Provisional National Defence Council (PNDC) days when Rawlings preached the gospel of a free-for-all and advocated a system of local initiatives to tackle the development problems of the country. Consequently, its philosophy was based on left-of-centre 'social democracy'. In several respects, the NRP was a failure at birth, being a conglomerate of disgruntled NDC insiders who, in the eyes of the public, were the brains behind Rawlings' extended regime that had resulted in hardship and poverty for ordinary Ghanaians [*consensual view of a focus group discussion*].

Although the intra-New Patriotic Party (NPP) democratic ethos was far from excellent, its selection procedure encouraged competition and fairness in comparison with that of the NDC. For instance, about seven candidates contested the presidential primary; in the constituencies, the primaries were keenly contested without any candidate suffering intimidation or denial of the right to stand. Thus, unlike the NDC, whose congress was marked by rancour and divisiveness, the NPP congress was characterized by harmony and unity because party organizers did not interfere with or discriminate against contestants in the party's primaries.

Another subtle manoeuvre that the NDC pursued against the opposition involved the buying of political clients in an attempt to discredit and weaken them. A few months before the polls, Kwame Pianim (former NPP presidential aspirant), Alhaji Inusah, Dr Wayo Seini, Kakra Essamuah (who earlier in the year had contested the NPP General Secretary position and lost to Dan Botwe) and Professor Gilbert Bluwey (an ardent NPP) and a host of other members resigned from the party with all but Pianim and Dr

Seini joining the ruling NDC; in 2004, however, the latter announced his membership of the NDC. In a bid to demoralize the opposition further, statements were taken from the defectors and broadcast in the media. Professor Bluwey, for instance, reportedly remarked that he joined the NDC because, 'it is the only party capable of making Ghana a middle income country by 2020' (Gyimah-Boadi 2001: 60).

In many constituencies, the NDC paraded the defectors on national television and used them in a dirty campaign against the opposition, particularly the NPP. To a large extent, however, 'the so-called defections were stage-managed with the intention of causing the total collapse of the opposition' [*interview with some leading members of the NPP*]. These defections heightened tension in the corridors of the campaign organizations as some of the defectors revealed confidential information about the campaign strategies of their former parties.

Adebayo Olukoshi's observation about incumbent–opposition relations is relevant to this analysis: 'in several documented cases, ruling parties infiltrated agents provocateurs into the main opposition parties to cause disruptions for them from within and, thus, limit the actual and potential challenges which they pose to the incumbent' (Olukoshi 1998: 30). Rawlings further exacerbated division and tension within the opposition camp by fomenting division in the Nkrumahists' family (one of the leading political traditions in Ghanaian politics). He propagated the idea that his NDC is ideologically related to Nkrumahism, even though ordinary Ghanaians could read the lies. His manipulative schemes led to a split in the Nkrumahists' family (Convention People's Party, Great Consolidated Popular Party, and People's National Convention) which has been struggling to reunite without any success. However, some regard the rupture in the Nkrumahist front as a result of their ineptitude rather than due to the cleverness of Rawlings and his NDC.

Rawlings, with his NDC, explored other avenues to antagonize his arch-opponents who remained indignant about his strategies. He directed his manipulative schemes towards the NRP with a view to breaking its sources of funding. Towards this goal, he ordered the army to demolish an international hotel belonging to Alhaji Yusif, a private businessman and a former NDC financier who had resisted several appeals made to him by the NDC to rescind his decision to 'defect' to the NRP [*interview with leading NRP members*]. Indeed, all the orchestrated attempts to silence the opposition and ensure the victory of the NDC in the elections were, to a considerable degree, a reflection of the unbridled ambition of Rawlings and his NDC to remain in power 'till thy kingdom come' [*interview with voters*]. Even by 2000, Rawlings had not abandoned his dislike of multi-party politics and the opposition, which was growing in confidence and importance, and continually castigated them as 'disgruntled politicians and punks' and 'wished that they never taste political power' [*opinion expressed at a focus group discussion*].

## The campaign process

Campaigns are the most conspicuous aspect of the electoral process and seek to market parties' products, articulate their future programmes to the electorate and solicit their votes. The campaign period is a time for all political parties and contestants to place their offers on the table to be viewed by an anxious electorate. The process involves peaceful rallies, advertising and personal appearances by candidates to convince voters that they are to be trusted on many issues of importance. It is characterized by an absence of violence and is usually issue-oriented (Penniman 1981; Bowler and Farrell 1992). Thus, unfair practices such as negative advertisements, expropriation of state resources by one party and personal attacks on opponents are an affront to civilized democratic campaigns.

In Ghana, the use of physical violence, intimidation and coercion to influence the outcome of elections is perhaps the most blatant perversion of the electoral process. Regrettably, these phenomena remained fixtures in the 1992 elections, and the 2000 elections were accompanied by a pervasive state of violence, including the harassment of opposition figures. For instance, three weeks before the 7 December polls, the obtrusiveness of the military/security apparatus escalated in ways that threatened the elections. Over two consecutive weekends, the army conducted what they called 'military exercises' in Accra and Tema to 'test their combat readiness' in case of an external attack (Gyimah-Boadi et al. 2000: 11). Although such occasional military exercises are normal, the deliberate timing of the manoeuvres heightened civilian anxieties about the possible disruption of the electoral process should the incumbent lose the elections. Also, the likelihood of violence erupting between pro-NDC and pro-opposition forces was so imminent that the Electoral Commission (EC) admonished peaceful polls. This move, however, proved futile as violence and intimidation occurred, directed mainly at preventing opposition supporters from voting by the state security apparatus loyal to Rawlings and the NDC on a scale reminiscent of the 1992 founding elections. Rawlings' private army, also known as 'commandos', in a destructive show of force fired guns to disperse opposition voters during the run-off in many polling centres. In the midst of the violence, an armed NDC supporter stabbed Kwamena Bartels, the NPP MP for Ablekuma North, in the chest while the police looked on helplessly.

In the Volta region, home of Rawlings, also known in Ghanaian electoral politics as 'NDC's World Bank' because the voting pattern shows its preference for the NDC with about 90 per cent of valid votes cast in his favour, incumbent party candidates with superior forces chased out or frightened voters loyal to the opposition while ensuring that the NDC supporters voted in peace. Also, on the eve of the elections, opposition party agents who had undergone election observation training and received accreditation from the EC to monitor the polls were severely beaten, intimidated and threatened with death by NDC sympathizers. This researcher witnessed voting harassment.

In many constituencies, however, some agents of the opposition were able to parry, thwart or counter such tactics by the NDC. The opposition parties also realized that it was necessary to have 'muscles' and 'thugs' to protect oneself even if there was no intention of intimidating opponents (Hayward and Dumbuya 1985: 74). But it was only in the opposition's strongholds in Ashanti that their militant supporters counteracted in equal measure the intimidation by the ruling NDC. This development is reminiscent of a comment made by Hayward and Dumbuya in respect of the 1982 Sierra Leone elections:

> Elections are not Fourah Bay College (gentlemanly). A candidate should have a gang of strong men to protect his wife and his supporters. It is kick for a kick. If you think your opponent is going to be violent, you must show that you are willing to be more violent. It is a hard way to campaign but you must meet your opponent physically if that is necessary. (ibid., p. 75)

For many Ghanaians, the actions of Rawlings and his NDC did not come as a surprise as they were wholly consistent with his authoritarian past during his ten years of military rule. But contrary to his socialist-oriented philosophy in the early 1980s, his NDC is ideologically related to western capitalism, to a privatized market economy.

The campaign process, which started peacefully, degenerated into conflict. For the most part, the economy was the focus of the campaign. The NDC counted on its past economic achievements. Indeed, since 1983 when Rawlings made a U-turn to court the friendship of the World Bank (WB) and the International Monetary Fund (IMF) and implemented structural adjustment programmes (SAPs), he had made nominal economic progress. Continuing the progress made during his nineteen-year rule was the central theme of his campaign message. Hence, its slogan was 'Continuity in Change and Progressive Change'. It promised to continue to build on Rawlings' economic and democratic legacies. In substance, there is no ideological difference between the NDC and the NPP, but only the Nkrumah-affiliated parties declared for the socialist solution to the country's socio-economic problems. Similar to the NDC campaign messages, the NPP offered the voters a free enterprise programme but 'within a proven expertise of its leadership'. This way, a 'Positive Change' from the NDC's past corruption, bad leadership, economic mismanagement and human rights abuses would help promote 'Development in Freedom' in the country. Thus, the rising cost of living, unemployment and the deteriorating socio-economic lives of the people were the holy grail of the opposition.

Surprisingly, the otherwise mundane campaign entered a deplorable phase. Although Rawlings was not a candidate in the elections, warnings to the opposition and personal attacks became the staple of his rhetoric throughout the campaigns. He portrayed the opposition politicians as failures – the NDC media advertisements sought to portray the NPP presidential candidate as a waffling 'ne'er-do-well', a failed businessman, lawyer and sports administrator and a rejected presidential candidate for the 1996 elections. His running mate, Alhaji Aliu Mahama, was depicted as a failed civil engineer of a failed parastatal and an unknown quantity in politics. The NPP responded by making several cutting remarks about the NDC presidential candidate. He was portrayed as a disappointed vice president, an incompetent tax administrator with weak morals – he was accused of failing to declare that he was the father of an eleven-year-old son born out of wedlock (Gyimah-Boadi 2001: 63).

Issue-oriented campaigns are the hallmark of electioneering; hence, whether the political force-feeding that takes place in campaigns actually educates the voters or only dulls their appetite depends on how a political party's product is presented and how interested the voters are in consuming it. It is important to emphasize that, over time, the Ghanaian electorate have become issue-conscious[3] and have little or no regard for campaigns that include personal attacks and insults. Consequently, many voters in NDC strongholds in Greater Accra, Central, Western and Brong Ahafo regions deserted the party and endorsed J. A. Kuofor, the NPP candidate, and replaced many NDC MPs with NPP parliamentary candidates.[4] The observation made by Ivor Crewe and J. J. Kirkpatrick is true of the Ghanaian elections: 'a party whose campaign platform ran counter to the views of its own sympathizers courts disaster at the polls' (cited by Penniman 1981: 135).

## Patronage and clientelist factors in the elections

During Rawlings' military regime, a conscious effort was made to promote patron–client relations — a phenomenon whereby officials seek control and influence over various organizations within the state (Sandbrook and Oelbaum 1999; Clapham 1985). Even in the constitutional era, Rawlings became preoccupied with the need to manage patronage, a need which made him intolerant of debate within his own government,[5] and increasingly resorted to the use of presidential power to impose centrally determined distribution of patronage on all factions. Throughout the electioneering, NDC electoral mobilization rested on clientelist politics in which local power-brokers such as district chief executives, Assembly-members, chiefs and cadres were incorporated into an informal party movement having access to state resources, and organized the rural electorate to vote for the NDC. Similarly, state institutions, including the District Assemblies, National Mobilization Programme, National Commission for Civic Education, National Disaster Management Organization and Ghana Private Roads Transport Union (an affiliate of the Trades Union Congress – TUC), became appendages of the NDC's rule. The bulk of human resource in these institutions were the cadres of the 'revolution'[6] who have been rewarded for their dedication and service to the cause of the 'revolution', and remained the foot-soldiers canvassing support in the rural areas for the NDC. The army was even denied its neutrality. Under the pretext of holding 'town hall meetings' to discuss security issues, Rawlings used the platform to denigrate the opposition and solicited their support for his party. As Gyimah-Boadi (2001: 60) reported: 'Indeed, on one such occasion, Rawlings was reported to have said that the opposition NPP was planning to cancel the economically and professionally lucrative engagement of Ghana soldiers in United Nations overseas peace missions.'

It is no secret that Rawlings carried into the constitutional regime certain traits of his 'revolution' by continually regarding politics and governance outside his domain as unrealistic enterprises that could only be contemplated by utopians [*popular opinion expressed at focus groups discussion*]. Consequently, he encouraged a personal rule that impeded the formation of any associations not based on patronage affiliations or kickbacks (Clapham 1985: 48–50). As one of his control mechanisms, Rawlings promoted some groups and organizations, such as the Progressive Voluntary Organizations (PVOs) and Association of Committees for the Defence of the Revolution (ACDR), that furthered his interests particularly during the elections and put his party at an undue advantage over the opposition parties. For instance, the 31 December Women Movement (DWM) headed by Mrs Nana Konadu Agyeman Rawlings, his wife, grew into a powerful organization under the guise of promoting the interests of Ghanaian women and the underprivileged in society to mobilize mass support for Rawlings and the NDC. Consequently, autonomous civil society groups could not flourish within this climate of patronage, thereby raising obvious obstacles to achieving electoral fairness (Lemarchand 1992: 104). Thus, while funds were channelled to DWM, the National Council on Women and Development (NCWD), the legitimate government institution responsible for women's affairs, was starved of funds and logistics.

As in many other African countries, the exploitation of incumbency under Rawlings involved the careful management of patron–client ties to cement mass–elite linkages that only helped to channel economic success into the NDC's support. The NDC adopted two interrelated approaches to the clientelist linkages. The first involved a centralized patronage network that revolved round Rawlings and his NDC that invariably grew into moral and organizational corruption where businesses required an NDC identification card in order to receive contracts with 10 per cent of the contract sum going into the party's treasury [*interview with some business executives*]. Seeking employment in state institutions and even private establishments required a recommendation from a big man in the NDC or the first family [*interview with youths and local businessmen*]. The second patronage strategy that Rawlings and his NDC manufactured involved a decentralized political control over resources and partial, even-handed disbursement of funds through a series of well-publicized 'development programmes' (usually in the form of building of public conveniences and bore-holes) to all districts irrespective of whether the district was an NDC or opposition stronghold.

While the latter strategy was intended to woo opposition supporters to the NDC, the former, however, was 'planned to "starve" opposition businesses of access to funds and ensure that only NDC clients obtained access to patronage resources' [*interviews with voters*]. At the grassroots level, for instance, district chief executives (DCEs), the political and administrative heads of the districts, implemented the NDC-crafted patronage web by ensuring that beneficiaries of the poverty alleviation funds were card-bearing NDC members. Not only did many of the DCEs prevent opposition MPs from using their share of the local government unit budget under the 'District Assembly Common Fund' to pursue any development in their constituencies, but also 'ensured that anti-NDC rural voters/communities were discriminated against and blacklisted in the distribution of state largesse' [*interview with rural voters*].

## The muddy electoral field and the ethnic conundrum

A credible electoral contest is the one that promotes optimum fairness in the process, including the degree to which money influences the election outcome, that provides unimpeded access to resources and an absence of those practices that disadvantage some contenders (Goodwin-Gill 1994;

Choe 1997; Debrah 1998). As the electioneering heated up, there was a clandestine move by Rawlings to utilize resources which were generally believed to be state resources to support his party's chances of success in the elections. For instance, Rawlings and his ministers campaigned in state vehicles without paying for their use. It was commonplace for ministers and district chief executives to attend NDC rallies and campaign in rural constituencies in state vehicles. In addition, the NDC purchased and distributed brand-new Toyota and Nissan pickups to all 2,000 constituencies [*interview with some aggrieved NDC cadres*]. Thus, whereas the NDC campaign was smooth because it enjoyed state resources, the electoral hemisphere of the opposition was deprived of the oxygen of funds. The poverty of the opposition was evident in the frequent breakdown of their campaign vehicles and the restriction of their campaigns to door-to-door canvassing rather than big rallies [*interviews with executive members of opposition parties*].

The incumbents' machinations were further manifested in starving opposition private businesses of resources so as to break their financial supplies. Many public officers associated with the NRP were also dismissed. Even more troubling, two siblings of the presumptive leader of the NRP, who held top management positions in a local subsidiary of a private foreign company, lost their jobs in the wake of the political reprisals that greeted the electioneering [*interview with NRP members*].

Other weapons the NDC used to 'massage' the electoral process were intimidation and harassment of opposition media practitioners. Although media pluralism was encouraged before and during the elections, the NDC was critical of the press that it tagged as anti-NDC and clamped down on opposition journalists. For instance, the *Crusading Guide*'s office was vandalized with human excreta and its editor, Kwaku Baako, received several anonymous letters and telephone calls conveying the warning that if he did not shut up, there would be more 'shit at his office' (Gyimah-Boadi et al. 2000: 9). Felix Odartey Willington, a lawyer and political commentator, was arrested after making a comment about Rawlings on a GTV morning show and Mawuko Zomerlo, a Joy FM radio host, lost his job for playing on his programme a controversial tape that chronicled Rawlings' past and revealed assassination plots against oppositionists whom the NDC considered a threat to its survival. Rawlings further ordered the Inspector General of Police (IGP) to supervise the removal of all party posters/ads within seventy-two hours and submit a detailed plan of action indicating how he would deal with any further provocation by the parties. Surprisingly, only opposition advertisement materials were removed while those of the NDC conspicuously remained [*excerpt from News File Joy FM discussions*].

It is becoming increasingly evident that ethnicity is a powerful and resilient phenomenon that helps shape the ideological contours of social and political lives in many African societies (Lumumba-Kasongo 2000: 101–2). For instance, in Ghana, ethnic mobilization for purposes of electoral competition entered the political lexicon in the mid-1980s when, in the search for legitimacy for his populist government, Rawlings saw ethnicity as the basis for interaction between elites at the centre and the rural masses (Barrows 1976: 246) at the periphery. Since then, ethnic voting has remained a key variable in the electoral process even though the phenomenon was prevalent in the 1969 and 1979 elections. In the electioneering process, Rawlings sought to portray Ashantis as an 'arrogant batch of people who would subjugate other ethnic groups if the electorate voted for the NPP'. The NDC propaganda machine in both the urban and rural areas spread falsehoods about the NPP and its presidential candidate, who is an Ashanti. References were frequently made to the pre-independence politics of attrition spearheaded by some Ashantis that led to the formation of the National Liberation Movement (NLM) and became the arch-rival of Dr Nkrumah's CPP. Ewes, the tribesmen of Rawlings, were told to reject the NPP because the Ashantis were predisposed to hate them. The NDC propaganda machine told the electorate that 'if NPP won the elections, all the "Zongo" dwellers would be expelled from the country' [*interview with leading northern opposition supporters*]. It is important to emphasize that in many cases such tribally-punctuated exchanges were uninformed, misleading and prejudicial, and sought only to undermine the spirit of fair play in the elections. Even in the top echelon of the NDC there were many Ashantis including, among others, the wife of Rawlings and Finance Minister Kwame Peprah.

The ethnic undercurrents in the elections were much pronounced during the presidential run-off. As Gyimah-Boadi (2001: 62) rightly observed, 'the NDC campaign strategy in the second round appeared to rest strongly on ethnic mobilization'. In a panic, Rawlings descended on Ga chiefs and prevailed upon them to influence their subjects to vote for the NDC candidate, warning them of the danger of an Ashanti becoming the next president: 'They will take over your lands and make you subordinates' [*interview with people in Accra*]. Similar cautions were addressed to the Fantis, the tribesmen of the NDC presidential candidate. He chastised the chiefs for allowing their people to reject their own 'native son' and vote for Kuofor, an Ashanti [*interview with voters*]. He called on them to 'wise up' and 'transfer' their votes to the NDC candidate. Rawlings also influenced and sponsored a high-powered delegation of chiefs from Eweland (Volta region), his tribe region, to visit their counterparts in the home region of the NDC candidate to persuade them to vote for him in the presidential run-off. In spite of the invocation of ethnic commonality, the instrumental values of reciprocity and utility also underscored Rawlings' overtures. Thus, the needs, values and aspirations of ethnic constituency should not be divorced from the benefits that the chiefs and their ethnic clients received in exchange for their votes.

Notwithstanding the intimidation, patronage and exploitation of ethnicity and incumbency by the NDC, the electorate disregarded all its manipulative strategies and voted to reject the party (43.1 per cent) and overwhelmingly voted for the NPP presidential candidate (56.9 per cent). The high voter turnout in the presidential run-off (60.4 per cent) which was very close to the first round (61.7 per cent) is suggestive of how eager Ghanaian voters were to show Rawlings and his NDC the exit from the corridors of power. It was political suicide and a miscalculation for Rawlings to play the ethnic card in the elections, knowing that Ewes (to whom he belongs) constitute the minority (12.7 per cent) of the population, while the Akans (69.1 per cent), who include Kuofor's Ashantis, form the largest proportion of voters.

## Conclusion

Since 1992, elections in Ghana have been characterized by excessive political partisanship and a lack of agreement on the 'rules of the game' for competitive 'democratic' elections. This has resulted in inflammatory campaigns, violence, coercion and other unfair practices by parties and contestants in the elections. The political partisanship tends to be intense between the ruling NDC and the largest opposition NPP because most of the membership of the latter had been victims of human right abuses perpetrated by the former. This helped to raise the stakes in Ghanaian electoral politics because of Rawlings' paranoia that the opposition's victory would lead to vengeance over their perceived enemies in his party [*interview with former NDC district chief executives*]. Therefore, contests among rival political groups for access to, and control of, public office have caused electoral politics to degenerate into fierce 'all or zero sum' games, thereby making the electoral process and the elections little more than state-sanctioned power struggles between competing leaders or factions.

Thus, instead of elections representing the means of resolving political crises or deadlocks, in Ghana they have reflected and amplified existing rivalries and unresolved animosities (NDI 1996: 10). One could see the pain in Rawlings' heart on relinquishing power in 2000 (as the constitution bars him from standing a third time). Before other contenders in his party had declared their intention of succeeding him, he unilaterally chose his successor, unopposed, as a move towards safeguarding his personal liberty and security. His exit from the political arena, therefore, must not be interpreted as a benevolent act, for 'no military junta which has controlled state largesse of the magnitude' that Rawlings has controlled for two decades would agree to leave the stage as an act of self-immolation (Jinadu 1995: 93).

Perhaps a more plausible explanation of Rawlings' NDC defeat at the polls was that, by 2000, the initial burst of popular enthusiasm ignited by the flame of democratization in 1992 had given way to widespread disillusionment. The persistent expression of authoritarian tendencies culminating in subtle human rights abuses, political corruption, mismanagement, incompetence, high unemployment and poverty became the barometer which voters employed when measuring the NDC's record. The general perception of a failed regime and the opposition's call to voters to examine their living conditions before casting their votes yielded a positive outcome at the polls.

## Notes

1 Steps for electoral process function: 1. Establishment of the legal framework for the electoral process; 2. Establishment of adequate organizational management structures, i.e. systems for managing the electoral process, including securing the adequate financial and other means; 3. Demarcation of constituencies and polling districts; 4. Voter education and information; 5. Voter registration; 6. Nomination and registration of political parties and candidates, i.e. providing ballot access; 7. Regulation of the electoral campaigns; 8. Polling; 9. Counting and tabulating the vote; 10. Resolution of electoral disputes and complaints, verification of final results, certification; 11. Election results implementation; 12. Post-election handling of election materials; production of the official statistics: archiving; closing the books (*Source*: Elklit 1999).

2 See the illuminating exposition on this by Mike Oquaye (1995), especially pp. 260–72. For a detailed account see the New Patriotic Party (1992).

3 See K. A. Ninsin (1993) who sheds new light on the scope for issue voting in Ghana. Amos Anyimadu further discusses the place of issue voting in Ghanaian politics in an unpublished article of 2001, 'The Place of Policy Issues in the Meaning of Ghana's First Second Elections: A Focus in the Sekondi and Takoradi Constituencies', showing that the Ghanaian electorate make choices based on the policy preferences of parties. This is in sharp contrast to early studies by Naomi Chazan (1987), and by Dennis Austin and John Dunn in Austin and Luckham (eds) (1975), which imply a lack of issue perspectives in Ghanaian voter choices.

4 See *Ghana Gazette*, January 2001, for a list of winning candidates as members of parliament to the Legislative House, showing a drastic reduction of 1996–2000 NDC candidates in parliament. In many constituencies in the Greater Accra, Brong Ahafo and Central regions, the NPP displaced NDC

incumbent MPs, some of whom were rushed to see physicians at the hospital after they had been pronounced losers in the elections. Also, the NPP presidential candidate, J. A. Kuofor, won astonishing victories in those regions as follows: Western, 60.90 per cent; Central, 60.31 per cent; Greater Accra, 59.95 per cent; Brong Ahafo, 58.30 per cent – all much greater than the NDC.

5  In 1996, Rawlings assaulted his deputy, Mr K. N. Arkaah, at a cabinet meeting for holding divergent views on the government approach to governance. He hit the vice-president in the groin, sending him (a sixty-five-year-old) to the floor.

6  He meant a radical transformation of the social and economic order of the country, and a system of popular democracy where government is based on the consent of the people – farmers, police, workers, soldiers – who would become part of the decision-making process. It would be a 'Holy War' against injustice, the bourgeois, profiteers and what he called economic saboteurs. For more on this, see Naomi Chazan (1998: 93–139).

## References

Adejumobi, S. (1998) 'Elections in Africa: A Fading Shadow of Democracy?', *Africa Development*, vol. xxii, no. 1: 41–61.

Apter, D. (1963) *Ghana in Transition* (New York: Athenaeum).

Austin, D. (1964) *Politics in Ghana, 1946–1960* (London: Oxford University Press).

Austin, D. and A. Luckham (eds) (1975) *Politicians and Soldiers in Ghana, 1966–72* (Manchester: Manchester University Press).

Ayee, J. R. A. (ed.) (1998) *The 1996 General Elections and Democratic Consolidation in Ghana* (Accra: Department of Political Science).

— (ed.) (2001) *Deepening Democracy in Ghana: Politics of 2000 Elections, Vol. 2* (Accra: Freedom Publications).

Barkan, J. D. and N. Ng'ethe (1998) 'Kenya Tries Again', *Journal of Democracy*, vol. 9, no. 2: 32–48.

Barrows, W. (1976) *Grassroots Politics in an African State* (New York: Africana Publishing).

Bowler, S. and D. M. Farrell (eds) (1992) *Electoral Strategies and Political Marketing* (New York: St Martin's Press).

Bratton, M. (1999) 'Second Elections in Africa' in L. Diamond and M. F. Plattner (eds) *Democratization in Africa* (Baltimore, MD and London: Johns Hopkins University Press).

Chazan, N. (1983) *Anatomy of Ghanaian Politics: Managing Political Recession, 1969–1982* (Boulder, CO: Westview Press).

— (1987) 'The Anomalies of Continuity: Perspectives on Ghanaian Elections since Independence' in F. M. Hayward (ed.), *Elections in Independent Africa* (Boulder, CO: Westview Press).

— (1998) 'Ghana: Problems of Governace and the Emergence of Civil Society', in L. Diamond et al. (eds), *Democracy in Developing Countries: Africa* (London: Adamantine Press).

Chazan, N., R. Mortimer, J. Ravenhill and D. Rothchild (1992) *Politics and Society in Contemporary Africa* (Boulder, CO: Lynne Rienner).

Choe, Y. (1997) *How to Manage Free and Fair Elections: A Comparison of Korea, Sweden and the United Kingdom* (Sweden: Kunjalv).

Clapham, C. (1985) *Third World Politics: An Introduction* (Wisconsin: University of Wisconsin Press).

Dahl, R. A. (1956) *A Preface to Democracy* (Chicago, MI and London: University of Chicago Press).

Debrah, E. (1998) *Indices of Free and Fair Elections: A Performance Appraisal of Ghana's Electoral Commission, 1993–1996*, Unpublished M. Phil. thesis (Accra: Department of Political Science).

— (2001) 'Mechanisms for Ensuring Free and Fair 2000 General Elections in Ghana', in J. R. A. Ayee (ed.), *Deepening Democracy in Ghana: Politics of 2000 Elections, Vol. 1* (Accra: Freedom Publications).

Diamond, L. (1999) 'Introduction', in L. Diamond and M. F. Plattner (eds), *Democratization in Africa* (Baltimore, MD and London: Johns Hopkins University Press).

Elklit, J. (1999) 'Electoral Institutional Change and Democratization: You Can Lead a Horse to Water, but You Can't Make It Drink', *Democratization*, vol. 6, no. 4 (Winter): 28–51.

Franco, J. C. (2001) *Elections and Democratization in the Philippines* (New York and London: Routledge).

Goodwin-Gill, G. Y. (1994) *Free and Fair Elections: Internal Law and Practice* (Geneva: IPU).

Gyimah-Boadi, E. (2001) 'The December 2000 Elections and Prospects for Democratic Consolidation', in J. R. A. Ayee (ed.), *Deepening Democracy in Ghana: Politics of 2000 Elections, Vol. 1* (Accra: Freedom Publications).

Gyimah-Boadi, E., B. Agyeman-Dua, A. Gadzekpo, K. Yankah and E. Selormey (eds) (2000) 'Towards Election 2000', *Democracy Watch*, vol. 2, no. 4 (Accra: Centre for Democratic Development): 2–12.

— (eds) (2001) 'Reflections on the Third Transition Elections', *Democracy Watch*, vol. 2, no. 1 (Accra: Centre for Democratic Development): 2–11.

Hayward, F. M. (ed.) (1987) *Elections in Independent Africa*, (Boulder CO: Westview Press).

Hayward, F. M. and A. Dumbuya (1985) 'Changing Electoral Pattern in Sierra Leone: The 1982 Single Party Elections', *African Studies Review*, vol. 28, no. 4 (December): 62–86.

Horowitz, D. L. (1985) *Ethnic Groups in Conflict* (Berkeley, CA: University of California Press).

Hutchinson, J. and A. Smith (1996) *Ethnicity* (Oxford: Oxford University Press).

Jeffries, R. (1998) 'The Ghanaian Elections of 1996: Towards the Consolidation of Democracy?', *African Affairs*, vol. 97, no. 387: 189–208.

Jinadu, A. (1995) 'Elections Administration in Africa: A Nigerian Case Study Under the Transition to Civil Rule', in S. Adejumobi and A. Momoh (eds), *The Political Economy of Nigeria Under Military Rule: 1984–1993* (Harare: Natprint).

Joseph, R. (1999a) 'Africa, 1990–1997: From Abertura to Closure', *Journal of Democracy*, vol. 9, no. 2: 3–17.

— (1999b) 'Africa, 1990–1997: From Abertura to Closure' in L. Diamond and M. F. Plattner (eds) *Democratization in Africa* (Baltimore, MD and London: Johns Hopkins University Press).

Katz, S. R. and R. Kolodny (1992) 'The USA: The 1990 Congressional Campaign', in S. Bowler and D. M. Farrell (eds), *Electoral Strategies and Political Marketing* (New York: St Martin's Press).

Kimberling, W. C. (1991) 'A Rational Approach to Evaluating Alternative Voter Registration Systems and Procedures', in J. Courtney (ed.), *Registering Voters: Comparative Perspectives* (Cambridge, MA: Centre for International Affairs, Harvard University Press).

Lemarchand, R. (1992) 'Africa's Troubled Transitions', *Journal of Democracy*, vol. 3, no. 4 (October): 98–109.

Lumumba-Kasongo, T. (1998) *Rise of Multipartyism and Democracy in the Global Context: The Case of Africa* (Westport, CT: Praeger).

— (2000) 'Reflection on Nationalistic Discourses and Ethnonationalism in the Struggles for Democracy in Africa', in L. Adele Jinadu (ed.), *The Political Economy of Peace and Security in Africa: Ethnocultural and Economic Perspectives* (Harare: AAPS Books).

Mozaffar, S. (2002) 'Electoral Governance in Africa Democracies', *International Political Science Review*, vol. 32, no. 1: 85–101.

National Democratic Institute (NDI) (1996) *Making Every Vote Count: Domestic Election Monitoring in Asia* (Washington, DC: NDI).

New Patriotic Party (NPP) (1992) *The Stolen Verdict: Ghana, November 1992 Presidential Election* (Accra: NPP).

Ninsin, K. A. (1993) 'The Electoral System, Elections and Democracy in Ghana', in K. A. Ninsin and A. Drah (eds), *Political Parties and Democracy in Ghana's Fourth Republic* (Accra: Woeli Publications).

Nugent, P. (1996) *Big Men, Small Boys and Politics in Ghana: Power, Ideology and the Burden of History, 1982–1994* (Accra: Asempa).

O'Donnell, G. (1993) 'On the State, Democratization and Some Conceptual Problems: A Latin American View with Glances at Some Post-communist Countries', *World Development*, vol. 21, no. 8: 1355–69.

Olukoshi, A. O. (1998) 'Economic Crisis, Multipartyism and Opposition Politics', in A. O. Olukoshi (ed.), *The Politics of Opposition in Contemporary Africa* (Uppsala, Sweden: Nordiska Afrikain Institut).

Oquaye, M. (1995) 'The Ghanaian Elections of 1992 – A Dissenting View', *African Affairs*, vol. 94: 259–75.

Penniman, H. R. (1981) 'Campaign Style and Methods', in A. Butler et al. (eds), *Democracy at the Polls: A Comparative Study of Competitive National Elections* (Washington, DC: American Enterprise Institute).

Pye, L. W. (1990) 'Political Science and the Crisis of Authoritarianism', *American Political Science Review*, vol. 84, no. 1 (March): 3–19.

Ranney, A. (1981) 'Candidate Selection', in A. Butler et al. (eds), *Democracy at the Polls: A Comparative Study of Competitive National Elections* (Washington, DC: American Enterprise Institute).

Rothchild, J. (1981) *Ethnopolitics: A Conceptual Approach* (New York: Colombia University Press).

Sandbrook, R. and J. Oelbaum (1999) 'Reforming the Political Kingdom: Governance and Development in Ghana's 4th Republic', *Critical Perspective* (Accra: Centre for Democracy and Development).

Schedler, A. (2002) 'The Nested Game of Democratization by Elections', *International Political Science Review*, vol. 32, no. 1: 103–22.

Shillington, K. (1992) *Ghana and the Rawlings Factor* (London: Macmillan).

Theobold, R. (1982) 'Patrimonialism', *World Politics*, no. 34: 548–59.

Twumasi, Y. (1975) 'The 1969 Election', in D. Austin and A. Luckham (eds), *Politicians and Soldiers in Ghana, 1966–72* (Manchester: Manchester University Press).

Weber, M. (1968) *Economy and Society* (New York: Bedminster Press).

Young, T. (1993) 'Elections and Electoral Politics in Africa', *Africa: Journal of the International Institute*, vol. 63, no. 3: 299–312.

## Other sources

Focus Group discussions, participants drawn from civil society groups, local notables, farmers, public servants, businesses and academia, May and June 2002.

Interviews with some executive members of political parties that participated in the 2000 elections and party activists in six of the ten regions (Gt Accra, Eastern, Ashanti, Upper East, Central and Brong Ahafo regions), June 2002.

Interviews with some Ghanaian voters and party poll watchers, May 2002.

# 7 | Voting without choosing: interrogating the crisis of 'electoral democracy' in Nigeria

## W. ALADE FAWOLE

'A truly representative system of government absolutely depends upon the integrity of elections.'[1]

Even though Nigeria has been independent for forty years and has conducted a number of elections since then, the general conception of politics by the practitioners of the art is curiously Hobbesian and violent, an enterprise in which the only *raison d'être* is the capturing and retention of state power. It is thus a Machiavellian contest for power in which all methods and tactics, no matter how mean, vile and ignoble, are freely deployed for the ultimate goal of seizing and/or retaining the reins of state power. State power is acquired for its own sake, not for the public good.

Nigerians are regularly called out, through intimidation, blackmail, bribery and even the deployment of threats and occasional use of state terror, to participate *en masse* in the electoral ritual of voting for contestants for state power without actually choosing or determining who the winners and losers will be. The vast majority of the Nigerian electorate do not really exercise the power of choice since they are often coerced, intimidated or blackmailed into merely confirming those candidates for office who have been selected for them. Once securely ensconced in the corridors of state power, the holders of this power operate arbitrarily without much input from or even consideration for the wishes, sentiments and aspirations of the electorate, and without ever being accountable to them. Governments are often too far removed, remote and distant from the voters and operate conveniently without them.

The implication is that the electoral process which should ordinarily open up the democratic space to the vast majority of the people so that they can control and influence their own political destinies is actually deliberately configured to marginalize them. What is foisted on them in the name of democracy is 'a version of liberal democracy reduced to the crude simplicity of multi-party elections ... [and] voting that never amounts to choosing, freedom which is patently spurious, and political equality which disguises higher unequal power relations' (Ake 1993: A7).

In Nigeria, political power guarantees unlimited and uncontrolled access to the resources of the state and society that are then appropriated for personal and parochial use and advantages. Nigeria's brand of civilian politicking is therefore no more than a prebendal enterprise engaged in largely for the crude appropriation of national resources.

As conceptualized above, elections and electoral processes intended to usher in and guarantee the integrity of democratic rule are fraught with contrived irregularities and fraudulent practices. The entire electoral process is manipulated through a plethora of ingenious and less-than-subtle devices such as outright and bare-faced rigging, pre-election ballot-stuffing, ballot box disappearance or substitution, destruction of ballot boxes and disruption of voting in opponents' strongholds, intimidation of voters, bribing of electoral officials, deployment of terror tactics and violence.

Apart from all these, there is also the outright disenfranchisement of the mass of the people in the formation and operation of political parties, and the establishment of the rules of electoral contest that are patently elitist and discriminatory. All these account for why the 'elected' office-holders can remain remote and distant from the people that they govern. This is no doubt a reflection of the fact that these office-holders know that they are in power not by virtue of a credible and unassailable electoral process but through the instrumentality of a mere charade called an election. Politicians are of the view that they would gain or retain power regardless of the votes of the electorate. In fact, winners and losers have often been determined upon before the contest, and voters merely go through the charade of confirming choices already made for them.

The chapter will trace Nigeria's electoral history from colonial times till the present, and utilize both empirical evidence and first-hand experience of the electoral process to prove that democratic rule, properly defined, is still alien to Nigeria.

### Defining the situation: the crisis of electoral democracy

The use of adult suffrage has been universally accepted as a credible means of mass participation in the determination of who is fit and proper to rule over a nation. Popular elections guarantee that all people who have attained the constitutionally defined adult age of eighteen years have the right to participate in determining the type of political arrangement and government under which they will live. Elections are therefore regarded as one of the most enduring democratic practices, allowing people to make informed choices as to who will govern them.

The adult franchise was introduced into Nigeria when the colonialists sought to involve some of the 'natives' in administration and governance, even if only symbolically at first. It was first used in the colony of Nigeria once the 1922 Clifford constitution granted a new concession for three unofficial representatives for Lagos and one unofficial representative for Calabar to be elected into the then Legislative Council (see Sklar 1963: 28). Elections were thus held for the Legislative Council from Lagos and Calabar in 1923 (Kirk-Greene 1996: 7). But this electoral practice did not become a serious means of choosing the executive and legislative leadership for some time to come; it was restricted until the early 1950s when the provisions of the 1951 constitution actually granted a substantial local autonomy to the three regions that made up the country to form and control their own governments. Only Lagos and Calabar residents who earned an income of about £100 per annum could participate, with the consequence that only about 3,000 male taxpayers in Lagos actually took part (Sklar 1963: 46). Even in the 1950s adult suffrage was not universal because women were largely denied voting rights in the predominantly Muslim Northern region. The first major national election was held in 1959, when colonial rule was winding down, to elect the government to whom the departing British would hand the reins of power upon their final exit on 1 October 1960. Nigeria has been conducting elections at all levels since then.

While it is assumed that the electoral process remains the most widely used means of popular participation in choosing leaders, its operation is often fraught with fraudulent practices that actually negate the declared objective. Do people actually choose their leaders or are they merely deceived by the mimicry, i.e. are elections for real or mere appearance without substance? One would assume, as Ahmadu Kurfi (quoted at the opening of this chapter) has observed, that a government which is truly representative of the wishes and aspirations of the majority must have been elected via the instrumentality of a credible electoral process. It means that even the rules for choosing leaders and governments must also have had the input of a majority of the adult population for their credibility to be ensured. The case of Nigeria seems to negate both prescriptions: i.e. elections have more often than not been mere exercises in bestowing popular confirmation and legitimacy on choices already made by faceless groups and foisted on the people;[2] and, secondly, that even the rules and procedures for elections have always been made without the input from the people.

The implication of the above scenarios is that what passes for democracy in the Nigerian context may only be a parody of the real thing. And this brings us to a definition of democracy. Democracy, as Diamond, Linz and Lipset have made clear, must include:

> Meaningful and extensive *competition* among individuals and organised groups (especially political parties) for all positions of government power,

at regular intervals and excluding the use of force; a highly inclusive level of *political participation* in the selection of leaders and policies, at least through regular and fair elections, such that no major (adult) social group is excluded and a level of *civil and political liberties* – freedom of expression, freedom of the press, freedom to form and join organisations sufficient to ensure the integrity of political competition and participation. (emphasis in original) (Diamond et al. 1988: xvi)

Georges Nzongola-Ntalaja (1997: 13–14) further provides an operational definition of democracy to include:

- the idea that the legitimacy of power derives from the people
- adherence to the rule of law as opposed to rule by force
- the notion that rulers are chosen by the people and are thus directly accountable to them
- the right of citizens to participate in the management of public affairs through free, transparent and democratic elections
- the right of the people to change a government that they no longer want.

For any system of government to be called democratic, to be described as a 'government of the people, by the people and for the people', it must exemplify and satisfy the above conditions. But it is, however, the right to vote and choose governments or remove unwanted ones that is the most emphasized aspect of democratic rule in Africa. The sheer irresponsibility of elected governments means that they do not hold themselves accountable to those who gave them the mandate to rule.

The implication of the above is that democracy fundamentally involves healthy competition for all governmental positions of power, mass participation by the adult population in the processes and procedures for choosing leaders and governments, and enjoyment of certain fundamental freedoms that are *sine qua non* to the exercise of the right to participate in the choice of leaders and policies. This broadly agrees with Salim A. Salim's position that democracy 'must involve not only free and unfettered exercise of fundamental freedoms of expression, association and political choice, but the ability of all citizens to participate in the process of national governance'.[3] The Nigerian experience has been more in the breach than in the observance of the above prescriptions. Political competition has been more of a zero-sum enterprise in which political gladiators employ all and any means to secure and retain power; mass participation has been a charade; while the requisite civil and political freedoms for participation in the political process have been treated as mere privileges to be dispensed at the whim of the rulers of the state. Thus, the development of an enduring democratic culture[4] has eluded Nigerians, and the various civilian governments since independence have been vulnerable to assault and disruption by the military.

One of the biggest obstacles to democracy in Nigeria has been the propensity not only of soldiers to topple civilian institutions but also the tendency of civilian politicians themselves to subvert the democratic process through an inability to guarantee credible elections. No elections have been relatively free except the ones conducted by the British rulers before independence and the ones organized, conducted and supervised by the military, to the extent that they were not marred by election-day violence. The first nation-wide general election of 1964 conducted by civilians ended in violence and a deep controversy that almost sundered the fragile democratic experiment; the western regional election of October 1965 was marred by rigging and outright fraud, and the resultant violence eventually brought about the military intervention of January 1966 (see Ademoyega 1981); the general elections of 1983 were similarly marked by fraud, rigging, intimidation, lawlessness and violence, also resulting in military intervention on 31 December 1983.[5] The NPN government of President Shehu Shagari was toppled by the military only three months after it was returned to power for a second term via a controversial 'landslide' victory. The 2003 general elections were equally fraudulent.

The point here is that even while Nigeria does not seem to have been successful at running a fully-fledged democracy, it also seems to have defaulted on electoral democracy. By 'electoral democracy' we mean the mere exercise of periodic popular elections that result in civilian rule. It is only a small prerequisite of democracy, and not democracy in its full ramifications as defined above. In any case, that seems to be the western prescription for Third World nations as even the most ruthless civilian governments in Africa are classified as democracies so long as the charade of 'popular' elections is periodically enacted to the applause of western public opinion. The implication is that since the western world is more interested in the appearance rather than the substance, most so-called African democracies merely fulfil the simplest prescription of conforming to electoral practices to qualify for the appellation. What Nigerians periodically enact is an electoral process that is superficially 'popular' and 'democratic', but that in actual fact robs them of the power to choose and control their own governments. The people are invariably disempowered in that they are: (i) not involved in establishing the rules and modalities of electoral contests and participation; (ii) often marginalized or simply ignored in the process of party formation and registration; (iii) neglected in the process of determining the suitability of candidates for elections; (iv) merely goaded or coerced by government into taking part in elections whose outcomes have been largely predetermined by the powers-that-be; (v) incapable of exercising control over governments once elected; and (vi) incapable of exercising the power to recall or remove unwanted governments. Nigeria's experience has been that unwanted governments are removable only by military intervention.

## Understanding the crisis of 'electoral democracy' in Nigeria

Any attempt to unravel the dynamics and problematic of electoral democracy in Nigeria must take a retrospective look at the country's political history and peek into the psychology of politics and power.

Being a colonial Leviathan created by force, Nigeria was largely held together only by the logic of armed force; little attempt was made by its creators to weld the disparate ethnic groups into a modern commonwealth. The colonial divide-and-rule philosophy cynically encouraged ethnic particularism. Sir Hugh Clifford, the colonial governor of Nigeria, said as far back as 1920 that his administration would secure 'to each separate people the right to maintain its identity, its individuality and its nationality, its chosen form of government; and the peculiar political and social institutions which have been evolved for it by the wisdom and accumulated experience of generations of its forebears' (Nnoli 1978: 112). As a consequence of this premeditated encouragement of ethnic particularism, what emerged was a zero-sum type of politics, a Hobbesian scenario where ethno-regional interests and concerns dominated political intercourse. As independence approached, the emergent political parties simply concretized into potent champions and defenders of ethnic and regional interests. This was the inevitable outcome of the intense regionalism that the British consciously promoted, especially from the time of the 1951 constitution. Under that constitution, the regions, according to Larry Diamond (1995: 421), became 'the most important locus of political life'. But then the 1954 constitution, which created a federal structure for the country and devolved enormous political powers to the regions to control their own governments and resources, further entrenched the political parties as veritable instruments of control in the hands of the major ethnic formations in each region. The major political parties were the National Council of Nigerian Citizens (NCNC), the Action Group (AG) and the Northern People's Congress (NPC), which held sway in the east, west and north respectively. In actual fact, both the AG and NPC initially started as parochial ethno-cultural associations. The AG emerged from the Egbe Omo Oduduwa, a pan-Yoruba association, while the NPC became a political party from the Jamiyyah Mutanen Arewa.

The three political parties with their ethnically-minded leaders successfully dominated political life in their regions and at the centre even during the gradual winding down of colonial rule in the post-Second World War period. It was this 'ethnic and regionally-based power politics', as IDEA has rightly noted, that eventually dissolved Nigeria's First Republic (1960–66) into 'a spiral of violence, vote-rigging, nepotism, corruption and mis-management' (International IDEA 2000: 47).

Those emergent nationalists, schooled in the politics of intense regionalism, intrigue and agitation against foreign rule, instead of the democratic ethic, were entrusted at independence with the enormous task of running a new democracy. Their political tutelage and involvement in the public affairs of the country were initially limited to defending their narrow regional interests against foreign rule. There is therefore no doubt that their ill-preparation for the gargantuan task of democratic rule eventually jeopardized civilian rule in the First Republic. The experiment collapsed under the barrel of the gun less than six full years into its operation.

Second, the very conceptualization of politics by the Nigerian elite is problematic. Politics is not regarded as a vocation or a calling into public service for the good of society but rather as a crude contest for state power and all its appurtenances, a zero-sum contest that allows winners to take all while losers lose everything. It is akin to a savage blood sport that leaves very little room for magnanimity in victory and gallantry in defeat. It is a game in which every election is fought as if it is the last one. This perhaps has to be so because of the prebendal character that politics has assumed in the Nigerian context. Prebendal politics, as brilliantly analysed by Richard Joseph, is based on the philosophy that the offices of the state should be exploited as 'benefices by the office holders' and thus it is conceptualized 'as an unremitting and unconstrained struggle for possession and access to state offices, with the chief aim of procuring direct material benefits to oneself and one's acknowledged communal or other sectional group' (Joseph 1987: 75).[6]

Politics as a source of primitive private wealth accumulation is characteristic of the patrimonial state in Africa, as Said Adejumobi has reminded us. The patrimonial state is the cheapest source of private wealth accumulation, and that may explain why elections for the control of the state and its apparatuses are fought with Hobbesian savagery (Adejumobi 1997: 126). Capturing the state is therefore the 'major avenue of upward mobility, status, power and wealth' (ibid.). The logic that the holders of state power and offices use them to appropriate vital resources was the very hallmark of colonial plunder. The colonial state created an array of coercive apparatuses to pacify the rising wave of local opposition to foreign

155

plunder. Unfortunately, this very authoritarian, violent and thieving character of the colonial contraption was eventually transferred wholesale into the post-colonial state. The state therefore became 'a resource, devoid of moral content or attachment, to be pursued, occupied, milked – and later plundered – for the individual politician and his support group' (Diamond 1995: 419). The emerging nationalists, having been waiting in the wings and learning from the masters, simply stepped into the shoes of the departed colonial plunderers. Politics in post-colonial Nigeria was conceptualized as a crude competition for appropriating the nation's wealth, a practice which made good governance and accountability an alien philosophy in the 1960s (Fawole 2001b: 3–8). As a result, political contestations between individual politicians and between political parties were marred by thuggery, violence and hooliganism; governments at all levels were unaccountable to the electorate, and constitutional checks and balances thrown overboard for lawlessness to reign supreme; human rights and fundamental freedoms were abused with impunity as incumbents of public offices employed crude methods of pacification to silence their opponents and remain in power; elections were rigged and governments functioned outside and in spite of the wishes of the people. In short, the quest for the control of the state and appropriation of its resources constitute 'the logic of electoral competition among the political parties' in post-colonial Nigeria (Adejumobi 1997: 126).

Having thus been reduced to this crude level, electoral contests cannot be expected to be the democratic means of choosing and removing governments. No wonder, then, that those to whom the departed British rulers gave power at independence continued to manifest authoritarianism through employment of state security apparatuses to repress and enfeeble opposition parties and groups. As politics increasingly approximated the zero-sum game, political 'rules of any kind became increasingly fragile and untenable, and democracy increasingly hollow and superficial' (Diamond 1995: 419). Politics in the 1960s was inevitably characterized by intrigues, suspicion, violence, intimidation and even assassination. Political gerrymandering became a potent weapon to weaken all opposition. The AG and the western regional crisis of 1962 had all the trappings of this brand of anti-democratic politicking. The creation of the Midwest region from the West in 1963 was an act of gerrymandering done purely for political vendetta by the ruling NPC at the federal centre to weaken the political hegemony of the AG and Chief Obafemi Awolowo in the West. Encouraged by the federal centre, Western Nigeria imploded in a way that ended the first experiment at democratic rule in January 1966.

The post-military Second Republic turned out to be a re-enactment of the politics of violence and banditry of the 1960s as old political parties and regional alliances resurfaced in new garbs but with the same political *dramatis personae* at the helm. The National Party of Nigeria, NPN (north), Unity Party of Nigeria, UPN (west), and Nigerian People's Party, NPP (east), simply approximated the NPC, AG and NCNC of the 1960s. With the exception of the NPN, which had a modicum of national spread, the others were largely regionalist parties, all of them peopled by politicians who had been well 'schooled in the politics of intrigues, insincerity, deceit and the manipulation of ethnic and regional sentiments to sustain themselves in power' (*Report of the Political Bureau* 1987: Ch. 2, p. 35). Just like the First Republic, prebendalism was the motive force behind political and electoral competitions. The NPN engaged in perhaps the most brazen plunder and mismanagement of the resources of the state between 1979 and 1983. This brought the economy to near total collapse by 1982, forcing the Shagari government to institute belt-tightening measures and even to seek an IMF loan facility of about 2 billion US dollars. To remain in power and continue the pillage, election rigging was so brazen that even the federal police under its inspector general, Sunday Adewusi, an NPN partisan, was massively deployed to intimidate the opposition in non-NPN-controlled states during the 1983 general elections.[7] The NPN recorded an unprecedented but questionable 'landslide' victory in the elections[8] but succumbed to a *coup d'état* a few months afterwards.

In general, 'elected' officials usually become unaccountable to the electorate once they get into power. Having bribed or manipulated the electorate, party machinery and election officials to get themselves into office, government officials feel no need for accountability and do not believe that they are there to 'serve at the pleasure of the electorate' (International IDEA 2000: 216). The electorate, largely poor and illiterate, are also powerless to demand accountability from public-office-holders.

To ensure favourable outcomes in elections, politicians and political parties are often more concerned about gaining control of state electoral machinery as a fundamental objective than about the actual votes they intend to win.[9] This is because election outcomes are easier to manipulate at the official level, no matter in what direction the electorate actually voted. Election machinery and election officials are neither neutral nor totally independent of overbearing government control.[10] More than anything else, the 'incumbency factor' is a potent weapon of election rigging for office-holders to succeed themselves. That may explain why civilian governments in the country have not been successful at organizing, conducting and supervising hitch-free and fair elections. Even the 2003 general elections were massively rigged.

## The Nigerian political process: parties and democratic contestations

The electoral process as a mechanism for choosing leaders is based on the party system. Political parties are formed as platforms for the articulation of objectives and aspirations and as mechanisms for the struggle to gain political power. The Nigerian electoral system, perhaps based on its British colonial provenance, has never seen fit to allow independent candidates to vie for political offices. All such aspirations have to be channelled through political parties, thus making membership of a political party compulsory for anyone wishing to stand for political office.

Party formation began with the Nigerian National Democratic Party (NNDP) formed by Herbert Macaulay and other members of the coastal elites in Lagos on 24 July 1923. It has since then remained an elitist pastime, the sole preoccupation of the local intelligentsia. All subsequent parties have always drawn their membership from the intelligentsia, the working class and the propertied class in the urban centres. From its localized origin in Lagos, the rise of post-Second World War nationalism all over West Africa gave birth to the first truly national party in Nigeria's history, the National Council of Nigeria and the Cameroons in 1944.[11] Other more ethnically and regionally oriented political parties were to emerge on the political scene in the 1950s. Even in Northern Nigeria the emergent associations that eventually coalesced into political parties had their roots in the Northern intelligentsia and educated youths from the privileged feudal aristocracy. The Jamiyyah Mutanen Arewa, formed in October 1948, which later metamorphosed into the Northern People's Congress, is an example. It can be safely said that the narrow ethnic and regional antecedents of party formation have survived to haunt Nigerian politics to this day.

Consequent upon the elitist and urban origins of political parties, grassroots mobilization was not really considered an important aspect of democratic politics for some time. Real grassroots mobilization and mass involvement in political party activities began only when opposition parties started to challenge the entrenched hegemony and dominance of ruling parties in their regional domains, especially in the early 1960s. Today, as a result of mass political awareness, membership of political parties cuts across regions, ethnic affiliations, professions, religious and ideological persuasions, age, gender, urban and rural dwellers.

But apart from the political parties of the First and Second Republics which emerged out of the shared values and desires of their members, parties since then have always invariably been legislated into existence by military fiat. General Ibrahim Babangida, Nigeria's military president from 1985 to 1993, started the practice of deliberately forming and imposing political parties on civilians. He established the Social Democratic Party (SDP) and the National Republican Convention (NRC) in the process of his promised disengagement from national governance. In doing so, he proscribed the thirteen political associations, whose application for registration had been duly screened and ranked, with six of them recommended to the Armed Forces Ruling Council by the National Electoral Commission (NEC).[12] Instead of selecting the two to be registered as expected, the regime simply abolished all of them and replaced them with its own (see Yakub 1992: 53).

Regardless of their merits, strengths and performance in the evaluation conducted by NEC, the military regime acted in the most undemocratic manner and against the wishes and desires of Nigerians by annulling the parties. Nigerians meekly acquiesced to this authoritarian directive and flocked to join the new government-established parties. Having sensed that Nigerians would settle for anything in order to be allowed to play politics, General Babangida proceeded to ban, un-ban and re-ban different categories of politicians according to his whims and fancy throughout the duration of his interminable transition to civil rule programme. The emergence of M. K. O. Abiola and Bashir Tofar as the presidential candidates of the SDP and NRC respectively was facilitated by the blanket ban that Babangida had earlier placed on twenty-three other presidential contenders from both parties. The use of military fiat in the affairs of political parties continued to prevail even during the Sani Abacha and Abdulsalami Abubakar regimes when only the political associations that enjoyed the blessing of the military authorities stood a chance of being registered. Abacha registered only five out of the several political associations that sought to operate[13] while Abubakar permitted only three to be registered.[14]

One significant aspect of party formation since the Second Republic is the tendency of the military autocrats to teleguide the process through strict and often cumbersome registration guidelines such as the requirement for a pan-Nigerian membership, operating functional party offices in two-thirds of the states of the federation, electing officers that meet the federal character criterion, etc.[15] The implication from this condensed history of party formation in the country is that political parties do not meet the criteria of being organically derived from the wishes of the people that come together in them as members. The absence of shared values and ideology make such parties unresponsive to popular aspirations and unaccountable to the ruled. Since winning elections is the sole *raison d'être* of their existence, the parties are often fatally defective in the crucial functions of 'educating, mobilizing and aggregating the demands of the electorate' which are fundamental functions of political parties in liberal democracies (Yakub 1992: 55).

## The monetization of politics and the influence of 'moneybags'[16]

Party formation is still very much the province of the well-to-do. To run a party is an expensive commitment and only people of means dictate the tunes while the masses are merely tolerated for the sheer numbers that they provide for the party. The influence of 'moneybags' is so pervasive and debilitating that Babangida at one time thought that politics could be sanitized if the government established political parties in which all participants would be equal. Even that experiment failed as the parties still fell to the depredations of those who had corruptly enriched themselves with national resources. They were hijacked by ex-military officers, retired bureaucrats and the propertied class to the exclusion of the masses of the people.

Once hijacked, even nomination for elected offices was a weapon in the hands of those who bankrolled the parties. During the First and Second Republics, political parties were formed around strong and influential personalities such as Chief Obafemi Awolowo, Sir Ahmadu Bello, Mallam Aminu Kano and Nnamdi Azikiwe, who brought their towering personalities to bear on the affairs of their political parties, and only their anointed candidates could contest elections. The Second Republic followed the same pattern. For example, of all the governorship candidates of the Unity Party of Nigeria (UPN) during the 1979 elections, only Bola Ige of Oyo state was not a personal nominee of the party leader, Chief Obafemi Awolowo.[17] The exit of those few powerful political figures from the national political scene after the Second Republic has ensured that various caucuses would emerge in each party to dictate the tunes. It was such a caucus of 'party elders' that nominated Chief Olu Falae as the presidential candidate of the Alliance for Democracy (AD) for the 1999 presidential election. The influence of money has also ensured that old and even discredited politicians and former bureaucrats are constantly recycled into power every time there is civilian rule. When that is not the case, party elders simply impose candidates on the party. The immediate past governor of Osun state in South-western Nigeria, Chief Bisi Akande, was so imposed, while that of Lagos state, Bola Ahmed Tinubu, did not win the primary election but nevertheless emerged as the candidate of the Alliance for Democracy. In Anambra state, an elected senator had to 'voluntarily' step down from his position to enable Chief Jim Nwobodo to contest the seat after the latter had failed to secure a presidential nomination.

But an even more potent means of excluding the poor masses from standing for office is the exorbitant party nomination fees which ensure that only moneybags or their anointed can pay. Whenever this would not work in favour of certain influential people, perhaps because of other contending moneybags, party executives employed other stratagems to ensure victory for favoured candidates. President Shehu Shagari's nominations for a second term as presidential candidate of the ruling National Party of Nigeria was rigged by the party's national officers who reportedly collected Shagari's nomination forms and supporting documents and promptly locked up the party's secretariat and disappeared into thin air till the close of nominations, thus ensuring that Shagari was the only validly nominated candidate. Sometimes the incumbent government directly intervenes in the determination of who is 'fit and proper' to contest elections by using security clearance as a weapon. For example, Chief Don Etiebet's presidential aspiration was scuttled when the Abacha regime refused registration for the political party that he had formed and later refused him clearance to stand for election even after he had joined another registered party.

## Electoral commissions and the electoral process

The establishment of an electoral commission to organize, conduct and supervise election into political offices has always been the sole responsibility of the government in Nigeria. From colonial times, successive governments have had the duty to set up the electoral commission by law, establish its rules and guidelines, and to appoint, train, deploy and discipline its officials. This body has emerged under different appellations and mandates, and enjoyed different levels of autonomy and freedom from the state.[18] The electoral commission constitutes a distinct bureaucracy charged with a unique responsibility but relying on the state for funding and other support. As Adele Jinadu, a fomer official of NEC, has pointed out: 'Apart from this specific bureaucracy, whose primary function is the administration of elections, there are agencies and institutions of the state, like the civil service, the police and security agencies and civil society groups whose support and cooperation through the provision of logistical support is vital to the operation of the electoral body' (Jinadu 1997: 2).

The usually pervasive and overbearing influence of the government in the functions of the commission does not guarantee its autonomy and the requisite impartiality. Its function, broadly defined as election administration, is multi-faceted, and generally includes registration of political parties, voter registration, screening of nominees, organizing and supervising the balloting and counting of ballots, declaration of election results, and such other ancillary functions as training of electoral officials, constituency

161

delimitation, voter education and supervision of party congresses and primaries (ibid.).

The influence of the government is responsible for the centralization of election administration, especially since military rule turned an otherwise *de jure* federal country into a *de facto* unitary one. Electoral officers are centrally appointed from the ranks of government bureaucrats, thus compromising the integrity and autonomy of the electoral body. This practice began in the colonial days when only a narrow and restricted franchise was extended to the intelligentsia and the propertied class, and this was strictly controlled by the government (Sklar 1963: 28). The successors to the colonial rulers saw the merit of controlling the electoral process to remain in power, and thus 'saw no reason to develop strong, independent electoral administrations that would only serve to undermine or subvert their hegemonic drive' (Jinadu 1997: 2). The military further capitalized on this to ensure that only civilians who receive their favour would ever be allowed to contest or win elections or even hold power.[19] Where, then, lies democracy in all this?

Since the control of the electoral machinery is the best means of ensuring victory, political parties as well as individual politicians always seek to exercise control over electoral personnel through manipulation, bribery, intimidation and even threats of violence. But government control is by far the most pervasive since it establishes the body, writes its rules and guidelines, appoints its officials and provides other ancillary services such as intelligence and security, communication and transportation. Politicians therefore struggle to make input into the process because those who control the electoral machinery determine the outcome of elections. Recognizing this unassailable truism, civilian governments since independence have seen the control of the machinery of elections as the most potent weapon against opposition and have thus manipulated it to stay in power. But this practice, we are led to believe, is not peculiar to Nigeria alone. Accordng to Adele Jinadu:

> In the Zambian elections of 1991 and the Kenyan and Ghanaian elections of 1992, opposition parties and civil society groups made the composition of and modality for the appointment of members of existing electoral bodies an issue in the pre-election discussions. At issue was their demand to make input into the process of appointing members of the electoral bodies, as a way of ensuring fair and equal access to, and the impartiality of these bodies. The concern, in other words, was to insulate the process for the appointment of the members of these bodies from undue interference by the executive branch of the state. (Jinadu 1997: 5)

Real election rigging to determine election outcomes normally begins at the stage of voter registration and constituency delimitation (ibid., p. 9). The voters' register usually contains the names of all adults who have attained voting age and have been duly registered. The compilation of the voters' list, often done on an *ad hoc* basis because of the absence of a national databank, is fraught with irregularities and contrived problems. Amadu Kurfi, chief electoral officer of FEDECO from 1976 to 1981 and who conducted a series of elections, has observed from a privileged position that 'experience has shown that Nigerians in general and political candidates or their agents, are capable of inflating the electoral register by the inclusion of ghost names in it for nefarious purposes at election time' (Kurfi 1989: 7). Other associated fraudulent practices include purchase of voters' registration cards from individual voters or bulk purchase from fraudulent electoral officials and community leaders for distribution to rented impersonators at election time (ibid., p. 15). Other election-rigging stratagems include gerrymandering, deliberate manipulation of the electoral register, misallocation of voters to voting districts, manipulation of the nomination process, manipulation of the allocation of polling stations and polling booths, ballot manipulation on polling day (through inflation, impersonation, disappearance of polling clerks for long periods during voting, etc.) (ibid., pp. 51–6). Others are ballot box disappearance, pre-election ballot box stuffing, outright falsification of election figures, deliberate cancellation of voting results in certain districts and so on.

## Political contestation and election rigging

Political contestation, as we have pointed out earlier, is conceptualized in purely Hobbesian terms, and is thus characterized by intimidation, threats and violence. It is important to emphasize that election rigging is not just an affair of the individual political contestant alone but a well co-ordinated practice within political parties and is divided into pre-election and actual election stages. At the pre-election stage is party formation which excludes the vast majority of the populace, voter registration, inflation of the electoral register,[20] constituency delimitation, candidate nomination, and so on. But perhaps the most absurd occurrence in Nigeria's political history was Abacha's doctoring of his transition programme to enable him to transform from military dictator to civilian president in 1998. He surreptitiously compelled the five registered political parties at the time to adopt him as their sole presidential candidate at hastily convened and teleguided party national congresses in April 1998. Fortunately, General Abacha died in controversial circumstances in early June 1998 before his political ambition could be realized and thus was the nation saved a potential bloodbath.

At election time, however, parties and politicians employ bribery, blackmail, intimidation, threats, violence, thuggery, murder, arson and other unwholesome acts to win. This practice predated independence in 1960. For example, massive political violence was unleashed in Kano (16 to 19 May 1953) in the wake of the Action Group's attempt to campaign in the North in support of the motion for self-government moved in the Federal House of Representatives by Chief Anthony Enahoro earlier on 31 March of that year. That violence resulted in 277 casualties, among them thirty-six deaths.[21] As Larry Diamond has also informed us, resort to violence to intimidate political opponents has been in use since the inception of serious electoral contests in 1951. It quickly spread all over the country and was actually a powerful tool in the 1959 general elections, especially in the north (Diamond 1995: 423). Recourse to violence by ruling parties against the opposition effectively turned the three regions into virtual single-party enclaves and the various regional elections of 1960 and 1961 helped to entrench and consolidate the dominance of the hegemonic parties and severely enfeebled the smaller parties in their regions. Violence has thus remained an integral element of national politics.

At election time, ruling parties are usually the most guilty of rigging as they use their powers of incumbency and control over the electoral commission and the information, propaganda and security paraphernalia of the state to ensure that their opponents do not win elections. This was the case in the regional elections of 1960 and 1961, the federal elections of 1964 and the Western regional elections of October 1965, all of them marred by violence and bloodletting. The Second Republic witnessed the use of state apparatus, especially the employment of the federal police by the NPN, to intimidate the electorate in states that were governed by opposition parties, especially the UPN-controlled states of Lagos, Ogun, Oyo, Bendel and Ondo. It was the same incumbency powers that General Abacha employed to get himself simultaneously nominated as presidential candidate in all the five political parties.

### Implications for democratic consolidation

Two pertinent questions that flow from the above analysis are: to what extent has the ritual of electoral democracy opened up the democratic space for the majority of Nigerians? And what is the impact of the above practice for the democratic consolidation in the country? By democratic consolidation we refer to how the practice of democracy will become so entrenched in the minds and psyche of the people that its smooth operation and effective functioning would be taken for granted. This, as Diamond (1994: 6) has observed, would 'involve such political challenges as constructing strong procedural commitments to constitutionalism and the rule of law, which lead people to value democracy even when it does not perform well economically'. Only the deliberate cultivation of the requisite attitudinal disposition towards democracy can deepen it in the minds of the people and thus ensure that its operation would become institutionalized to the extent that it becomes 'the only game in town'. Nigerian society would still be largely susceptible to experimenting with other systems unless democracy is acceptable at the elite and mass levels as the best option for governing the nation. But the acceptance is contingent upon the democratic system satisfying the basic needs and expectations of the people such as welfare needs, food security, provision of adequate security for life and property, provision and maintenance of essential modern infrastructure, guarantee of economic rights, and respect for fundamental human rights and basic freedoms. These, in the current Nigerian political parlance, represent the dividends they expect to derive from democratic rule.

The critical question to ponder is whether Nigeria's current romance with the democratic idea has any chance of surviving or enduring beyond the level of mere infatuation. If not, then the dangers of reversal are ever present. What needs to be done to prevent a reversal and ensure that the current illiberal civilian rule transforms into an actual and functioning liberal democracy? How much of the tenets of liberal democracy have Nigerians learnt and imbibed from the five years of experiment in civilian rule?

## Conceptualizing democratic consolidation

In analysing democratic consolidation, we take our cue from Larry Diamond (1997: 15) who has observed: 'It is the deep, unquestioned, routinised commitment to democracy and its procedures at elite and mass levels that produces a crucial element of consolidation, a reduction in the uncertainties of democracy, regarding not so much the outcomes as the rules and methods of political competition.'

One of the hallowed 'procedures' of democracy is the electoral contest to determine who will be allowed to hold public offices at all levels. An important ingredient of this procedure, as Diamond would have us believe, is the strict adherence to the rules of the electoral system. The implication is that adherence to the laid-down rules and procedures, which makes acceptance of electoral outcomes less problematic even when it fails to favour one, is more crucial to democratic consolidation than the actual outcomes of elections. Fairness and objectivity are irreducible prerequisites for democratic consolidation. For any society to adhere strictly to the hallowed rules of the political game demands a critical attitudinal overhaul on the part of both the elites and the masses, the development of the attitude that the outcomes of any election would be judged to be acceptable so long as all the rules and procedures of fair contests have been observed. It is such an acceptance that allows losers to accept their fate gallantly and for their supporters to refrain from violence. Since this has to do with the cultivation of an attitudinal disposition that is necessary for enhancing the survival and thriving of democratic governance, a 'stable democracy also requires a belief in the legitimacy of democracy' (Diamond 1994: 13). People must accept in their minds and without coercion that for there to be good governance, there can be no alternative to democracy.

It is obvious from the preceding analysis that the advent of civilian rule in Nigeria in 1999 after a decade and a half of military dictatorship has not automatically translated into democratic governance, *in stricto sensu*. This, as Naomi Chazan (1994: 72) has so aptly observed, is because 'democratic institutions and norms require time to take root and thrive, to form liberals determined to uphold them'. The decades of military rule and the indelible authoritarian imprints it left upon the psyche of Nigerians has stunted the development of the requisite attitude and correct disposition that can make democracy thrive and deepen. Instead, and as Adamu Ciroma has observed, 'the long period of military dictatorship has dulled the democratic sensibilities of Nigerians'.[22] There is no doubt therefore that 'dictatorship seems to have become a culture from which every Nigerian needs to be purged'.[23] Secondly, the largely illiterate population of Nigeria, having subscribed to the contemporary political psychology described above, cannot be said to comprehend, much less uphold, the basic tenets of democracy in all its ramifications. And since old habits die hard, it might be premature, if not presumptuous, to assume that Nigerians who could not be trusted with a fair operation of the electoral system would have divested themselves of long-imbibed authoritarian, predatory and prebendal notions of governance. These authoritarian and anti-democratic practices, we must hasten to add, are deeply rooted in the political culture with which the Nigerian Leviathan was created and nurtured.[24] The colonial enterprise that brought Nigeria into being by force, maintained it by force for close to a century, later bequeathed it to the world as a sovereign state in 1960. Unfortunately the essentially authoritarian and predatory character of the colonial state was also bequeathed to Nigerians in its pristine and unrefined form.[25] This national character is a basic impediment to evolving a proper democratic culture that would transcend the current façade of elections and infatuation with the democratic ideal.

## Conclusion

One inescapable conclusion from the preceding analysis is that the generality of Nigerians do not actively participate in the actual choice of those who rule them. Taking part in the charade of elections only disguises popular dis-empowerment of a more invidious type. The electorate are marginalized in the choice of leaders who, invariably, are neither accountable to them nor removable by them. Government is perceived as a distant contraption that has no relevance for the daily existence of the vast majority of the people since it does not respond to their needs or yearnings. The majority of Nigerians thus exist without and in spite of the state, and are thus willing to sell their votes at election time because they are not given a real opportunity to be relevant in governance. Politics remains a prebend as long as the rulers of the state know that they have bought or rigged themselves into power and could thus dispense with the electorate until another election time. Less than a year into Obasanjo's second term, Nigerian politicians already began frantic preparation for the year 2007 general elections. The whole country was awash with campaign groups, and sponsored newspaper and magazine articles touting the 'democracy dividends' that they will bestow on hapless Nigerians.

Democracy, even of the electoral variety, has suffered terrible mockery as those who claim to be democrats and who now operate the democratic system barely understand what democracy actually entails. For them, regular elections are perhaps what democracy is all about.

The question therefore is: If the practice of electoral democracy has been reduced to such mockery, would democracy in all its ramifications ever become a reality in Nigeria? If yes, what must be done realize it? To be frank, there does not seem to be a simple solution to these questions. Perhaps if the Nigerian politicians would simply realize that the danger of military intervention is ever-present, they might be persuaded to make political contestation a healthy affair and not the zero-sum and violent enterprise that it has become. This is because the dangers of reversal would be too difficult to recover from. If they tread carefully and do not conceptualize elections as do-or-die contests, the country might be on the road to consolidating democracy in the minds of the people and thus ensure that it would go through the necessary refinements along the way. Because of mass illiteracy and a general lack of political consciousness, the numerous pro-democracy groups, the human rights community and civil society organizations in the country have a lot of work to do to sensitize Nigerians to the dangers lying in wait for them if they allow the current experiment to be subverted. Nigeria might then have a chance of moving from mere electoral democracy to the real thing in a matter of years.

Voting without choosing

## Notes

1 Ahmadu Kurfi, Executive Secretary of the Federal Electoral Commission (FEDECO) for the 1979 Nigerian general elections, quoted in Joseph (1987: 153).

2 Alhaji Shehu Shagari, a senatorial aspirant in 1979, was subsequently imposed by powerful elements in the National Party of Nigeria (NPN) as the presidential candidate. Chief Obafemi Awolowo, founder and national chairman of his own Unity Party of Nigeria (UPN), was also its presidential candidate in the 1979 elections. Similarly, Chief Olu Falae was anointed presidential candidate of the Alliance for Democracy (AD) for the 1999 election by a caucus of twenty-three 'party elders' at a meeting in Ibadan.

3 OAU Secretary General Salim Ahmed Salim, quoted in *Africa Recovery*, July–September 1990, p. 29.

4 For an analysis and critique of the Babangida regime's attempt at engineering a democratic political culture, see Adigun Agbaje (1996: 143–74).

5 See analysis of the 1983 elections in Richard Joseph (1987), esp. ch. 10, 'The Challenge of the 1983 Elections: A Republic in Peril', pp. 153–69.

6 Ibid. Joseph provides a more rigorous and elaborate conceptual discourse of prebendalism in ch. 5, pp. 55–68.

7 The act of election rigging in the 1983 general election conducted under NPN supervision included: inflation of voter registration figures, deliberate shortage of ballot papers at the polling booths, election officials not arriving at polling stations, loss of ballot boxes, contrived communication breakdowns, etc. *New African*, September 1983, p. 11.

8 The elections, especially for the governorship positions, were marred by large-scale violence especially in the Yoruba states of Oyo and Ondo where NPN rigging was too obvious. Large-scale arson and killing took place in both states with at least thirty people reportedly dead in Oyo state alone. See *New African*, September 1983, p. 11.

9 Joseph (1987: 155) cites evidence from the work of Haroun Adamu and Alaba Ogunsanwo. For details see Adamu and Ogunsanwo (1983).

10 To underscore the lack of independence of the election machinery, the Babangida regime for example removed Professor Eme Awa, a renowned political scientist, as chairman of the National Electoral Commission on account of his refusal to bend to the will of government to remove the then duly elected chairman of Enugu Local Government in 1988. See his account in Eme Awa (1996: 133–4). His successor as chairman, Professor Humphrey Nwosu, was later removed by fiat by General Babangida in 1993 in the wake of the annulment of the 12 June presidential elections of that year.

11 For details on the birth and rise of the NCNC see Sklar (1963: 55–64).

12 The six parties recommended by the National Electoral Commission for consideration were the People's Solidarity Party (PSP), the Nigerian National Congress (NNC), the People's Front of Nigeria (PFN), the Liberal Convention (LC), the Nigerian Labour Party (NLP), and the Republic Party of Nigeria (RPN). See Yaqub (1992: 53).

13 The parties were the United Nigeria Congress Party (UNCP), Congress

for National Consensus (CNC), National Centre Party of Nigeria (NCPN), Grassroots Democratic Party (GDM).

14  Those registered include the Alliance for Democracy (AD), the All People's Party (APP) and the People's Democratic Party (PDP).

15  For example, out of the more than forty political associations that applied for registration as political parties in 1978, the FEDECO registered only five (Joseph 1987: 154).

16  The term 'moneybags' is a Nigerian-coined euphemism for wealthy people.

17  Bola Ige actually defeated Chief Awolowo's preferred candidate at the party primaries. See Joseph (1987: 115).

18  The names include Federal Electoral Commission (FEDECO), National Electoral Commission (NEC), National Electoral Commission of Nigeria (NECON) and the present Independent National Electoral Commission (INEC).

19  Military rulers, such as Generals Ibrahim Babangida, Sani Abacha and Abdulsalami Abubakar, perfected this practice through banning, un-banning and re-banning of politicians, clever manipulation of the electoral rules, denial of registration to political associations, use of security clearance to exclude some people from contesting elections, and so on. A typical example was the blanket ban that Babangida placed on all public officers and politicians who had held political or public office from 1 October 1960 to January 1966, and from 1 October 1979 to 30 September 1983, while all those who had been convicted of misdeeds in public office were banned for life. See Awa (1996: 129).

20  For example, in the 1983 elections, Modakeke town, a small community in the then Oyo state, returned an outrageous figure of more than 200,000 votes, thus giving the NPN a dubious victory.

21  See Sklar (1963: 132), citing the *Daily Times* (Lagos), 22 May 1953.

22  Alhaji Adamu Ciroma, frontline politician and Nigeria's current Minister of Finance, made this statement at a book launch at the University of Jos. See *Guardian-on-Sunday* (Lagos), 25 May 1997, p. A14.

23  Mrs Catherine Acholonu, quoted in *TELL* newsmagazine (Lagos), no. 19 (8 May 2000): 12.

24  For a more thorough conceptual and analytical discourse on the authoritarian imperative in Nigerian and African politics, see W. Alade Fawole (2000).

25  For details on the character of the Nigerian state, see W. Alade Fawole (2001b).

## References

Adamu, H. and A. Ogunsanwo (1983) *Nigeria: The Making of the Presidential System: 1979 General Elections* (Kano: Triumph Publishing).

Adejumobi, S. (1997) 'The Two Political Parties and the Electoral Process in Nigeria, 1989–1993', in G. Nzongola-Ntalaja and M. C. Lee (eds), *The State and Democracy in Africa* (Harare: AAPS Books).

Ademoyega, W. (1981) *Why We Struck: The Story of the First Nigerian Coup* (Ibadan: Evans Brothers Nigeria).

Agbaje, A. (1996) 'Mobilizing for a New Political Culture', in L. Diamond, A. Kirk-Greene and O. Oyediran (eds), *Transition without End: Nigerian Politics and Civil Society under Babangida* (Ibadan: Vantage).

Ake, C. (1993) 'Is Africa Democaratizing?' Guardian Annual Lecture, *Guardian-on-Sunday*, 12 December.

Awa, E. (1996) 'Electoral Administration in the Early Transition', in L. Diamond, A. Kirk-Greene and O. Oyediran (eds), *Transition without End: Nigerian Politics and Civil Society under Babangida* (Ibadan: Vantage).

Chazan, N. (1994) 'Between Liberalism and Statism: African Political Cultures and Democracy', in L. Diamond (ed.), *Political Culture and Democracy in Developing Countries* (Textbook Edition) (Boulder, CO and London: Lynne Rienner).

Diamond, L. (1994) 'Political Culture and Democracy', in L. Diamond (ed.), *Political Culture and Democracy in Developing Countries* (Boulder, CO and London: Lynne Rienner).

— (1995) 'Nigeria: The Uncivic Society and the Descent into Praetorianism', in L. Diamond, J. Linz and S. M. Lipset (eds), *Politics in Developing Countries: Comparing Experiences with Democracy*, 2nd edn (Boulder, CO: Lynne Rienner).

— (1997) 'Consolidating Democracy in the Americas', ANNALS, AAPSS, 550 (March).

Diamond, L., J. Linz and S. M. Lipset (1988) *Democracy in Developing Countries, Vol. 2: Africa* (Boulder, CO: Lynne Rienner).

Fawole, W. A. (2000) 'Institutionalising Democracy in Nigeria: The Mindset and the Attitide', text of seminar presented at the African Studies Centre, Leiden, Netherlands, 16 November.

— (2001a) 'Will Democracy Survive Beyond 2003?' *Nigerian Tribune* (Ibadan), 17 and 18 July, pp. 12 and 12 respectively.

— (2001b) 'The Problematic of Democratization and Democratic Governance in Nigeria: An Overview', in W. A. Fawole (ed.), *Beyond the Transition to Civil Rule: Consolidating Democracy in Post-Military Nigeria* (Lagos: Amkra Books).

International IDEA (2000) *Democracy in Nigeria: Continuing Dialogue(s) for Nation-Building*, Capacity-Building Series no. 10 (International IDEA).

Jinadu, A. L. (1997) 'Matters Arising: African Elections and the Problem of Electoral Administration', *African Journal of Political Science*, Special Issue: *Elections in Africa*, New Series, vol. 2, no. 1.

Joseph, R. A. (1987) *Democracy and Prebendal Politics in Nigeria: The Rise and Fall of the Second Republic* (Ibadan: Spectrum).

Kirk-Greene, A. (1996) 'Remedial Imperatives of the Nigerian Constitution', in L. Diamond, A. Kirk-Greene and O. Oyediran (eds), *Transition without End: Nigerian Politics and Civil Society under Babangida* (Ibadan: Vantage).

Kurfi, A. (1989) *Election Contest: Candidate's Companion* (Ibadan: Spectrum).

Nnoli, O. (1978) *Ethnic Politics in Nigeria* (Enugu: Fourth Dimension).

Nzongola-Ntalaja, G. (1997) 'The State and Democracy in Africa', in G.

Nzongola-Ntalaja and M. C. Lee (eds), *The State and Democracy in Africa* (Harare: AAPS Books).

*Report of the Political Bureau* (1987) (Abuja: MAMSER).

Sklar, R. (1963) *Nigerian Political Parties: Power in an Emergent African Nation* (Princeton, NJ: Princeton University Press).

Yaqub, N. (1992) 'The Third Republic, the Military and the Institutionalisation of Democracy', *Studies in Politics and Society* (Journal of the Nigerian Political Science Association), no. 7 (August).

# 8 | The electoral process in the Central African Republic in 1993 and 1999: protagonists and challenges

AIMÉ SAMUEL SABA

## Background and underpinnings of the democratization process

In this chapter, I critically examine within a historical perspective the nature of the electoral process and its challenges in the Central African Republic (CAR) during both the 1993 transitional period and the period of the establishment of institutions of democracy in 1999. The main purpose is to carry out a cross-analysis of both periods with a view to gauging the progress achieved, if any. My main objective here is to identify and to understand the factors congenial to a successful transition and the difficulties encountered by the regime during the democratization era. This study is an introductory part of a large research work on the political sociology of the CAR.

For some years now, the winds of democratic change have been sweeping across all regions of the world at a speed that probably suggests the process is irreversible. Governments of socialist countries have not been spared by this trend; they either had to adapt to its dictates or perish. Similarly, in capitalist countries of the Third World, the clamour for democratization has taken on the same popular dimension, although it remains the privilege of urban societies. This trend 'signals significant progress in the democratization of political systems in many Third World countries' (Amin 1989).

The demand for democratization has been accompanied by another global trend that started in the 1970s, namely market liberalization. The combination of both trends, according to Samir Amin, is making our generation 'an era of intense confusion'. Democratization is considered as the outcome of submission to the logic of the world market. But what does democracy mean? Some authors claim that the term 'democracy' should denote only one unique form of democracy: direct democracy. Generally they would prefer to substitute the qualifier 'democratic' with 'republican' which, in their opinion, would apply better to an elected government. Others instead prefer to add the qualifier 'participatory' to 'democracy' to emphasize the role of the citizen in decision-making and to suggest that such a role should be strengthened.

The term 'democracy' is derived from two Greek words: *demos* which means people and *kratos* which also can be translated as 'government'. The concept therefore applies to government by the people, and may pertain to direct, participatory or representative forms of popular government. Today, the term has a positive connotation worldwide, such that many political regimes with a very small or no coefficient of popular representation are described as democratic (Macpherson 1995).

According to Y. Assogba (1996), democracy may be viewed from several angles: (i) its popular legitimacy, which is related to two practices – the expression of the will of the people or all the citizens of a country as voiced through genuine and regular elections, and the political or legislative role of elected officials either by representation or by delegation of sovereign popular power; (ii) political competition which involves the organization of such competition by means of elections; (iii) the existence of at least two political parties; and lastly, (iv) civil, political and social rights and respect of the latter.

Democratization is therefore a long and complex socio-political process by which a country attains democracy. What are the origins of the democratic revolution in Africa? What are the strategies for liberating people from dictatorships, and the models of transition to democracy?

A number of analysts have rightly established the link between the democratic implosion in Africa and the profound changes in Eastern Europe. Such changes have influenced developments in Africa: the cessation of rivalries between the two superpowers dissuaded certain states from continuing to engage in diplomatic blackmail by threatening to ask of one superpower what they could not obtain from the other. With the collapse of the communist system and the inability of eastern bloc countries to continue acting as a model of socialism, African Marxist countries were discouraged; inversely, too, the countries that had hitherto been in the western sphere of influence availed themselves of the upheavals in the eastern bloc to demand political pluralism, as they were convinced that western countries could not simultaneously approve the advent of democracy in the eastern bloc while refusing to Africa the same (Nzouankeu 1991: 399).

In this analysis, which is by no means comprehensive, we identify three factors that promoted the emergence of democratic pluralism on the continent and, by extrapolation, in the CAR: first, the failure of participatory democracy which had promoted a mythical vision of Africa, symbolized by the legendary *arbre à palabre* (tree beneath which elders talk to resolve matters of general interest to the community); second, the failure of the one-party system which turned out to be the main obstacle to national unity as it imposes an ideological monolith; third, the failure of an African concept of human rights which condones large-scale human rights abuses that have contributed, to a very large extent, to rock authoritarian African regimes; torture, arbitrary arrests and imprisonment, intolerable restrictions to freedom of movement, severe repression of all manifestations of freedom – these are part and parcel of the political scene in several African states (Nzouankeu 1991).

In the late 1970s, the Bretton Woods institutions, notably the World Bank and the International Monetary Fund (IMF), and scholars began highlighting the failure of development projects in sub-Saharan African states respectively in official assessment reports and research work. Since then, the international financial institutions, which are the so-called donors to African states, have had a tendency to distance themselves from the traditional approach to funding African states and are now planning 'to apply a more interventionist policy against recalcitrant and predatory governments skilled in the art of evasion and diplomatic manipulation whenever efforts are made to convince them of the benefits of the market economy' (Willame 1993).

In 1984–85, when the Lomé Accords were about to be renewed, democracy and the rule of law had already been imposed as preconditions for donor assistance. It should be recalled that the Lomé Accords are a legal instrument for regulating co-operation between the European Union and African, Caribbean and Pacific (ACP) countries.

In CAR, for instance, the proposed privatization plan targeted mainly corporations that were symbols of national sovereignty, such as the SNE (National Water Corporation), the Central African Energy Corporation (ENERCA) and the Central African Telecommunications Corporation (SOCATEL). Whereas, at the time, the CAR government urgently needed to pay long-standing salary arrears, pensions and scholarships, Bretton Woods specialists thought they could solve the problems by calling for a retrenchment of thousands of state employees, thereby merely transferring the problem to another sector of society.

Debt servicing, one of the numerous preconditions of SAPs, exceeded the total amount required to meet the most urgent social needs. Consequently, developing countries have a high incidence of infant and maternal mortality and infectious diseases, accompanied by the collapse of local industries, increased illiteracy, a growing dependence on food imports, run-down social services and the widening of the gap between rich and poor.

As is well known, SAPs increased poverty among the already destitute masses, exacerbated the misery in urban areas, and stepped up unemployment among middle social groups. SAPs shattered the hitherto possible foundations of proprietary and clientelist practices typical of autocratic regimes in post-colonial African states (Médard 1991).

General Kolingba's regime was no exception to the rule. Furthermore, SAPs highlighted the massive scale of embezzlement and looting initiated by that regime. As early as 1985–88, the assisted early retirement (DVA) programme was already being applied. However, this programme did not yield the expected results because beneficiaries had received no prior training and the millions squandered did not serve any purpose. To make matters worse, in 1990, SAPs were again imposed. It is worth noting that SAPs upset the country's economic and financial systems. The reduction of the public service budget turned the government into a beggar on the doorstep of private donors – a situation which aggravated corruption at the public treasury, since bribes had to be paid before debts owed by the government were settled.

The adjustments carried out during the decade of 1980–90 did not succeed in creating a favourable environment for sustainable growth. Furthermore, given the fragile macro-financial stability, there was seemingly a strong case for returning to the situation prior to the adoption of the SAPs.

It should be noted that although the macro-financial results of the SAPs ultimately were rather fragile in economic terms, they were socially sustainable. According to G. Blardone (1990: 7), 'the implementation of SAPs destroyed the vital link between economic policy and social policy which had up until then been interwoven. The restoration of macro-financial stability sacrificed social stability, thereby putting at risk the country's social model based on dignity and social justice.'

At the end of the period covered by structural adjustment, the need to safeguard national unity raised the burning issue of redefining a social policy linked to an economic recovery policy, as part of the establishment of a market economy. In this perspective, it should be noted that the economy had exhausted its growth reserves and CAR society also depleted its spontaneous reserves of solidarity. Growth reserves were exhausted through disinvestment, and restructuring coupled with unfair competition has led to unbridled economic liberalization; meanwhile, reserves of solidarity have been spent as a result of the sharp fall in purchasing power, rising unemployment without any prospects of finding work and the significant social deficits recorded.

The dilapidated state of several public and social services contributed to narrowing the social reproduction base and weighing heavily on household resources, given the increase in service access costs. The price paid for adjustment has severely weakened the national economy, shattering prospects of recovery and improvement in the short term, while the number of challenges remains very high.

Following the imposition of SAPs, people began to bring pressure to bear on the government, for workers' salaries were no longer paid on time – a situation that was unprecedented. Political liberalization and national dialogue were therefore the only way out. To achieve this, the government of the time had to institute political transition.

However, the hopes kindled by the advent of democracy in the CAR were short-lived. Very early in 1996, people realized that the problem of salary arrears was a time-bomb that could easily trigger a violent expression of pent-up social frustrations. Ethnic and political conflict was another catalyst capable of unleashing implosive social tensions. This corroborated the thesis that democracy and, above all, its introduction are prone to conflict, irrespective of time and place (Assogba 1996: 63).

## The political process in the CAR

A brief historical description of the state formation may help contextualize our arguments. 'Discovered' in 1870, the first colonial post was established on the left bank of the river Oubangui in 1889. Called Bangui, it is now the capital of the country. The constitution of the colony touched off fierce fighting between the colonizers and the chiefs of the cantons and kingdoms that existed at the time.

In 1905, the Oubangui-Chari colony was founded and the French Central African territories were organized into a federation in 1910: French Equatorial Africa, of which Oubangui-Chari was a part. During the Second World War, Oubangui-Chari was one of the first colonies to side with Free France in 1940. It may be recalled that, in the same year, the AEF, into which Oubangui-Chari was integrated, acquired significance for the colonizers on account of its geographical location. 'Before then,' wrote Jacques Lique (1993), 'the country had hardly changed, even under the Popular Front. The only note-worthy events which had any lasting impact on the life of that region were the introduction of cotton growing in 1926 by Félix Eboué, Governor of the AEF, and gold and diamond mining in the '30s.' Chad's joining of the resistance, of course, under Félix Eboué's banner, prompted the AEF territories, including Oubangui-Chari, to rally behind General De Gaulle.

After the war, with the increase in colonial constraints, the Oubangui-Chari colony elected its first representative, Barthélemy Boganda, to the French National Assembly. With the blessing of Mgr Grandin, Barthélemy Boganda ran in the legislative elections and was thus elected, in the second round, the first representative of Oubangui-Chari to the French parliament on 10 November 1946. This marked the start of a new stage in his life. He joined the MRP which, according to him, was the group with which he had the greatest affinity, given his Christian and social background. However, in 1950 he decided to form his own party, the MESAN (Movement for the Social Development of Black Africa), as he realized that the MRP was out of touch with the situation in the AEF.

His main objective was to establish a United States of Latin Africa. Boganda, though outraged by the colonial abuses, insisted that western Christian values and human rights must be upheld in Central Africa, as in France, but the road to reconciliation would be long and thorny. He wanted a revision of frontiers defined by the colonizers and decried the partitioning of Africa (*'la balkanisation de l'Afrique'*) as a crime against humanity.

Central African Republic was proclaimed after the 1958 referendum. Following the death of Boganda, Abel Goumba was elected acting president during the 1959 presidential campaign. On 5 April, legislative elections were held, but 45 per cent of the electorate abstained. David Dacko was elected with the collusion and support of the French who pushed aside his heir apparent and legitimate successor, Abel Goumba. That situation prompted the opposition to establish the MEDAC (Movement for the Development of Central Africa). On 13 August 1960, the country gained independence. The political process in the CAR is characterized by strong, persistent one-party regimes, such as the MESAN founded by Boganda, succeeded by Dacko and strengthened by Jean Bedel Bokassa.

However, the failures of the Dacko administration brought the military to power. These failures included economic mismanagement, the corruption of the political class, rivalry between the country's various security services, the Chinese influence and, more importantly, Dacko's mistrust of the Central African army commanded at the time by Jean Bedel Bokassa. The people fault David Dacko particularly for his weakness and lack of control. His laxity led to disorder and the widening of the social and economic gap between civil servants and the peasantry. As a result of unbridled corruption, loans allocated to numerous public investment projects were systematically siphoned off by ministers and used for the construction of private villas.

David Dacko made economic recovery his main objective. He wanted to be realistic and open, and his economic and industrial development objectives were designed to please the European colonialists who manipulated such objectives so as to protect their interests and privileges. The people called Dacko '*Moundjou voko*' (Black Whiteman). The perpetuation of his policy after Boganda's death marked the unredeemable failure of the compromise between African traditions and western civilization. He was immediately perceived as a lame duck, incapable of standing his ground against the Europeans.

After the disagreement between Dacko and Bokassa over allegations that

Bokassa, the army chief of staff, was plotting to overthrow the president, Dacko summoned him in November 1965 and ordered him to keep quiet, threatening to demote him. The meeting closed with Bokassa taking an oath 'over the heads of their common aunts' not to make an attempt on Dacko's life. Dacko soon forgot about the oath and decided not to maintain Bokassa as personal adviser to the Minister of Defence, a ministerial post which he combined with that of president, though he would maintain him as army chief of staff.

Dacko decided to appoint Jean Izamo as his personal adviser and intended to make expedient appointments in the army so as to put Banza and Bokassa out of the way. Bokassa learned about this in a Bobangui village where Dacko had carelessly confided in the village sage. Feeling betrayed, Bokassa devised a daring strategy to take over state power. On 31 December 1965, he carried out this strategy in collusion with Banza and overthrew Dacko while he was out of Bangui.

Shortly after the putsch staged on 1 January 1966, Colonel Bokassa was perceived to be a unifier and nationalist. He very quickly won the confidence of the Central African people with his first public statements, followed these with concrete actions such as raising the salaries of state employees, and took measures to fight unemployment: seizure and nationalization of all property that was ill-gotten or acquired at the expense of the people, abolition of unpopular taxes, abolition of the single-shift system, ban on excision, abolition of renting of property by the administration, and so on. It is the view of this author that, regardless of what people have said or still say, Bokassa remains the true catalyst of the 'development' of CAR.

It should be emphasized that Bokassa's first years in power were not as dramatic as presented in the western media. Even today Bokassa continues to be viewed by many Central Africans as the most nationalist of all the presidents of the CAR.

This assessment in no way conceals the gruesome reality of the last years of Bokassa's reign. After having caused MESAN to proclaim him the 'life-president', his government became increasingly corrupt and degenerated day by day. He imposed an autocratic regime with a new constitution that endowed him with both executive and legislative power. His 'political folly' led him towards a monarchy and he crowned himself emperor of the Central African Empire. The pomp of the coronation, the despotism, the arbitrariness of the regime and the degradation of the economy stirred up popular unrest. However, his sense of nationalism – condemnation of embezzlement and France's stranglehold over the country, protection of national interests – was disapproved of by France.

That is why the French army, which had always 'made' the CAR presidents, took advantage of a trip abroad by 'the emperor' and invaded Bangui in 'Operation Barracuda'. The French army looted Bokassa's various palaces and reinstated David Dacko who restored the republic, endowing it with a presidential regime.

The CAR did not wait for the Baule statement by Mitterrand in 1990 before organizing democratic elections. But in what context can one situate the Baule statement? Changes in the former Soviet Union and in Eastern Europe, riots, demonstrations and strikes in a number of French-speaking African countries, developments in some Latin American states, Asia, the Maghreb and South Africa seemed to justify a change of French policy in sub-Saharan Africa. Thus, since 1990, the notion of good governance is in fashion in various parts of Black Africa. Such a notion, which, according to Niandou Souley (1995), 'should not be watered down and robbed of its substance or real meaning', is based on four fundamental principles, namely: transparency, responsibility, popular participation and efficiency. The application of these principles was the cornerstone of the condition-alities imposed by donors and partners in the development of African states. Very quickly, the link between democracy and good governance was established.

Similarly, democratization was also made a prerequisite for the granting of public development assistance, a condition clearly spelt out by the late French president, François Mitterrand, in his speech at the Baule African and French Heads of States Summit: 'When I say democracy, I, of course, have a ready-made model in mind: a representative system, free elections, the multi-party system, a free press, an independent judiciary, the abolition of censorship ... this is the model we have.' He added, 'France will tie its entire contribution to the efforts that will be made as part of the quest for greater freedom' (Souley 1995: 48).

The above position or statement was issued at a time when the eco-nomic base of most African countries was fast shrinking, causing acute cash shortages in most countries. Democracy was premised on a strong social and political demand that those states could not satisfy. Viewed from another standpoint, African states looked like eternal novices needing to be spoon-fed, at times forcibly. As democracy was not taking root in those countries, it was incumbent on their leaders to prove the contrary by adapting it to the continent's numerous, complex realities.

Although one may be sceptical with regard to the real possibilities for sustainable democratization of political systems in sub-Saharan Africa, France's position on the subject should be unambiguous. As a matter of fact, the contribution the French president was referring to was unfor-tunately made on a non-transparent and selective basis. France failed to assist sustainably several legitimate governments, such as that of Ange Félix Patassé in CAR.

The problem of democracy in sub-Saharan Africa can be understood only from a historical perspective, mainly because it is perceived from that standpoint by Africans themselves, and democratic progress is, at least to a certain extent, dependent on Africa's historical background, as disheartening as it may seem.

Moreover, although the Baule statement failed to cause the much anticipated radical changes in African politics, it nevertheless contributed to rekindling African's democratic aspirations. That speech created a new situation requiring the gradual institution of democratic instruments to guarantee the freedoms and lay the foundations for the rule of law.

CAR could pride itself on being among the first African states to try its hand at liberal democratization. Lack of literature on the 1981 elections, in which several opposition parties participated, seems to have relegated this country to oblivion.

After coming to power in 1979, thanks to Operation Barracuda, President David Dacko, under pressure from the political class, organized legislative and presidential elections. Unfortunately, the gods did not smile on him. Declared the winner of the presidential elections, his victory was contested by Ange Félix Patassé and his party, the MLPC (Mouvement de Libération du Peuple Centrafricain), which orchestrated street demonstrations followed by disturbances and looting which forced him again to hand over power to the military. This time, a general unknown to the Central African people, André Kolingba, came to power without any bloodshed.

General Kolingba's two-phase rule enabled him to stay in power for a long time. Soon after the handover, likened to a military takeover, he set up a military junta: the Comité Militaire de Redressement National (CMRN). Under the cover of the new constitution of 1986, he gave himself a six-year mandate to rule.

The second phase of the Kolingba regime was marked by all sorts of fierce social protest movements. First, the Baule statement, which had rekindled the people's democratic aspirations, thereby contributing to the ushering in of democracy, spurred on opposition political parties that had up until then been operating underground; those parties now demanded a sovereign national conference. Such clamouring resulted in the organization of a broad-based national debate in 1992, at the end of which the political system was liberalized. However, such liberalization tolled the death-knell of the regime, already weakened by trade union strikes. That was the background to the 1993 presidential elections, which brought Patassé to power.

Such a turbulent political situation raised several questions among political scientists who did not seem to understand the nature of the instability in the CAR political scene. As of 2004, the political class in CAR consists of over fifty parties, including those that are firmly established nationwide, such as the MLPC, the FPP (Patriotic Front for Progress), the RDC (Central African Democratic Movement), the MDD (Movement for Democracy and Development), the PSD (Social Democratic Party) and the PUN (National Unity Party). The remaining parties are small ones with alliances, and owing allegiance, to the ruling party.

It is also worth noting that Patassé played a negative role by encouraging division and obstructing the democratization process in CAR. In the view of many, his name is associated with all the blood-letting and disturbances in the country. He orchestrated the killings in 1979, masterminded Dacko's untimely departure in 1981, attempted a coup against Kolingba and is at the root of all the crises rocking the CAR today.

## Democratic transition and the stakes of the electoral process in the CAR

The beginning of the electoral process in the CAR was marked by violence. It was all the more disastrous as the country was on the verge of economic bankruptcy. Despite the pressures brought to bear on the country in the wake of the sovereign national conference, the RDC (Central African Democratic Movement) refused to accept multi-party politics and President Kolingba replaced the conference with a broad-based national debate. The protagonists in the process were:

- Opposition parties: brought together in the Coordination Committee for the Convening of the National Conference (CCCN); they published two open letters in which they violently attacked General Kolingba's regime
- Trade unions: a group of affiliated trade unions and Central African Workers' Trade Union (USTC) initiated social unrest over non-payment of their salary arrears. The National Association of Students of the Central African Republic (ANECA) backed the workers' movements by organizing a series of protests and struggles with the forces of law and order
- Civil society: human rights associations, NGOs and youth movements became increasingly critical of the actions of Kolingba's regime, and wanted a political and democratic transition
- The church: the Central African episcopacy, acting through the Central African Bishops' Conference and the Association of Central African Pastors, started dissociating themselves from the regime, which found itself increasingly isolated

- International community: bilateral partners, such as France, which supported the regime, stood aloof and demanded democratic reforms, with the European Union exerting more pressure on Kolingba to democratize his government.

In fact, the protagonists in the CAR electoral process were grouped into two categories. On the one hand were national public opinion and the active forces, and on the other hand was international opinion, including sponsors and donors. The RDC found itself muzzled. Faced with enormous internal and external pressures, President Kolingba accepted multi-party politics in April 1991. Political prisoners were freed; political parties were legalized on 31 August 1991; and the right to form trade unions was restored.

### The Joint Independent Electoral Commission (CEMI) and the 1993 and 1999 elections

As noted above, President Kolingba initiated the democratization process under pressure, after the 'broad-based national debate', which was boycotted by part of the opposition. Multi-party elections were organized as part of this process. However, to avoid a repeat of the 1986 scenario with the election of Kolingba, which could not be differentiated from the constitutional referendum, the opposition insisted on the creation of an independent body to control and supervise elections. That is how the Joint Independent Electoral Commission (CEMI) was established.

The CEMI consisted of representatives of all parties participating in the parliamentary and presidential elections. Civil society, trade unions and youth movements were all represented in the commission, which set up branches in the hinterland.

Despite the establishment of the CEMI, the elections slated for October 1992 were called off after the regime in power realized, during the campaign, that the electorate had refused to vote for it. This attitude was interpreted as acts of rejection and sabotage. President Kolingba's wife was stoned and booed as she alighted from a plane, and T-shirts bearing Kolingba's name were worn by dogs and sheep.

The organization of presidential and parliamentary elections within a multi-party system on 22 August and 19 September 1993 took place under the strict supervision of the international community, particularly France whose Special Representative, Michel Luven, co-ordinated the international observers' mission, while the French troops stationed in the country at the two permanent bases, Bangui and Bouar, were exceptionally placed under his command and mobilized to assist in the elections.

Bokassa's former prime minister, Ange Félix Patassé, was elected on 19 September 1993 with 53.45 per cent of the votes, ahead of Abel Goumba, the candidate of the Consultation of Democratic Forces (CFD); the former president having been eliminated in the first round, with only 11 per cent of the votes. The president's party, the MLPC, which won thirty-three seats in the parliamentary elections, had to take advantage of the split of the CFD to obtain a comfortable majority in parliament. The seven MPs of Abel Goumba's Patriotic Front for Progress (FPP), a member of the Socialist International, and the fourteen MPs of the Central African Democratic Movement (RDC), the former single party, were clearly in the opposition. The new constitution adopted by referendum on 28 December 1994, by 82 per cent of votes cast, though with a mere 40 per cent voter turnout, was enacted into law by the decree of 14 January 1995.

The political situation crystallized very rapidly. Seven opposition parties came together to form the Democratic Council of the Central African Opposition (CODEPO) in November 1995; and it criticized the authoritarian and ethno-centric nature of Ange Patassé's government. The nature of the Patassé regime was self-evident in the concentration of the management of state affairs in the hands of Patassé and his close associates. Furthermore, some articles of the 1995 constitution, revised by the nation's active forces, were unilaterally amended by President Patassé, who carved out most of the powers for himself, to the detriment of the legislature and the judiciary. The following statement encapsulates Patassé's authoritarian and ethnocentric spirit: 'Keep your hands off my militants.' By 'militants' he meant his relatives, friends, and 'northerners'. Rejection of dialogue, negotiation and compromise became the norm.

Political and economic problems fed into one another; part of the army revolted in April 1996, demanding payment of their salaries. French troops intervened and put an end to the mutiny. However, in spite of threats against the soldiers who had participated in the revolt, and the head of state's promise of amnesty, another mutiny was staged in May and this time it took on a political dimension. It was again quelled, thanks to another French intervention, and President Patassé promised to form a government of national unity. At the end of May, the mutiny was transformed into a civil war between the royalist and French troops, on the one hand, and the mutineers, on the other.

The various crises prompted Chad, Gabon, Burkina Faso and Mali to initiate several mediation efforts. With their support, the Central African Commission for Consultation and Dialogue reached a reconciliation agreement. The Bangui accords (AB), signed on 25 January 1997, made provision for the creation of the Inter-African Mission for the Monitoring of Bangui

Agreements (MISAB) and the United Nations International Follow-up Committee (CIS). MISAB, consisting of soldiers of mediating countries and supported by France, was installed on 12 February 1997. A new administration with a mandate to defend democracy was formed. The entire political class was represented in this new administration. The clashes between the mutineers and MISAB in March and June almost derailed the Bangui accords.

The United Nations set up the United Nations Mission in Central African Republic (MINURCA), consisting of 1,400 soldiers, with a mandate to enforce the agreements signed between the various parties. France, which gave its logistic and military support to MINURCA from the time of its creation in 1998, decided to stop supporting the mission in January 1999. A cloud of uncertainty also hung over the renewal of the mission's mandate, given the August and September 1999 presidential elections.

The presence of an international committee to monitor the Bangui accords was all the more crucial as elections were potentially conflict-ridden as a result of the deep-seated political and ethnic identity divisions. The last parliamentary elections held in December 1998 were further contested. Disorganization during the first round almost derailed the elections in spite of the fact that they were conducted by the CEMI in which all parties were represented. In the second round of voting held on 13 December, the opposition won an absolute majority, with fifty-five seats. President Patassé, who was faithful to his delaying tactics, avoided cohabitation by appointing his former finance minister, Anicet G. Dologuele, to the post of prime minister. The opposition contested what it considered as corruption and the buying over of an MP.

The opposition, furthermore, had been clamouring for institutional reforms for several years. It believed that power-sharing favoured the head of state and put democracy at risk. However, none of the earmarked reforms was carried out apart from the increase in the number of MPs from eighty-five to 107.

During the 1998 parliamentary elections, the president's party won an absolute majority through a system of alliances described as 'manipulation' by the opposition. The end of the electoral cycle did not mean the end of political and institutional uncertainties. In April 2000, the opposition in parliament, which had fifty out of the 109 MPs, passed a vote of no confidence against Dologuele's government. The presidential majority rejected the vote of no confidence, prompting the opposition parties to take their political struggle to the street, with the support of civil society which in turn called on the head of state to step down.

## Electoral attitudes

Can French-speaking sub-Saharan Africa accede to democracy and develop through democratic practices? Democratization is a long and complex social and political process. However, it is immediately evident that the initiation of the democratization process 'has turned out to be the trigger of implosive, social tensions and the key opening a Pandora's box of old African evil practices, real or mythical: tribal/regional/ethnic and political conflicts' (Bakary and Ela 1996).

Moreover, democracy as a potential source of all types of conflicts should not be automatically associated with the *leitmotiv* of the 'exceptional nature of African societies' in history. Indeed, democracy and, above all, its implementation are potentially conflicting, irrespective of time and space. At the turn of the century, a careful study of Tocqueville's analyses of American democracy reveals 'the complex and sometimes chaotic democratic system', in a way that makes us realize that beyond the multiplicity of individual positions held, there is a common logic (Jacques 1995: 12).

In this perspective, we understand why the democratization process initiated in sub-Saharan states in the late 1980s began with jolts and socio-political violence (Mbembe 1993). In the space of three years, from 1990 to 1993, through conferences and national discussions, more or less free and fair elections were organized.

In a democracy, the primary objective of a representative regime is to enable citizens to participate in political decisions. Since a people's representative cannot be allowed to exercise his duties for life, it is necessary to look for a way that can help the said people either to maintain their representative in power or vote him out of office. Hence, the institution of regular elections. Many experts consider the electoral system as a key characteristic of democracy (Mayo 1960).

The process starts with the selection of candidates. The methods used to choose candidates vary from country to country and even within the same country. In some countries, the system is completely under the supervision of political parties and citizens keen to influence the choice of candidates and to become active members of political parties. In other cases, though political parties maintain their independence, elections are organized (known as the primaries in the United States) with a view to reducing the number of candidates. In this case, citizens can influence the final list of candidates by voting effectively. Of course, giving money or actively campaigning for a candidate can have an impact on the outcome of the election (Spitz 1984).

Electoral attitudes give rise to two types of theories. The first theory, derived from the liberal economy, considers elections to be a means of choosing the most suitable policy or candidate likely to meet expectations. The second theory, which is more specifically sociological, views an election as the expression of a constituent conflict of social identities. Representative democracy is therefore viewed as a pacified system, since it is governed by social contradictions (Montoussé and Renouard 1997).

Voters' attitudes depend, first and foremost, on the political context and configuration. The type of election (e.g. presidential, municipal), the kind of election (single or two-round ballot) and the contesting parties constitute a political offer which voters are obliged to accept.

The political stakes of the election also contribute to determining the election results. Focusing the electoral campaign on a given theme to the detriment of others can sway some voters in favour of the candidate or party that appears to be most credible, in this regard.

According to Montoussé and Renouard, 'the vote is, above all, a sign of loyalty to, and solidarity with, other members of the social group and is evidence of the recognition of a class, religious, ethnic or other identity. The vote is therefore a ritual by which a social group revives its identity.'

The analysis of electoral attitudes in the CAR can be understood in the light of two major parameters: the campaign and the vote. Although a campaign can be taken to mean a process of persuading and seducing voters through a government's programme or legislation, it is also defined as a material and financial support system. Thus, the electoral campaign is a whole strategy, an arsenal and a mechanism designed to attract votes.

Although the CAR constitution recognizes political parties' right to state funding, this provision is still a principle and benefits only the ruling party, in spite of complaints by the opposition. Such open and unfair confiscation of state resources is evidence of the ruling party's appropriation of state resources. The Kolingba regime indulged in such practices, as did the government of Patassé who took over from him.

Notwithstanding these imbalances, the opposition parties, rallying under the banner of the Coordination des Forces Démocratiques (Coordination of Democratic Forces, CFD), succeeded in mobilizing significant resources for their campaign.

In 1993, General Kolingba's RDC placed bicycles, mopeds and vehicles at the disposal of the party leadership. T-shirts displaying the incumbent president's effigy, posters and large quantities of coloured pictures were handed out to the various sections of the party. These material campaign aids were, of course, followed up with media hype on radio and television that pulled in crowds of idlers, whereas the other parties with meagre resources campaigned with only the little they could garner from friends, relatives and foreign partners. This was the case with Goumba's FPP, which was assisted by his friends of the Socialist International, Dérand Lakoué's PSD, which was also supported by President Sassou Nguesso of Congo.

Since 1993, a new trend within the electoral process has been emerging that no one has been able to withstand. The quality of the RDC's campaign, coupled with all that had been invested, could not change the choice of the people. The campaign was marred by acts of violence between political opponents. For instance, in 1999 there were clashes between RDC supporters and those of the MLPC, resulting in deaths.

Electoral campaigns are also characterized by the distribution of gifts in the form of food (sugar, milk, oil, rice, salt) or basic necessities (soap, clothes, hoes and machetes). Of course, voters welcome these gifts since they consider them as merely a part of their taxes given back to them. Some candidates go to the extent of giving cash to buy votes. This scenario was witnessed during the last electoral campaign in 1999, when the MLPC, which was losing popularity, began buying votes (FCFA10,000 for a vote for Patassé) on the eve of and during the election.

Unfortunately, these campaigns do not focus on the real problems of the people. The vision for society presented by candidates or parties taking part in elections is not feasible. Consequently, demagogy replaces the truth. For instance, Patassé said during his campaign that: 'The Central African Republic is a paradise flowing with milk and honey.' Such demagogy sowed the seeds of dishonesty in voters. It was translated into common expressions such as 'Let us go and eat, but let us not vote'. People attended rallies but did not seem to care what they were about. They came only to help themselves and to eat, then they voted for another candidate. General Kolingba is familiar with this.

This attitude, paradoxically, changed in 1999. That is why the MLPC lost the majority in the legislative elections. The electorate was not interested in MPs who did nothing at all during the first legislative year. The MLPC became a minority party in the National Assembly overnight, leaving Patassé with no choice but to resort to co-habitation. Even then, the president had to make strenuous efforts to turn the tide in his favour, with an opposition MP crossing over to join the MLPC.

Of course, the blueprint for society presented by the opposition parties during the 1999 elections had changed. It was no longer a question of a blueprint for society – far from it. Everybody was asking the regime to present a balance sheet of its stewardship. And that is precisely why the MLPC lost the parliamentary majority: no MP was able to defend the promises made to voters. Everything was blamed on political and military instability. The people could not believe in this.

Moreover, had the presidential election been regular, President Patassé would not have won. I can claim that everyone knew this situation. For the sake of peace, the international community present in the country, notably Kofi Annan's representative and the Nigerian, Adepojo, played into Patassé's hands. Unfortunately, the peace which the United Nations very much wanted to maintain turned into mutinies, repeated *coups d'état* and the subjection of Central Africans to misery and abject poverty.

Still with regard to the international community, one should say that it bears its own share of responsibility for the series of crises the CAR is going through. This country has never benefited from the accompanying measures to the democratization process promised by the financial institutions and France, in particular. Given its meagre national budgetary resources, the Patassé regime could not pay the salary arrears of civil servants and the military, retired workers' pension arrears and students' scholarships while investing in the country's major reconstruction projects.

The IMF policy consists in extorting the scanty resources that the state has managed to glean from taxes. Examples abound to prove the lack of interest in the Patassé regime: Sassou Nguesso's regime is not more democratic than Patassé's; elections in Chad are not as regular as those organized in the CAR, neither is Kabila's regime more legitimate, and so on. Yet the authorities in these countries have received millions of United States dollars from the IMF and the World Bank to be used in various 'development' programmes. This is a typical example of the double standards practised by the IMF and the World Bank. The CAR is under a veiled embargo – a situation which basically calls into question the Baule statement. The difficult negotiations with the IMF and the World Bank, the repeated postponement of IMF schedules and the pressures brought to bear on the government to pay its debts when the economy is in decline, all speak for themselves.

Electoral attitudes in the CAR are influenced by several factors, including the popularity of candidates, the breadth of their experience on the political scene backed by concrete acts and the message conveyed during electoral campaigns (the blueprint for society). Such factors have been associated with socio-cultural parameters such as ethnic origin, regionalism and religion.

## Ethnicity and the electoral process

Raising ethnic issues in the CAR poses a problem. One can even argue that it is a taboo, as well as a complex, issue. Yet today, and since the advent of Kolingba and Patassé at the helm of the state as well as the dawn of the democratization process, the CAR's political history has become an integral part of the ethnic reality.

The ethnic factor is, in itself, not a bad thing. It is a homogeneous socio-cultural space, an essential basis for a living cultural expression and sociological consolidation. As Lumumba-Kasongo (2000: 101) stated: 'Most people define themselves in terms of their geographical location, their language, their religion, and their local history whether it is a glorious history or one of defeat. The ethnic affiliation is based on common economic, political and socio-cultural characteristics. These characteristics are shaped by geography, history of political struggles, and metaphysical values (preservation of some moral values).' Having suffered the consequences of colonization and the political and economic changes which have affected Africa, the ethnic fact remains a reality to be reckoned with. However, the main important question is: What does this concept really conceal?

Today, the expression 'ethnic group' is widely used in place of the word 'tribe' with colonial and even racist coloration. However, it is still applied to human groupings considered to be inferior or backward – subjects for the study not of sociology but of ethnology and anthropology. The expression 'ethnic group', which comes from the Greek word *ethnos*, means 'people' or a 'nation' and came into use in 1896 at the acme of colonization.

Jean-Loup Amselle and Elikian Mbokolo (1985) maintain that, 'though these terms have acquired a wider usage at the expense of other words such as nation, there is no doubt that it has to do with separately classifying some Amerindian, African and Asian societies as groups apart and different from ours while ridding them of those characteristics that can help them to belong to the same community of mankind'.

All that has been demonstrated, so far, only goes to show how difficult it is to grasp the concept of the ethnic group within a scope other than the dialectic framework. People do not simply emerge as an ethnic group, but they become one in comparison with another ethnic group and as opposed to it. Ethnicity can be used as an instrument of political process. It is specifically for this reason that, in the CAR, the political manipulation of the ethnic group by the ruling party, the MLPC, is seen as the cause of the various crises and tragic excesses which weaken the country and compromise the democratization process.

The ethnic reality which, during the worst days of the empire, passed unnoticed is now highlighted in order to pit the various political parties against each other. For some years now, the votes of the citizens have no longer been reflecting the choices of individuals. Rather, they have been reflecting ethnic manipulation. 'This is a situation which has transformed the political pluralism so much called for into ethnic pluralism' (Sine 1997).

The political landscape in the CAR has taken on a configuration of ethnic pluralism. This pluralism is not yet as glaring as what one finds in other African countries. In the Republic of Niger, for instance, political leaders use the ethnic phenomenon as a means of legitimizing their power or guaranteeing their rise to political prominence within the power structure.

Unlike in Niger where this most dreadful factor devalued political parties with the 'tribalistic' orientation of votes, the CAR is still forging ahead through trial and error. Despite this experimentation, party membership begins with the party leaders' ethnic group, with family roots. Therefore, the CAR has witnessed the emergence of regional political parties such as Dacko's MDD, the MLPC national party of yesteryear and the FODEM. Electoral results consequently reflect these regional configurations. The ethnic reality and political party membership in the CAR underpin the conduct of elections.

Unlike in Niger, where ethnicity appears to be used (the President of the Republic, the prime minister and even the speaker of the National Assembly have to come from different ethnic groups), access to top administrative posts in CAR is not based on such criteria.

It should be noted that it is only since the 1990s that ethnicity has become part and parcel of the political scene. The socio-cultural platform, the national language, Sango, constitutes a strong link in the country's unity. It is incredible that the democratic process and its attendant political competitions have given birth to this phenomenon.

In the meantime, the CAR has no legislative provisions that allow for the regulation of the use of ethnicity. It is clear that the ethnic group is considered to be a basic and decisive piece of information in African institutional history. It is also an expression of societal dynamics, and necessitates a collective awareness. In the CAR today, the danger lies in ethnicity, which constitutes a perverse and tendentious reading of people's loyalty to a given sociological group.

Ethnicity, which is gradually taking root in the CAR, stimulates another phenomenon, which equally has a negative impact on the democratic process: namely, military intervention along ethnic lines, in the political process in the CAR.

### The army and the electoral process in the CAR

The CAR is one of the African countries with an unusually high number of military takeovers. Such takeovers are staged alternately by soldiers and civilians. In 1966, Colonel Bokassa overthrew President Dacko before being in turn overthrown fourteen years later by the same Dacko, though this time with the support of the French army (Operation Barracuda). Under pressure from the street and the MLPC, which believed it had been robbed of victory, President Dacko gave back power to General Kolingba in 1981. In the meantime, the Bokassa regime was rocked by a series of aborted coups, including those led by General Obrou, Banza and others. For some years, the Patassé regime suffered from a series of coup attempts that repeatedly disrupted the functioning of state institutions.

A recap of such events would help situate the role of the army in the political process. The army has always been present, exerting its influence on the political administration of the CAR. For instance, Bokassa's empire was a highly militarized regime. The first phase of the Kolingba regime was named the National Recovery Military Committee (CMRN). In that regime, all ministers were soldiers. But what was the role and status of the army in the democratization process?

The CAR constitution allows soldiers to vote. This implies that soldiers have a say in the choice of their leaders. Apart from being entitled to vote, they are also under a duty to provide for security during elections. The fact that the composition of the army admittedly does not reflect the country's geographical and ethnic configuration leaves the door wide open to political manipulation. The president, who holds the reins of power, tailors his army and the presidential guard, including the police and gendarmerie hierarchy, to suit himself.

For instance, General Kolingba had a very well trained commando unit which played the dual role of standing army and presidential guard. The Eléments Blindés Autonomes (autonomous armoured force, EBA) consisted only of people from the Kolingba's Yakoma ethnic group. This system was maintained and reinforced by Patassé's 'caraco' and 'codo'.

Such a military system is not conducive to democratic progress. Furthermore, the 1992 presidential elections were cancelled not only because they were poorly organized, but also because army officers close to President Kolingba did not want to loosen their grip on power. Immediately after the General lost the 1993 elections, the swearing in of the president elect, Ange Félix Patassé, gave the nation a dreadful fright. It is alleged that those officers had asked Kolingba to seize power, but he turned down the offer, preferring to put before them a *fait accompli*.

In the exercise of its duties, the army has been politically manipulated time and time again. The democratization process, marked by twists and turns, illustrates this point very well. No sooner was Patassé elected president than he forgot the promises made to the army whose rank and file live in the same abject poverty as civil servants and the rest of CAR society.

Such misery has promoted 'the development of a military unionism which has stepped up social pressure on political institutions' (Kone

1996). The army is obliged to bring the government to reason by force of arms.

Since Patassé came to power, the army, whose unity began to flag under his predecessor, has become even more divided. Efforts to reform it, following the various hostilities against the government, have instead ended up transforming the army into a corps composed solely of members of President Patassé's ethnic group, his region or party. This situation has further complicated the problem of the army and opened the door to people whose sole intention is to cause disorder so as to take advantage of the country's resources.

The army, faced with Patassé's intransigence in addressing its grievances, demanded his resignation, thereby putting the newly established democratic institutions at risk. Today it can be unequivocally said that the CAR has no army. All that is left of the army are small splinter groups of soldiers faithful to charismatic leaders such as Kolingba, Bozize and Patassé.

The military mutinies express in a nutshell the immediate grievances of the masses who today support the army, thereby showing the extent of the Patassé regime's isolation. At the time of publication of this book, only the presidential guard and the paramilitary units (the '*caraco*' and '*codo*'), recruited solely for the purpose of counterbalancing the army, seemed to have been spared by the crisis; the president suspects the army of consisting solely of members of the Yakoma ethnic group.

Today, the army's sole role is civilian monitoring, since it is disarmed, as opposed to the presidential guard, which is armed. Moreover, the presidential guard is responsible for the maintenance of law and order, distribution of election material and security during elections.

Reports on the latest legislative and presidential elections show that the presidential guard committed large-scale abuses by forcing voters to put only ballots for President Patassé in ballot boxes. Those who disobeyed such instructions were beaten up. This reopens the debate on the role of international observers in Africa and, in particular, in the CAR.

It can be said in all objectivity that the CAR army has truly not contributed to the development and strengthening of the democratization process. All its actions during the democratization period served only more or less to erode the democratic progress achieved.

This attitude is aggravated by the war-mongering of Patassé's collaborators. The CAR army seems to have forgotten its constitutional role: to protect national sovereignty. The indiscipline that is characteristic of the army keeps those in power in the CAR in a permanent state of fear, preventing the emergence of a democratic culture premised on debate, negotiation and national consensus among political protagonists.

In the CAR, the government, weakened by the recurrent military crises, has become increasingly estranged from the people. Most of the regime's efforts are devoted to protecting the president, who is compelled to disband the presidential guard in favour of foreign troops and mercenaries (Libyans, Sudanese and Bemba's rebels from DRC).

The current state of the democratization process in the CAR is peculiar, as President Patassé, who enjoyed wide popular support in 1993, eroded his own support by flouting basic democratic principles. The systematic exclusion of other political groupings from public management, the intransigence and refusal to engage in political dialogue, the adoption of unorthodox government practices (corruption, political patronage, masked dictatorship) promoted, if not triggered, a violent reaction by a disorganized army which, according to the government, was on a witch-hunt.

In spite of several national and international meetings aimed at pulling the CAR out of its socio-political woes (National Reconciliation Conference, deployment of the Mission to Monitor the Bangui Accords, United Nations' Mission for the Central African Republic), the regime did not want to change its policy, as is evident in the various statements made by the president's spokesman, Ndouba.

The army has lost confidence in its supreme commander, the president, who, according to the former, does not keep his promises. In short, the army needs to be reformed, taking into account the regional configuration of the country. The army's legitimate demands must be seriously and expeditiously examined, as should those of the police and the gendarmerie. The CAR needs a republican army which contributes to the development of democracy.

## Conclusion

The electoral process in the CAR from 1993 to 1999 has been in two phases. The first phase was part of a popular clamouring for the democratization of the country's political process. This phase, known as the democratic transition, conformed to the rules. It was marked by:

- the decline of the Kolingba regime rocked by socio-economic crises which sapped the CAR's resilience and strength
- the mobilization of students, workers and pressure groups as part of the demand for political reform and change and the establishment of a more democratic system
- the decision to carry out reforms which are a logical consequence of the mobilization. General Kolingba decided to institute multi-party politics, freedom of expression and some basic democratic procedures

- the formulation of reforms involving the drawing up and adoption of a transition programme, including the drafting of a new, more democratic electoral code, setting up of the CEMI and, lastly, the organization of general elections in 1993, after the establishment of an electoral list, registration of political parties, electoral campaigns, voting and proclamation of results.

The above transitional stages put an end to Kolingba's one-party regime and turned the page from the transition to political change. Political change, which is peaceful transfer of power through elections (Diouf 1988), was hitch-free.

However, events which occurred in the immediate aftermath of the change of government undermined the achievements of the transition. The CAR's hard-won democracy, achieved after the protracted collective struggle of the nation's active population, was nipped in the bud by President Patassé's government and the MLPC. This relegated the CAR to the position of an eternal apprentice, whereas this country is among the first African states to have opened up to democracy.

The elections held during the wave of democratization did not follow the rules of the game. They were fraught with irregularities, fraud and falsification of results, all of which foiled the political processs.

Today, the CAR can be likened to a jungle where the fittest eliminate and crush the weakest. The CAR's democracy is marking time, for all the achievements of the transition are being eroded day by day as a result of the series of political and military crises rocking the country.

## References

Amin, S. (1989) 'La question démocratique dans le tiers monde contemporain', *Afrique et Développement*, vol. XIV, no. 2: 6.

Amselle, J. L. and E. Mbokolo (1985) 'Aspects politiques et sociaux des pays en voie de développement', *Revue politique africaine*, no. 25.

Assogba, Y. (1996) 'Problématique de la gouvernance en Afrique au Sud du Sahara. Tendance générale en Afrique noire', *Revue Canadienne d'études du développement*, spécial issue.

Assogba, Y. and J.-M. Ela (1996) 'La politique africaine de la France sous Mitterrand. Précarité de rupture et continuité du néocolonialisme en Afrique noire' *Le Devoir*, 27–8 January.

Bakary, T. and J.-M. Ela (1996) *La politique africaine de la France sous François Mitterrand. Précarité des ruptures et continuité du néocolonialisme en Afrique noire*, Le devoir, 27–8 January) 1996, p. A9.

Bigo, D. (1988) *Pouvoir et obéissance en Centrafrique* (Paris: Karthala).

Blardone, G. (1990) *Le Fonds Monétaire International, l'ajustement et les coûts de l'homme* (Paris: De L'épargne).

Diouf, M. (1988) *Sénégal, l'Etat d'Abdou Diouf ou le temps d'incertitude* (Dakar: NEA).

Jacques, S. D. (1995) *Tocqueville et la modernité. La question de l'individualité dans le démocratie en Amérique* (Montreal: Boréal).

Kone, I. (1996) 'Walf Adjri', *Quotidien*, no. 310.

Kozlov, V. (1979) *La nouvelle critique*, no. 70, January 1974, p. 26; cited by Paul Mercier in *La nouvelle Edition sociale*, p. 48.

Lallement, M. (1993) *Histoire des idées sociologiques*, vol. 1 (Paris: Nathan), p. 205.

— (2000) *Histoire des idées sociologiques*, vol. 1 (Paris: Nathan).

Lique, R.-J. (1993) *Bokassa 1$^{er}$ la grande mystification*, vol. 6 (Paris: Chaka), p. 18.

Lumumba-Kasongo, T. (2000) 'A Reflection on Nationalistic Discourses and Ethnonationalism in Struggles for Democracy in Africa', in L. A. Jinadu (ed.), *The Political Economy of Peace and Security in Africa: Ethnocultural and Economic Perspectives* (Harare: African Association of Political Science).

Macpherson, C. B. (1995) *Principes et limites de la démocratie libérale* (Montreal: La Découverte).

Maquet, J. (1974) *Les Pygmées*, in *Encyclopaedia Universalis*.

Mayo, H. B. (1960) *Introduction to Democratic Theory* (New York: Oxford University Press), pp. 72–106.

Mbembe, A. (1993) 'Déconfiture de l'Etat et risque de la transition démocratique', *Le Monde Diplomatique*, no. 470: 16–17.

Médard, J. F. (1991) 'Autorisation et démocratie en Afrique noire', *Politique africaine*, no. 43: 92–104.

Mercier, P. (1961) 'Remarque sur la signification du tribalisme actuel en Afrique noire', in *Cahiers internationaux de sociolgie*, vol. XXI, July–December: 61–80.

Montoussé, M. and G. Renouard (1997) *100 fiches pour comprendre la sociologie* (Rome: Boréal).

Nzouankeu, J. J. (1991) 'L'Afrique devant l'idée de démocratie', *Revue internationale des sciences sociales* (Paris: Edimédia).

Penel, J.-D. (1995) *Barthélémy Boganda, écrite et discours 1946–1951: la lutte décisive* (Paris: L'Harmattan), p. 20.

Rapport du gouverneur de la BEAC présenté à la conférence des chefs d'Etat de la CEMAC (2000), Ndjaména, 14 December.

Sine, L. (1997) 'Tribalisme et parti unique en Afrique Noire', *Revue politique africaine*, no. 5: 217–50,

Souley, N.-A. (1995) 'L'Afrique subsaharienne sous les injonctions occidentales', *Revue le courrier*, no. 171: 48.

Spitz, E. (1984) *Majority Rule* (Chatham, NJ: Chatham House).

Willame, J. C. (1993) 'Aller et démocratiser toutes les nations', *La Revue Nouvelle*, vol. 1501, nos 1–2: 113.

# 9 | Conclusion: beyond the current discourse on democracy and democratic process in Africa

TUKUMBI LUMUMBA-KASONGO

With the exception of Chapter 1, which intentionally focused on general theoretical issues within the political science literature related to various dimensions of the current practices of democracy and democratic processes in Africa, the authors have examined, using case studies, how democracy and various democratic processes have been perceived, debated, adopted, produced and challenged in Algeria, Cameroon, the Central African Republic (CAR), Republic of Congo (Congo-Brazzaville), Ghana, Kenya and Nigeria.

This book is essentially a critique of a system of governance and its relationships with society at large, discussing how to improve or change this system for the betterment of the majority of people. It has examined the contradictions related to the practices and values of electoral and representative democracy and the mechanisms of its reproduction in an African context. It deals with how the norms and rules of liberal democracy are reproduced and with the quality of these norms and rules. It also examines the questions of who invents, manages and controls the norms and rules of this democracy in Africa and who supports these mechanisms of liberal democracy culturally, financially and institutionally. In short, whose interests are being articulated within democracy and the democratic process in Africa?

The authors have also incorporated, comparatively and historically, in their analyses and perspectives, illustrations from other parts of Africa to make their arguments intellectually comprehensive and politically generalizable. The examples from other parts of the world, including those from the global North, were used to help contrast how democracy and the democratic process are being expressed in Africa by women, the youth, lumpen-intellectuals, lumpen-proletarians, traditional politicians and the military class. Each author has also touched on the question of the meanings of African political particularities and their policy implications within the context of both national policies and politics and international imperatives.

Liberal democracy is a system of governance that relies on the dynamics of certain established stages in articulating its values and producing its actions. Some aspects of these stages, which are part of the process, include the production of a national constitution, the selection of candidates by political parties, the raising and allocation of funds for campaigns, the free movement of citizens and voters, freedom of assembly, the composition of an electoral commission to determine electoral laws, and the supervision of the elections. Within this system, it is assumed that the final outcome of this process of producing candidates or elected officials will be based on concepts of fairness and freedom. The notion of 'free' and 'fair' elections as the measurement of an electoral process is central to liberal democracy. What do 'free and fair elections' mean in Africa? Who determines what is fair and what is free, and for what purposes?

It is clear that all the authors have expressed the need to project this study more within the areas of policy and the national political economy. Democracy and the democratic process must have real social and economic meanings beyond technicalities, legalism and the sentiments of feeling good about participating in a political process. They should have a positive impact on the living conditions of citizens. They must empower the people to participate in the process that should be theirs, through which they can obtain the feedback needed for identifying people's needs, interests and vision of society. Within the context of liberal globalization – the rise of the new monopolization of both liberal democracy in terms of funds and its direction and the so-called free market by a few forces and institutions located mainly in the global North, rampant poverty in most parts of Africa, and the increasing demand and struggles for democracy in Africa – the main question is: Where do we go from here?

It should be emphasized that this study has challenged theoretically and empirically the functioning, the meanings and the quality of democracy and the democratic process that started in the 1990s in Africa. The authors have distinguished between the views of the external forces of democracy and the internal established mechanisms and culture of democracy. They have also made a distinction between what the majority of the African people, through social and popular movements, have been pushing for (real democracy) and what was either imposed by or compromised with the African political elite (truncated democracy and its truncated processes). In fact, the notion of democracy itself as currently used in Africa was seriously questioned. The questions are: Do democracy and the democratic process in Africa reflect the people's struggles? How much have people participated, and what kind of participation has it been? Even in relative terms, do present-day African democracy and its processes reflect theoretically and practically what their prophets have advocated?

The authors agree that democracy and the democratic process in Africa are vital as political, legal, social and civil instruments that articulate development policies and institutionalize the rules of political games. Through democracy and the democratic process various forces of the civil societies should be able to engage the states and their apparatuses, and this engagement should pave the way for political dialogue between the state and people. This institutionalization is important to the process of creating political routinization, which may make African democratic practices reliable and relevant. The authors also emphasized that Africans, like people the world over, do appreciate democracy and the democratic process as mechanisms for transforming their societies. At the same time, however, they have all questioned whether the existing perceptions and definitions of liberal democracy and its process will be able to address adequately people's needs and interests.

We cannot generalize about the outcomes of the democratic process. This process may be quick, clear and clean, depending on the nature of the state formation and that of state–societal relations in their struggles for managing and controlling resources. The process is a reflection of, and is shaped by, the various articulations of individual or class interests, the energies of which come from the masses and their institutions, and the nature of the location of the state within the imperative of peripheral capitalism.

Superficiality in the electoral process in Cameroon as reflected in the elections in 1990 and 1992 is not uniquely Cameroonian. Constituents participated in the process not because they believed in the national interest promoted through liberal democracy, but because of some 'unquantified' or 'intangible' immediate interests associated with the possible victory of some supportive candidates. Thus, ethnicity and regionalism become the close and manipulated instruments upon which these interests can be articulated. As in other African countries, interests based on ethnicity and regionalism in general are foggy, undefined, imprecise and generally elastic and thus can be sustained orally for a longer period of time during the elections through fictive promises. Electoral behaviour is not an objectified political phenomenon. It is not a function of the calculation of ideological input. It is linked to what has been characterized in this book as the political economy of the liberal democratic process.

In the case of the Central African Republic (CAR), the author examined how political reform, especially the democratization process, was established within the historical context of state formation, political reforms in other countries and Cold War politics. Within the context of a 'unique' political culture of absolutism, which Jean-Bendel Bokassa created by declaring himself emperor – similar to Mobutu of the Democratic Republic of Congo who did not declare himself emperor but who *de facto* behaved as one – the transitional period to liberal democracy presented a different political reading in the country based on mass mobilization. Massive popular demands and the decline of the Kolingba regime rocked by socio-economic crises sapped the CAR's resilience and strength, and with the mobilization of students, workers and pressure groups, political reforms were finally carried out. General Kolingba was forced to institute multi-party politics, freedom of expression and some basic democratic procedures. But because of the presence of the military culture as a result of a history of so many *coups d'état* in the CAR, the establishment of civil political institutions was not guaranteed. Despite the weaknesses of the institutions, they succeeded in one important thing: the end of the one-party state of Kolingba. However, a lack of respect for the rules of democratic games, the corruption of political leaders and the fragility of the political institutions have characterized the quality of the democratic process. There is a less frequently expressed optimism among the majority now about the democratization process in CAR than was the case when the process started in the early 1990s.

In the case of Ghana, the author, who focused on the electoral process in the 2000 general elections, locates the analysis within the country's broader electoral history. He shows how Rawlings' military regime and political intrigues grafted patron–client relations with a conscious effort – a phenomenon whereby modern state officials seek control and influence over various organizations within the state through the political system. Even in the constitutional era, Rawlings remained preoccupied with the need to manage patronage. This process is the basis of the causes of the corruption and social and political manipulations that shaped electoral laws and candidate selection, which his regime and his political party, the National Democratic Party (NDP), were known to champion. Despite the buying of opposition parties by the NDP elites, however, the determination of the opposition parties was not totally shaken up. With the internal structural weaknesses of the ruling party, and despite a muddy electoral process and faulty and corrupt campaign processes, unlike in other cases in Africa, the unexpected election of a member of the opposition to the presidency can be considered a step forward in representative or procedural democracy in Ghana. To a certain extent, despite weak political institutions, massive corruption and military warnings, the electoral process worked well because of the support of the courts, the fatigue of the Ghanaian people faced with uniforms in power, and the arrogance of the ruling party.

The current practices of liberal democracy and its process have failed women in Kenya. Affirmative action was recommended in the political process and institutions to ensure more female participation in political institutions. Gender equity and equality must be part of the democratic process. There will not be any viable democracy in Kenya, or anywhere in Africa for that matter, as long as the majority of people, women, who are at the centre of social and economic reproduction, are still marginalized. A combination of gender parity and critically selective African traditions and practices must be explored, and the concept of African contributions to global democracy must be revisited. It is not enough to reform the democratic process without relating it to the political economy of democracy in Africa. Democracy involves the transformation of economic, political and social structures and of citizens' conditions. Democratization must be effectively translated into participation in economic, political and socio-cultural sectors. If the democratic process becomes truly democratic, this will call for more participation by women and poor people and the process can then accelerate the democratization of social and cultural institutions.

In the case of Nigeria, some of the characteristics of the author's arguments are localized in mapping the processes of how the formation of the Nigerian state can be considered as one of the bases of its permanent conflicts; the development and consolidation of the military culture and military economic interests, and the nature of the democratic process that has been produced during the so-called era of democracy. The author defines democracy in its social form as a phenomenon that originates from the people. It is a right of people to participate in the management of their economic, social and political affairs. The Nigerian case is unique because it has produced a strong military culture and has expanded military class interests. The articulation of these interests and the management of this culture have engendered an excessive case of corruption. Politics is the one area where one can acquire both wealth and influence quickly. The issue here is about how various parts of the political elites and their parties are struggling to gain access to the political power associated with the state.

In the Congo, there was initially a certain high level of optimism associated with the organization of the national conference in Brazzaville, which once succeeded in weakening the presidency, isolating the executive president, and creating a space for dialogue among various members of the civil society. However, the fragility of political culture, the monolithic nature of ethno-parties, the lack of clear national ideology and the political culture of the militias significantly shaped the political discourse in the 'transitional period'. Political alliances were not ideologically based. They were ethno-regional and strategically individualistic means for politicians and aspiring politicians to acquire power. Concerning problems associated with democracy and ethnicity, the author believes that some lessons related to the legal framework of parties in the Congo can be learned from the experiences of South Africa, Botswana and Mauritius; the latter two countries have inserted into the law clauses designed to prevent ethnic contradictions from paralysing the functioning of multi-partyism.

In the case of Algeria, the author demonstrates that the nature of the crisis in the Algerian state is serious and multi-dimensional. The current democracy and democratic process have been mainly articulating the interests of a mostly corrupt political elite rather than advancing democracy in Algeria and the rest of the Arab world. The transition to democracy has yet to come. It will be difficult for the people to negotiate with the groups of political leaders who do not believe in democracy. Political and social institutions of the so-called transition to democracy were not created with the purpose of allowing dissent against government policies. Rather, they are a mechanism for the regime to co-opt any opposition. Conflict thus becomes routine within a context in which state redeployment has succeeded in depoliticizing protests and social movements.

African people are not allergic to liberal democracy. Although the majority of Africans have not yet had any clear understanding about its content and philosophical foundations, they have enthusiastically welcomed liberal democracy because they expected it to solve social problems related to poverty, social injustice and gender inequality. The general conclusion has been that current democratic practice and process have been dysfunctional in Africa. The democratic process has been essentially a combination of up-down mechanisms created by a coalition of political elites in order to position their own interests in the state's power by isolating any possible challenges, including those which legitimately derive from the people's demands. As the material resources are badly distributed and scarce at the national level, as part of the nature of the incapacity of the African state to be public, those who have participated in this fragile process have been mainly the clients of the ruling parties and their management has been very much based on struggles rooted in a survival mentality. That is to say, the notion of national interest, in the process of creating rules and norms, has been in most cases either absent or weak. This is not because African people do not like or appreciate liberal democracy. It is so because:

- liberal democracy and its processes have been hijacked by the political elite
- the African state is still essentially a monopolistic agency of an 'oligarchic' class with some characteristics of a peripheral class
- some dimensions of African culture on gender have complicated the implementation of an already aberrant process

- this democracy and its processes have not been able to address the core issues of African societies, such as equal distribution of resources, social justice, employment, gender equality and individual and collective rights
- political institutions are characterized by widespread rigidity and personification
- militarization and the political culture of the militias in many cases dominate African politics
- there are low formal education and literacy rates
- high levels of corruption within the fragile institutions of democracy persist.

In short, we cannot study democracy and the democratic process outside the dynamics of the global economic and ideological context in which they function. The major player in this context is an African state which itself is incapable of producing institutions that can protect democracy and democratic values and processes. This study shows that *ad hoc* institutional reforms such as constitutional reforms, the establishment of an independent judiciary and legislative procedures will not bring much change to the nature of the democratic process in Africa. Africa has produced too many constitutions. Not only are these constitutions not fully implemented, but they are also consistently amended to support the heads of state for new terms in office. Recently, constitutional amendments have been adopted in Togo, Gabon, Uganda, Chad, Cameroon, Guinea Conakry and Equatorial Guinea where the Eyademas, the Bongos, the Debys, the Biyas and the Contés wanted power for themselves once again. In this work, the authors call for the democratization of the African state and within it its elites and the dominant political culture.

Whether in Algeria or Nigeria, where the outcomes of the elections are predictable, it is clear that liberal democracy as reflected in its current practices and processes is not enough to produce democracy in Africa, be it measured by representation, participation or rights related to resource management and distribution. That is to say, the mere presence of multi-party democracy alone may not be a solution to all the problems that continue to plague Kenyan women, peasants, farmers and lumpen-proletarians.

Thus, we have systematically and critically to go beyond the logic and practices associated with the current democracy and democratic processes in examining what the values of social democracy in Africa within a pan-African perspective might be. The features of the democracy that are badly needed in Africa are social and popular, with decentralized institutions, for the simple reason that liberal democracy is failing the majority of Africans, as did the structural adjustment programmes of the World Bank and the IMF. To institute this kind of democracy, multi-partyism has to be transformed into 'consociationalism' within pan-African visions and programmes. A strong state with a comprehensive social agenda is needed. Democracy and democratic processes in Africa will be more socially meaningful and politically acceptable if the majority of African people participate in them, not through their imposition by a corrupt political elite and its manipulated clients (based on class, ethnicity, religion and the like). Further, the democratic institutions and their processes must produce good jobs and relevant universal education, eradicate gender inequality and poverty, protect individual and collective rights, and judge and punish the leaders who betray the citizens within the policies and politics of the African welfare state supported by African traditions and value systems. The legitimacy of democracy and the democratic process must be based on performance, accountability and respectability. Finally, the process of building or developing democracy must be considered as a process of struggles, contests and protests. These struggles, in all their various expressions, must be incorporated into the democratic process and should have permanent legal, social and political space. In my view, democracy implies that people are able to own the state and the state apparatuses. This ownership is not possible in the current representative or procedural democracy as practised in Africa.

Conclusion

# Index